D0475532

BATTLESTATIONS!

AMERICAN WARSHIPS OF WWII

MBI Publishing Company

NICHOLAS A. VERONICO
ARMAND H. VERONICO

First published in 2001 by MBI Publishing Company, 380 Jackson Street, Suite 200, St. Paul, MN 55101-3885 USA

© Nicholas A. Veronico and Armand H. Veronico, 2001

All rights reserved. With the exception of quoting brief passages for the purposes of review, no part of this publication may be reproduced without prior written permission from the Publisher.

The information in this book is true and complete to the best of our knowledge. All recommendations are made without any guarantee on the part of the author or Publisher, who also disclaim any liability incurred in connection with the use of this data or specific details.

We recognize that some words, model names and designations, for example, mentioned herein are the property of the trademark holder. We use them for identification purposes only. This is not an official publication.

MBI Publishing Company books are also available at discounts in bulk quantity for industrial or sales-promotional use. For details write to Special Sales Manager at Motorbooks International Wholesalers & Distributors, 380 Jackson Street, Suite 200, St. Paul, MN 55101-3885 USA

Library of Congress Cataloging-in-Publication Data Available
ISBN 0-7603-0954-X

Edited by Michael Haemggi
Designed by Dan Poppie

On the Front Cover: *Missouri* (BB-63) seen on her shakedown cruise in August 1944 in a colorful camouflage paint scheme. After transiting to the Pacific and a repainting in San Francisco, the battleship arrived at Ulithi Atoll on January 13, 1945. The ship's nine 16-inch guns provided shore bombardment support for the Iwo Jima and Okinawa landings, as well as attacks against the Japanese home islands of Honshu and Hokkaido. The starboard quarterdeck of *Missouri* was the site of the Japanese surrender on September 2, 1945 in Tokyo Bay. *National Archives*

On the Frontispiece: A vigilant submarine lookout in the periscope shears keeps watch for approaching ships or aircraft. An entire crew's fate depends upon the alertness of its lookouts. Upon sighting the enemy, a submarine must immediately dive to avoid detection. *National Archives*

On the Title Page: *Indiana* (BB-58) fires a salvo at Kamashi, Honshu Island, 250 miles north of Tokyo, site of Imperial Japanese Iron Works. This is the first bombardment of the Japanese home islands, and is seen from the battleship *South Dakota*. *National Archives*

On the Back Cover: A battleship's 5-inch gun crews prepare to fire on the beaches at Saipan during fire support for the June 15, 1944 invasion. Fourteen men on deck pass and handle ammunition while the gun crew awaits the order to commence firing. Bombardment from ships off shore usually obliterates beach obstacles and any enemy waiting for the Army and Marines en route. *National Archives*

Printed in Hong Kong

CONTENTS

DEDICATION

For Desirae with love: The bond between a sailor and the sea is
only eclipsed by that of a father and daughter.

Also by Nicholas A. Veronico

Military Aircraft Boneyards (with A. Kevin Grantham and Scott Thompson)*

Blue Angels: 50 Years of Precision Flight (with Marga B. Fritze)*

Giant Cargo Planes (with Jim Dunn)*

Airliners in Flight: A Gallery of Air-to-Air Photography (with George Hall)*

Vought F4U Corsair: The Combat, Development, and Racing History of the Corsair (with John M. and Donna Campbell)*

Airliner Tech, Vol. 9: Boeing 377 Stratocruiser

Raceplanes Tech, Vol. 1: Griffon-Powered Mustangs (with A. Kevin Grantham)

Raceplanes Tech, Vol. 2: Racing Bearcats and Corsairs (with A. Kevin Grantham)

Fly Past Fly Present: A Celebration of Preserved Aviation (with Walter Boyne, et. al.)

Douglas DC-3: Sixty Years and Counting (with Ed Davies and Scott Thompson)

Wreck Chasing: A Guide to Finding Aircraft Crash Sites (with Ed Davies, et. al)

Wreck Chasing 2: Commercial Aircraft Crashes (with Ed Davies, et. al.)

Travis Air Force Museum (A Guide to the aircraft of)

March Field Museum (A Guide to the aircraft of)

Castle Air Museum (A Guide to the aircraft of)

*—Published by MBI Publishing Company

ACKNOWLEDGMENTS

This portrait of the U.S. Navy's engagements during World War II carries the names of the authors, but behind the scenes many people generously gave of their time, information, and access to photographic collections that contributed greatly to this book. For this, the authors are indebted to the following people and organizations: Holly Amundson; Jerry Ancher; Harvey Beigel; Molly Biddle, Wisconsin Maritime Museum; Barbara Callison, Crescent City Public Library; Caroline and Ray Bingham; Ed Davies; Jill Dunbar; Jim Dunn; Norm and Gail Felchle; Laura Graedel, Museum of Science and Industry, Chicago; Karen Haack; Michael Haenggi; Marty Hart, American Widescreen Museum; Jeff Hull, Matson Navigation; Chris Kleiber; Bill Kooiman, San Francisco Maritime Museum/J. Porter Shaw Library; Tillie and William T. Larkins; Hubert Marlow; Michael Marlow; Stephanie Mitchell, Pima Air & Space Museum; Gabriel Prado, Matson Navigation; L. Ray; the staff of the Sausalito Historical Society; Donna Schwein; Hank Silka; Becky Simmons, George Eastman House; Gina Timmons, Matson Navigation; Marifrances Trivelli, Los Angeles Maritime Museum; Betty S. Veronico; Jack Whitmeyer, Los Angeles Maritime Museum. Special thanks to Boris and Natascha.

Nicholas A. Veronico
San Carlos, California

Armand H. Veronico
Los Angeles, California

IMAGES OF WAR

Swordfish (SS-193) was launched with appropriate fanfare on April 3, 1939, at Mare Island, California, Naval Shipyard. In the days after the Pearl Harbor attack, the sub made a number of attacks and believed it had sunk a trio of cargo ships but was unable to confirm any of the sinkings. Swordfish became the first American submarine credited with sinking a Japanese ship on December 15 when three torpedoes sent the 8,663-ton Atsutusan Maru to the bottom near Hainan Island. SS-193 was lost south of Okinawa on January 12, 1945. (National Archives/80-GK-1379)

To many, World War II was fought in black and white. For the most part, the conflict was fought abroad, and most Americans experienced the battles through newspapers and newsreels—both monochromatic mediums. In all actuality, many of the photographs shot by combat cameramen during World War II were taken in color. Most war photographers carried three cameras when on assignment—a Speedgraphic shooting 4x5-inch sheets of film, a Bell & Howell "Eymo" 35mm movie camera, and a Kodak 16mm turret-lens movie camera exposing film magazines. After a battle, exposed film was sent to headquarters for processing and censoring. If the film passed the censors, it usually ended up in movie houses as the prefeature newsreel or on the pages of newspapers and magazines of the period.

A combat cameraman could easily get his hands on Kodachrome still color film, but was often frustrated by the results. Film stock was sent from Kodak's Rochester, New York, plant to depots (later in the Pacific war located at Guam, and Subic Bay, Philippines) that would issue the cameraman his supplies. During the film's journey from the states and across the Pacific deep in the belly of a transport ship, the film was often subjected to temperatures as high as 140 degrees. This caused "heat fogging" to occur on the unexposed color film. After developing, the photograph would appear as if the viewer was looking at the image through a mist. Many times a color image with heat fogging could be saved by printing the photograph in black and white.

In the years since World War II, most of the surviving color images seen today languished in the services' archives, in footlockers in many a serviceman's closet, and eventually in the National Archives. When the cost of reproducing color images for the print media began to decline in the mid-1990s, a new interest was born in the work of combat cameramen the world over.

Roger Fenton, an Englishman, is the first war photographer whose work has been chronicled. Fenton's descriptions of the effort to capture images of the Crimean War (1853, Great Britain, France, Turkey, and Sardinia versus Russia) conveys the difficulties of early war photography. The subject matter was battlegrounds, camps, forts, and posed generals. Why generals? "If I refuse to take them, I get no facilities for conveying my van from one locality to another," Fenton said. The van is what defines the task of pioneering war photography. To carry the photographic process from the laboratory into the field required horse-drawn carts to carry 36 cases of equipment, including 700 unsensitized glass plates. For Fenton to capture a single image, he first had to clean and polish a glass plate, and then coat it with various chemicals that dried to form an emulsion. Next, the plate was dipped in a solution of silver nitrate that turned yellow, making it light sensitive. The still-damp plate was placed in a lightproof holder, taken to the subject to be photographed, and exposed. After exposure, Fenton rushed back to the darkened van, rinsed the plate in tanks of chemicals that developed and fixed the image, passed it over an open flame to dry, and finished the plate by varnishing it to preserve the precious image.

America's Civil War was the first conflict to be extensively documented by photography. Matthew Brady, an American portrait photographer, realized the importance of a visual record of the struggle. Although many photographers photographed war, it is Brady whose name is associated with Civil War pictures. Brady was the quintessential organizer. He formed a team of photographers, and had up to 22 horse-drawn wagons following the action. Although Brady coordinated the operation from Washington, he was also involved in the actual fieldwork. The team used the same process as Fenton had, and faced the same problems. The exposure times for this process varied from 6 to 10 seconds, which precluded any sort of action or movement. Dead soldiers made excellent subjects and, for the first time, Brady's team documented the true horror of battle. Brady and his men are considered the first real photographers of war.

Every entrepreneur must cover his or her expenses and Brady was no different. His business plan was to sell photographs and stereographs (three-dimensional pictures that were viewed with a special viewer, common in most households during the late 1800s) of the battle scenes. He also attempted to sell the pictures to the government at the end of the war in 1865. Unfortunately, none of Brady's attempts at commercialization succeeded, and he was forced to declare bankruptcy. Brady's team produced nearly 7,000 images, making his name synonymous with Civil War photography.

The images produced by Fenton and Brady were not accessible to the general public in their original form. They were available in books that consisted of actual photographic prints, painstakingly pasted on pages. Newspapers and magazines of the time would have an artist make a woodcut, using the photograph as a guide, and then print what amounted to a line drawing. The invention of the halftone printing process allowed mechanical reproduction of a photograph for the first time. On January 21, 1897, the *New York Tribune* published the first halftone in a mass-circulation newspaper.

By World War I, camera and film technology was advancing, although equipment remained bulky and cumbersome. Photographs were still choreographed, although they brought the viewer closer to the atmosphere of war. True candid war scenes would have to wait for better, faster, more compact equipment. In the second decade of the twentieth century, the halftone process was commonplace, and there was a huge market for photographs. When U.S. troops were sent to Europe in 1917, photographers were waiting to cover their arrival. The *New York Times* Sunday edition had a special section known as *Rotogravure* (a type of printing press, particularly adept for halftone printing) that provided extensive photographic coverage throughout the war. In 1919, two New York newspapers collaborated to scoop their competitors with photos of President Woodrow Wilson signing the Treaty of Versailles. The photographs were rushed from Paris to the United States, and thus the era of competitive journalism was born.

Photojournalism made its "Quantum Leap" in 1924, when Lietz of Germany introduced the "Leica," a 24x36mm camera. Exposures were made on 35mm motion picture film, and the camera was very reliable, portable, and easy to operate. Photojournalists had everything they wanted except one final piece of realism—color.

On April 15, 1935, Kodak began selling "Kodachrome," a new film for motion pictures. The following year, Kodachrome was released in rolls for still cameras. The marriage of the new Leica-type cameras and Kodachrome film gave World War II photographers the tools to provide rapid, true-color, documentary photojournalism. In 1942, Kodak's Rochester facility was awarded the Army-Navy "E" for high achievement in the production of equipment and films for the war effort.

Kodachrome's end product was a positive color transparency that had to be held up to light to be viewed. Kodak decided to return the processed film in 2x2-inch cardboard holders, and the slide show was born. A few months after the debut of Kodachrome, the German company Agfa brought out "Agfacolor," a competing color technology. Near the end of World War II, the U.S. Army captured the Agfa factory near Leipzig, Germany. Included were the patents and techniques for Agfacolor film and its developing process. This information was deemed a war indemnity and given to film manufacturers worldwide. By the 1950s Agfacolor became the basis for color processes used by amateur and professional photographers.

The Navy used color photography widely in World War II, particularly in motion pictures. The majority of wartime movie footage depicting the Navy in action was originally Kodachrome, but was duplicated in black and white because there was little need for color until television began using it in the 1960s. Navy and Army Air Corps gun camera film also used color as well as black and white, depending upon which type of stock was available.

Photography's greatest role in World War II was as a weapon: the most obvious being propaganda, both negative and positive. In 1942, President Roosevelt established the Office of War Information (OWI) headed by CBS radio commentator Elmer Davis. The OWI censored all war material, yet Davis felt the American public was not seeing the realities of war. Through his efforts, in 1943, *Life* magazine published a color photo taken by George Strock (in December 1942) of three dead American soldiers, facedown on a beach at Buna, New Guinea. Publishing this type of photo could have had a negative affect on civilian morale. In this instance, the reality of combat motivated American resolve to win the war.

The Naval services (U.S. Navy, Coast Guard, and Marines) were fortunate enough to attract thousands of top-notch photographers to the service, among them the following: Horace Bristol, Dwight Long, Victor Jorgensen, Fenno Jacobs, Charles Kerlee, Jerry Anker, Charles Kerlee, Wayne Miller, and Edward Steichen. When the talents of these men— each an excellent photographer in his own right—were combined, they produced one of the greatest visual records of modern warfare. Although many had built reputations as commercial or magazine photographers before America entered the war, the images produced by combat cameramen were not only a documentary record of the Naval services, involvement in war, but could simultaneously be emotionally moving and patriotic. The stories told by the faces of Marines waiting to assault a beach, or the urgency of men fighting fire on the deck of an aircraft carrier, were brought home to the American public by the select few combat cameramen. In many instances the photographer gave his life to capture an image, the tale of death in battle only told when a buddy had the foresight to retrieve the film.

In addition to men on the ground capturing the action on film, aerial photography was used extensively for mapping, battle planning, and assessment of battle damage. Prior to the invasion of Normandy, millions of photographs were taken of the coast. Even the darkness of night failed to deter imaging of the enemy. Using flash bombs of almost a billion candlepower, troop movements and repositioning of hardware under cover of darkness were photographed by aerial still cameras. A Royal Air Force photograph of the German battleship *Bismarck* preparing to sortie was the first step in the pursuit that led to its sinking.

War forced American and Allied industry to improve many areas of photography, including microfilm for document storage and transport, cartography, aerial photography, and x-rays for the detection of shrapnel, as well as advancements in still and motion picture cameras used in battle.

The pictures that follow in this book are the result of combat photography's long evolutionary process. Tragically, photos of war do not come without a price. Many men and women, both in front of and behind the camera, perished in the making of these photographs. Let these images be a monument to their supreme sacrifice.

NEUTRALITY IS NOT AN OPTION

Fog-shrouded battleship New York (BB-34) was the fifth U.S. Navy ship to bear the name, and was launched on October 30, 1912. In the opening months of World War II, New York escorted convoys to Iceland and across the North Atlantic. The battleship provided shore bombardment, silencing the French cannons of Batterie Railleuse, for troops landing at Safi, French Morrocco, on November 8, 1942, during Operation Torch. New York joined the Pacific Fleet in time for the invasion of Iwo Jima. (*National Archives/80GK-14562*)

The 1930s were a decade of change and worldwide upheaval. America was gripped by an economic depression of catastrophic proportions. Many European nations suffered the same fate. To boost its flagging economy, the Nazi government of Germany began an armaments construction program in violation of the 1918 Versailles Treaty. Armaments construction put Germany's unemployed to work while simultaneously advancing its state-of-the-art military weaponry. To test its advances in armament technology, the 1936 civil war in Spain was used as a proving ground for Germany's aircraft and artillery designs. Bolstered by German war materiel, Francisco Franco's Nationalist forces succeeded in overthrowing Spain's left-wing Republican government in 1939.

While war raged in Spain, Nazi Germany's Chancellor Adolf Hitler continued to build an army, navy, and air arm of unequaled power. The industrial complex of Hitler's war machine turned out tanks, aircraft, and submarines, while the Nazi dictator lulled his future enemies into a false sense of security. Hitler formed alliances with Russia, Italy, and Japan, and signed non-aggression treaties with France and Great Britain.

On the eve of signing the September 28, 1931 Munich Pact with Hitler, British Prime Minister Neville Chamberlain proclaimed, "We, the German Führer and Chancellor, and the British Prime Minister, have had a further meeting today and are agreed in recognizing that the question of Anglo-German relations is of the first importance for our two countries and for Europe. We regard the agreement signed last night and the Anglo-German Naval Agreement as symbolic of the desire of our two peoples never to go to war with one another again. We are resolved that the method of consultation shall be the method adopted to deal with any other questions that may concern our two countries, and we are determined to continue our efforts to remove possible sources of difference, and thus to contribute to assure the peace of Europe.

"My good friends, for the second time in our history, a British Prime Minister has returned from Germany bringing peace with honor. I believe it is peace for our time . . ." Chamberlain avoided war and the Munich Pact ceded the Sudentenland region of Czechoslovakia to Germany. Unchallenged by Western powers, Hitler made his first territory conquest with the stroke of a pen while America maintained an isolationist policy toward involvement in European political affairs.

Japanese Expansion in the Pacific

In the Far East, Japan flexed its military muscle in its quest to acquire natural resources while developing an economically self-sufficient empire. Its scheme of conquest called for the expulsion of Western influences from the Pacific, and an "Asia belongs to the Asians" philosophy. As a member of the Allied cause during World War I, Japan reaped the spoils of victory and acquired vanquished German territories in the Pacific, including the Caroline and Marshall island groups as well as the Marianas Islands with the exception of Guam.

While Japan expanded its empire through World War I's victory—no matter how small the island nation's participation—the United States was giving up the right to fortify its Pacific bases (excluding Pearl Harbor). As a signatory power at the 1922 Conference on the Limitation of Armament (also known as the Washington Naval Arms Limitation Treaty of 1922), the United States could not increase the defenses of Guam or the Philippines. Britain gave up the right to fortify any island possessions east of the 110° east longitude meridian including the great naval base at Singapore, as well as Hong Kong. The Washington Treaty allowed the United States to maintain a fleet with a total of 525,850 tons—approximately 18 battleships ranging in size from the 21,825-ton *Utah* to the 32,600-ton *Maryland*. Britain's naval armada was limited to 558,950 tons, and Japan was kept to 301,230 tons. America was leading the cause for naval disarmament, and negotiation of the treaty appeared to be a victory for the Western powers. The West would maintain its powerful navies in exchange for promising Japan not to increase the fortifications of its Pacific territories.

For eight years, Japan, the United States, and Great Britain managed a peaceful coexistence. In 1930, the signatories to the Washington Naval Treaty met in London to extend naval construction limitations. At the conference, an agreement was reached for a 10:10:6 ratio of cruisers between the United States, Great Britain, and Japan, and a 10:10:7 ratio for destroyers. The pact was ratified by the Japanese Diet, but the Imperial Navy believed the treaty's restrictions were too limiting and thought that the Diet had severely restricted its ability to wage war. On November 14, 1930, a member of the right-wing nationalist party tried to assassinate Prime Minister Hamaguchi for his part in ratifying the extension to the naval treaty. Hamaguchi eventually died from wounds suffered in the attack in July 1931.

In spite of the restrictions on naval ship and base construction, the Japanese army had expansionist plans of its own. On September 18, 1931, a South Manchurian Railroad bridge was blown up at Mukden by the Japanese Kwantung Army. Officers claimed Chinese partisans had blown up the bridge and attacked the Army; this incident was used to justify Japan's invasion of Manchuria. In January 1932, the army moved into Shanghai, and two months later established its

occupied territory in Manchuria as the state of Manchuko with former Chinese Emperor Henri Pu-Yi as head of the puppet government.

Four months later, on May 15, 1932, Japanese Prime Minister Tsuyoshi Inukai, who had attempted to halt the Army's advance through Manchuria, paid for his actions with his life. He was assassinated at his residence by nine soldiers. At the time, the Japanese prime minister and the ministers of the Army and Navy had equal power and equal access to the emperor. The death of Inukai effectively ended party rule in Japan. The military replaced the government with a cabinet of 11 seats—eight military officers and three civilians—and appointed Admiral Makoto Saito as prime minister.

With the military firmly in control, the Kwantung Army marched into Inner Mongolia. Under the protests of the United States and The League of Nations, Japan refused to withdraw from China. In March 1933, The League of Nations issued the Lytton Report, reiterating the call for a Japanese withdrawal and an official statement refusing to recognize Manchuko as a legitimate government. Bowing to Army pressure, Japan withdrew from The League of Nations. Coincidentally, on October 14, 1933, Germany gave notice that it, too, was withdrawing from the League. The following year, in December 1934, Japan officially renounced its recognition of the Washington Naval Treaty and began a ship-construction program in secret. Plans called for the construction of seven battleships of the *Yamato* class, each displacing an estimated 69,000 tons—larger than any other

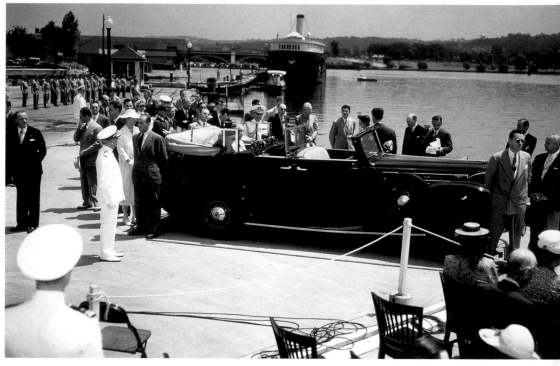

President Franklin D. Roosevelt addresses a crowd gathered at the Washington Navy Yard for the presentation of an unidentified ship to a foreign navy. Eleanor Roosevelt looks on from behind the convertible's bumper. Roosevelt led the nation through the Great Depression, the early dark days of the war, through negotiations and war planning with the nation's Allies, until his death on April 12, 1945. He was responsible for uniting the Allies with his January 1, 1942, "Declaration of the United Nations" calling for all countries fighting the Axis not to make separate peace agreements. (*National Archives/80GK-13832*)

New Mexico (BB-40) was launched April 13, 1917, and overhauled and modernized during 1931 to 1933. Part of the Atlantic Fleet when Japan attacked Pearl Harbor, the battleship was quickly transferred to the Pacific to serve as an escort for troop convoys. On July 21, 1943, New Mexico was part of the force that routed the Japanese from the Aleutians. The ship loads 14-inch shells for its next operation in the Pacific, most likely the June 14–16, 1944, bombardments of Tinian, Saipan, and Guam. (National Archives/80GK-1710)

ship afloat, each with a main battery of nine 18-inch guns, capable of speeds in excess of 30 knots, and a range of 8,000 nautical miles at 18 knots. (Only three of the class were eventually completed, *Yamato, Mushashi*, and *Shinano*.)

Vowing to fight the enemy, that is, communism, Japan and Germany signed the Anti-Comintern Pact on November 26, 1936. A year later, Mussolini joined the Pact, thus forming the first vestiges of an Axis alliance.

From Manchuria, the Japanese Army marched into China on July 7, 1937, after a minor engagement near Peiping that became known as the Marco Polo Bridge Incident. The advance was brutal, with the army taking control of Shanghai and then butchering the citizens of Nanking in December 1937 when more than 200,000 lost their lives. The Army's acquisition of Chinese lands ran into stiff opposition from Kuomintang and Chinese Communist partisans and, in May 1939, the Russian army as well. During the border war with Russia along the Siberia, Manchuria, and Korea frontiers, the Japanese lost 500 aircraft and more than 150 pilots. The Russians stopped the Japanese advance and in September both nations agreed to a cease-fire.

Choosing Sides: The Axis Seek a New World Order

Japan's war with China was of little concern to Hitler, half a world away. Hitler faced only verbal opposition from Britain and France in March 1936 when his troops occupied and began fortifying the Rhineland. The West paid only lip

service when Hitler proclaimed the union of Germany and Austria, and shortly thereafter annexed the Sudentenland. Sensing that the Allied nations of western Europe did not have the resolve to stop Hitler with force, the German Wehrmacht (army) rolled across the border into Czechoslovakia on March 14, 1939, to occupy that once sovereign nation.

Watching the European balance of power swing toward Hitler's Germany, President Franklin D. Roosevelt could not allow America's isolationist policies to dictate foreign policy any longer. In an address to Congress on September 21, 1939, Roosevelt sought the repeal of the arms embargo that withheld American guns, ships, tanks, and planes from being sold to France and Great Britain. As Congress mulled over the possible implications of lifting the arms embargo, Germany and Russia forced America's legislative branch to act.

In the early-morning hours of September 1, the German Wehrmacht rolled across the border into Poland. The Luftwaffe quickly gained air superiority and then turned its attention to supporting ground forces. This two-pronged, lightning-fast attack was dubbed the "Blitzkrieg," and within 20 days Poland's armed forces had been bombed and strafed into submission. Witnessing Hitler's decimation of Poland stirred the Congress of the United States to pass the November 4, 1939, Neutrality Act, which allowed America's defense industry to provide arms to Allied countries on a "cash and carry" basis.

The spring of 1940 saw the U.S. Navy's Pacific Fleet sortie from the West Coast for maneuvers in Hawaiian waters. Once the exercise was completed, Roosevelt directed that the fleet remain stationed at Pearl Harbor as a deterrent to the Japanese. In theory, the Pacific Fleet would be seven sailing days closer to any Pacific conflict, and would temper Japanese expansion plans to the south.

In Europe, Hitler invaded the Low Countries and France on May 10. France was quickly conquered, and by June 22 the Germans had divided the country into two sections, the northern half by the occupying Wehrmacht and the southern half by the Vichy-based government of Marshal Philippe Pétain. Japan quickly put pressure on the Vichy government to stem the flow of arms through France's Indochina colony to Chinese rebels led by Chiang Kai-shek. To ensure its position, Japan sent military units into northern French Indochina to police the border area. Seen as another expansionist move, Roosevelt swiftly reacted by cutting off Japan's supply of American oil, steel, and scrap iron—all were elements needed to wage war.

The following month, Konoe Fumimaro became the Japanese prime minister. The "Major Principles of Basic National Policy" were approved that solidified Japan's Asia-first policy. This called for an expansion to the south in an effort to gain territory that would help Japan's war economy become self-sufficient regardless of the consequences.

While Japan was planning its future, America was slowly taking steps to protect its shores. On September 2 an agreement was reached with the British whereby the island nation would receive 50, ex-World War I four-stack destroyers from America's mothball fleet in exchange for naval and air base leases in Newfoundland, Bermuda, and the Caribbean. By the end of the month, Japan, Germany, and Italy had signed the Tripartite Pact, solidifying their intent to cooperatively "maintain a new order. . . calculated to promote the mutual prosperity and welfare" of their nations. Within a week of signing the Tripartite Pact, Japanese Prime Minister Konoe said in a newspaper interview: "If the United States refuses to understand the real intentions of Japan, Germany, and Italy, and continues persistently its challenging attitude and acts. . . those powers will be forced to go to war. Japan is now endeavoring to adjust Russo-Japanese political and economic relations and will make every effort to reduce friction between Japan and Russia. Japan is now engaged in diplomatic maneuvers to induce Russia, Britain, and the United States to suspend their operations in assisting the Chiang regime."

The Axis powers sent a clear message of their intent to dominate the United States and its interests abroad. In reply, Roosevelt called upon U.S. citizens and businesses to become the "Arsenal of Democracy" to supply Allied nations with war materiel, while avoiding involvement in an armed conflict. Roosevelt said: "The proposed 'new order' is the very opposite of a United States of Europe or a United States of Asia. It is not a government based upon the consent of the governed. It is not a union of ordinary, self-respecting men and women to protect themselves and their freedom and their dignity from oppression. It is an unholy alliance of power and pelf to dominate and enslave the human race.

"Thinking in terms of today and tomorrow, I make the direct statement to the American people that there is far less chance of the United States getting into war if we do all we can now to support the nations defending themselves against attack by the Axis, than if we acquiesce in their defeat, submit tamely to an Axis victory, and wait our turn to be the object of attack in another war later on.

"We must be the great arsenal of democracy. For us this is an emergency as serious as war itself. We must apply ourselves to our task with the same resolution, the same sense of urgency, the same spirit of patriotism and sacrifice, as we would show were we at war."

1941: Steering a Course Toward War

The first steps to what would ultimately lead to a betrayal of trust between nations, a sneak attack on an American naval base, and the loss of more than 2,388 killed and 1,178 wounded in less than three hours, were taken on February 14, 1941. On that day, President Roosevelt received the Japanese Ambassador to the United States, Admiral

Kichisaburo Nomura. The two discussed the deterioration of Japanese-American relations, and Roosevelt suggested that the admiral frankly and openly discuss the troubles with Secretary of State Cordell Hull. Thus began a frustrating 10-month series of negotiations where Secretary Hull attempted to ascertain Japan's "willingness and power to abandon its present doctrine of conquest by force" and to respect the sovereignty of all nations. While Hull sought the answer, Admiral Nomura continued to intimate that peace between both nations could be achieved.

Negotiations in Washington with the Japanese continued as the German navy began attacks against shipping farther and farther from the European coastline. The Germans were attempting a naval blockade of England using its limited fleet of U-boats and were enjoying much success. To increase aid to England while maintaining some semblance of neutrality, Roosevelt signed the Lend-Lease bill into law on March 11, 1941. The bill provided increased spending on armament for self-defense while enabling the British to acquire vast amounts of shipping, aircraft, and other war materiel on a credit basis. Roosevelt stated that the materiel sent overseas kept the dictators from American shores while the nation continued to build a reserve of tanks, planes, and ships. American factories took on another lend-lease customer on June 22, 1941, when Hitler attacked Russia.

When America entered the war, the nation's citizens rallied to the cause. On the home front, everyone participated in the war effort in some manner. Many people had never seen the inside of a shipyard, let alone the vast oceans where the thousands of emergency ships would ply their trade. For those entering the maritime trades, new shipyards had to educate workers, maintain and boost morale, while each person had to conserve resources to meet the needs of the war industry. Clockwise from top: Calship produced the Calship Log to inform workers about the shipyard's activities; ration books contained stamps redeemable for food and fuel; Coca Cola boosted morale with patriotic trading cards depicting U.S. Navy aircraft in action; workers of shipyards producing at peak capacity were awarded "Ships for Victory" pins; each worker was issued an identification card or badge, this one from Calship in Wilmington, California; even the matchbook from the Philadelphia Naval Shipyard employee's cafeteria had messages on it—buy group life insurance and read the shipyard's publication The Beacon; education programs were set up to teach new shipyard workers such skills as welding and burning—welder's glasses rest on top of instruction booklets from Kaiser's Richmond, California, yards number one and three. (Nicholas A. Veronico)

Every U.S. industry converted to war materiel production shortly after America's entry to the conflict. Thousands of women and minorities joined the workforce to replace able-bodied men who had been drafted into military service. This defense worker adjusts the warhead section of a Naval Mk. XIII torpedo at a Pontiac Motor Division (General Motors) plant in the Midwest. *(National Archives/80GK-14117)*

Admiral Nomura had engaged Secretary Hull in a number of meetings to discuss peace during the first half of the year. In July, Nomura and the Japanese foreign minister were repeatedly voicing their nation's desire for peace as the Japanese army marched into the southern areas of French Indochina. Unable to make any progress on a Japanese withdrawal from China, and faced with further expansion in Indochina, Roosevelt was forced to hit Japan where it hurt the most—in the wallet. The president signed an executive order on July 26, freezing all of Japan's financial assets in the United States and barring all import and export transactions that had Japanese interests.

Negotiations with Japan continued, while in the Atlantic, a number of incidents involving Germany were slowly drawing America closer to a two-front war. On September 4, *U-652* fired torpedoes at the U.S. Navy's *Greer* (DD-145) while the destroyer was sailing en route to Argentia, Newfoundland. *Greer* became the first U.S. Naval vessel to attack the Germans when the ship dropped 19 depth charges against *U-652*. Roosevelt used the encounter between the sub and American man o'war to rally the nation claiming, "This was piracy legally and morally. It was not the first nor the last act of piracy which the Nazi Government has committed against the American flag in this war." Less than a month later, the *Kearny* (DD-432) was escorting a convoy to England on the night of October 16 when three of her charges were torpedoed by a U-boat wolf pack. The following morning, *Kearny* was struck by a torpedo from *U-568* in the forward fire room. Thirty-three of *Kearny's* crew lost their lives in the attack. The destroyer limped to Greenland for temporary repairs and eventually proceeded to the East Coast for permanent repairs. Although *Kearny* was a ship in a neutral navy, the destroyer was escorting ships laden with cargo for a nation at war—justification to fire from the U-boat commander's perspective. From Roosevelt's perspective, the attack on *Kearny* was reason enough to order the Navy to "shoot on sight" any Axis vessel in U.S. waters or acting in a belligerent manner.

The peace process with the Japanese took a turn for the worse on October 16, when the Konoe Cabinet toppled and was superseded by a cabinet headed by General Hideki Tojo. The Tojo cabinet expected America to make all concessions toward peace while Japan maintained its positions in French Indochina and Mainland China. Major General Kiyofuku Okamoto expressed the new cabinet's position in a statement released October 17: "Despite the different view advanced on

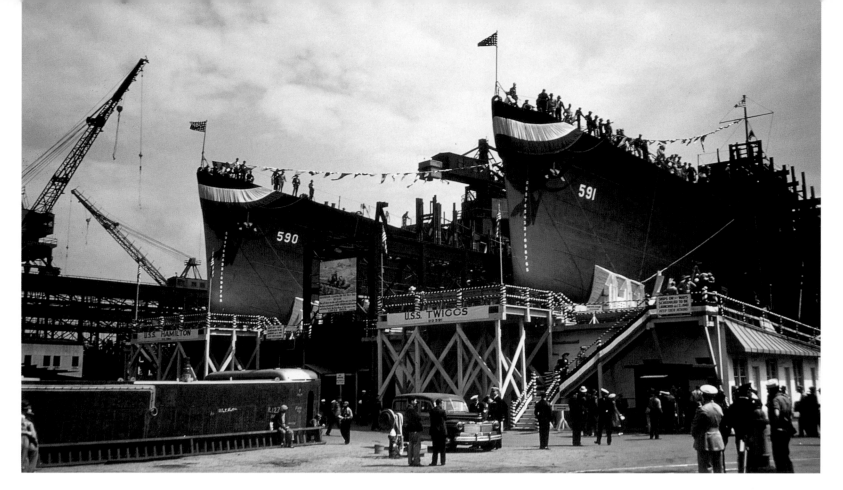

The introduction of assembly-line techniques to ship production saw launching out-pace ship losses. By 1943, yards often launched more than one ship per day. On January 20, 1943, both Paul Hamilton (DD-590) and Twiggs (DD-591) were laid down at the Charleston (South Carolina) Navy Yard. Less than four months later, both ships slid down the ways on April 7. Both destroyers sailed similar paths during the war, and each participated in the invasions of the Philippines, Iwo Jima, and Okinawa. (National Archives/80GK-13833)

the Japanese-American question, our national policy for solution of the China affair and establishment of a common co-prosperity sphere in East Asia remains unaltered. For fulfillment of this national policy, this country has sought to reach an agreement of views with the United States by diplomatic means. There is, however, a limit to our concessions, and the negotiations may end in a break with the worst possible situation following." Gen. Kiyofuku's statement was made as Admiral Nomura continued to present the hope of peace to Secretary Hull.

On November 3, Admiral Osami Nagano, chief of the Naval General Staff, and Admiral Isoroku Yamamoto finalized the plan of attack for Pearl Harbor. The Emperor was aware of the plan to strike once the final ultimatum was delivered to the United States on December 7. This decision set in motion a number of deadlines, both diplomatic and military, that led to war. The United States Pacific Fleet was to be "rendered impotent" in Hawaii to afford the Japanese military time to invade the Philippines, the oil-rich Dutch East Indies, the Malay Peninsula, and the naval base at Singapore, and bolster its forces in the mandated islands.

The strike force, under the command of Vice Admiral Chuichi Nagumo, gathered in Hitokappu Bay near Etorfu Island in the Kurile Islands. The Strike force consisted of six aircraft carriers (*Akagi, Hiryu, Kaga, Shokaku, Soryu,* and *Zuikaku*) with 423 combat planes aboard, two battleships (*Hiei* and *Kirishima*), two heavy cruisers (*Chikuma* and *Tone*), plus the light cruiser *Abukma*, 11 destroyers (two—*Sazanami* and *Ushio*—would split off and shell the airbase at Midway Island), three submarines (*I-19, I-21,* and *I-23*) to serve as advance lookouts for the strike force, and eight tankers. An Advance Expeditionary Force of twenty-seven additional submarines would join in the attack, having sortied from Kure and Yokosuka between November 18 and 20. The subs refueled and resupplied at Kwajalein before proceeding on the mission. *I-26* left the pack to monitor shipping in the Aleutians, and *I-10* guarded the flank in the Samoa area. The remaining 25 I-boats set sail for Hawaiian waters to launch five, two-man midget submarines and to harass shipping. At 6 A.M., on November 26 (Tokyo time), the fleet sailed for Pearl Harbor following a northern course to avoid detection by commercial ships. If negotiations with the United States were successful, the attacking force could be recalled, and war avoided. If there were not a breakthrough in negotiations, the strike force would launch its aircraft at 6 A.M., one hour before sunrise, on Sunday morning, December 7, Honolulu time (December 8—Tokyo time).

Unknown to Admiral Nomura, the fleet had sailed and diplomatic negotiations had been put on a strict timetable. Through diplomatic channels, the United States forwarded a

▲ Mrs. Edward J. Kelly, wife of Chicago Mayor E. J. Kelly, christens the heavy cruiser Chicago (CA-136) at the Philadelphia Navy Yard on August 20, 1944. The cruiser was the third ship to be named after the Illinois city, and was commissioned on January 10, 1945. Chicago reached the Far East on July 8, and bombarded the Japanese home islands until the ceasefire on August 15. *(National Archives/80GK-14405)*

▶ LSM-126 and -127, the first and second Landing Ship Medium types built at the Charleston Navy Yard, were also launched on the same day. The yard's band has assembled on the left of the viewing area, while the crowd of invited shipyard workers and dignitaries stand for the invocation prior to launching. During the battle for Iwo Jima, on February 18, 1945, destroyer/minelayer Gamble (DM-15) was struck by two 250-pound bombs, which flooded both fire rooms and killed six men. Gamble was towed by Dorsey (DD-117) until relieved by LSM-126, which towed the damaged destroyer to Saipan for repairs. *(National Archives/80GK-14465)*

document titled "Outline of Proposed Basis for Agreement Between The United States and Japan" on November 26 calling for peace between the two nations. The document demanded Japan withdraw from Indochina and China; and once China was a sovereign nation, it called for the recognition of Chiang Kai-shek's National Government. The outline, which became known as the "November 26 Note," was an olive branch from the United States to Japan additionally offering to release all frozen assets and to negotiate a reciprocal, most-favored-nation trade agreement.

Tokyo responded to Adm. Normura with comments on the "November 26 Note" two days later. In dispatch No. 844, Tokyo informed the admiral and fellow diplomat Saburo Kurusu: "The United States has gone ahead and presented this humiliating proposal. This was quite unexpected and extremely regrettable. The Imperial Government can by no means use it as a basis for negotiations. Therefore, with a report of the view of the Imperial Government on this American proposal, which I will send you in two or three days, the negotiations will be *de facto* ruptured. This is inevitable. However, I do not wish you to give the impression that the negotiations are broken off. Merely say to them that you are awaiting instructions and that although the opinions of your government are not yet clear to you, to your own way of thinking the Imperial Government has always made just claims and has borne great sacrifices for the sake of peace in the Pacific. Say that we have always demonstrated a long-suffering and conciliatory attitude, but that, on the other hand, the United States has been unbending, making it impossible for Japan to establish negotiations." In addition, the Japanese

diplomats were informed that a response to the "November 26 Note" would be forthcoming, sent by cable in 14 parts.

On the evening of December 6 in Washington, U.S. cryptanalysts had decoded and prepared the first 13 parts of the message for distribution to the War Council that included the president, secretaries of State, War, and Navy, as well as the chief of staff and the chief of Naval Operations. What they read was a lengthy reiteration of Japan's reasons for conquest and why it should hold its territories, and blaming the United States for pushing both nations toward war. The last sentence of the 13th part read, "Therefore, viewed in its entirety, the Japanese Government regrets that it cannot accept the proposal (American proposal of November 26) as a basis of negotiations."

The 14th part had been decoded and was in the process of being distributed at 8 A.M., on the morning of December 7. It read: ". . . obviously it is the intention of the American Government to conspire with Great Britain and other countries to obstruct Japan's efforts toward the establishment of peace through the creation of a New Order in East Asia,

U.S. Navy Ship Force Levels, 1938-1945

Date	6/30/39	6/30/40	12/7/41	12/31/42	12/31/43	12/31/44	8/14/45*
Battleships	15	15	17	19	21	23	23
Carriers, Fleet	5	6	7	4	19	25	28
Carriers, Escort	0	0	1	12	25	65	71
Cruisers	36	37	37	39	48	61	72
Destroyers	127	185	171	224	332	367	377
Frigates	0	0	0	0	234	376	361
Submarines	58	64	112	133	172	230	232
Mine Warfare	29	36	135	323	551	614	586
Patrol	20	19	100	515	1050	1183	1204
Auxiliary	104	116	210	392	564	993	1267
Surface Warships	178	237	225	282	635	827	833
Total Active	380	394	478	790	1782	3699	6768

Events:
• World War II begins in Europe when Germany and the USSR invade Poland September 1939.
• World War II in Europe ends May 8, 1945.
• V-J Day August 14, 1945 (August 15 in the Western Pacific).
• * Pacific War formally ends September 2, 1945.
Source: *Naval Historical Center*

and especially to preserve Anglo-American rights and interests by keeping Japan and China at war.

"The Japanese Government regrets to have to notify hereby the American Government that in view of the attitude of the American Government it cannot but consider that it is impossible to reach an agreement through further negotiations."

Upon review, the message simply stated that negotiations could not proceed at this juncture. Nowhere did the message state that diplomatic relations between the two nations should be or were broken, nor did the message declare war upon the United States.

Although the War Council had read it, the Japanese delegation was having difficulties decoding and preparing the lengthy message for presentation to Secretary Hull. Along with the text, the cable instructed the diplomats to deliver the message at 1 P.M., Washington time. They did indeed set an appointment to deliver the message at 1 P.M., but later called and moved the appointment to 2 P.M., unaware of the timing significance.

The bow section of West Point (AP-23) was repaired at New York. The section was removed from the ship and placed in a dock side warehouse. The bow was inverted to allow workers better access to the ceiling areas. *(National Archives/80GK-6686)*

CHAPTER 1

1941: UNDER ATTACK: A WORLD IN FLAMES

In the quiet early-morning hours of December 7, 1941, at 3:42 A.M., Ensign R. C. McCloy aboard the U.S. Navy minesweeper *Condor* spotted something that appeared out of place. Near the entrance buoys to Pearl Harbor, McCloy sighted a periscope in an area where U.S. submarines were prohibited from traveling submerged. Around 3:55 A.M., *Condor* reported its sighting to the destroyer *Ward* (DD-139) by signal light. *Ward* pursued the submarine, but after an hour and a half, was unable to locate it. *Ward* requested the sighting information from *Condor* again and renewed the search. By 6 A.M., *Ward* had broken off the search and resumed its regular patrol pattern off the entrance to Pearl Harbor. Lt. William W. Outerbridge, skipper of *Ward*, understood the significance of a Japanese submarine lurking off the harbor's entrance, but did not report the phantom submarine sighting to higher command at Pearl Harbor's 14th Naval District.

Thirty minutes later, the general stores issue ship *Antares* (AKS-3) arrived off Pearl Harbor with a barge in tow. Lying-to near the harbor entrance awaiting a pilot, an object resembling a small submarine was sighted 1,500 yards off *Antares'* starboard side. *Ward* was once again called in to investigate and at 6:33 A.M., a Navy PBY Catalina patrol bomber from VP-14 marked the sub's location with smoke bombs. The destroyer ran down the track and began shelling the midget submarine. Mortally wounded by cannon fire, the submarine passed under *Ward*, which then dropped a pattern of depth charges, sealing the fate of the Japanese midget sub and its two-man crew. Destroyer *Ward* had drawn first blood, but the significance of the morning's actions would not be known until later in the day.

At 6:51 A.M., Lt. Outerbridge reported to the 14th Naval District, "We have dropped depth charges upon subs operating in the defensive sea area." Feeling this was not direct enough, two minutes later Outerbridge transmitted, "We have attacked, fired upon, and dropped depth charges upon submarine operating in defensive sea area."

While the Japanese midget submarine made its final 1,200-foot plunge to the bottom of the Pacific, Privates Joseph Lockard and George Elliott were nearing the end

of their duty shift at the Opana Point aircraft warning station, on the northern point of Oahu. Gen. Walter Short had put the Army radar stations, and the information centers they report to, on alert during what he considered, ". . . the most dangerous hour of the day for an air attack, from four o'clock to seven o'clock A.M. daily." Although slated to return to base for breakfast at 7 A.M., Lockard kept the radar set on to give Elliott some additional training while the pair waited for their ride back to base. Moments before 7 A.M., Lockard saw a huge formation on the radar's screen. Thinking the machine had developed a fault, he readjusted the set and then determined that it was working properly. At 7:02 A.M., Lockard began tracking a large formation of aircraft 132 miles north of Oahu, heading toward the island from three degrees east.

Meanwhile, the information center had shut down and its crew headed for breakfast. Only Pvt. Joseph McDonald, a telephone operator, and Lt. Kermit A. Taylor, a fighter pilot sent to the center for liaison training and observation, remained on duty. The telephone operator received a call from Lockard at 7:20 A.M., and, with no one of authority on duty, transferred the call to Lt. Taylor. Hearing Lockard's report, Taylor told him, "Don't worry about it," believing the radar was tracking a flight of 12 B-17s expected to arrive that morning from Hamilton Field, California.

"Air Raid Pearl Harbor, This Is No Drill"

Privates Lockard and Elliott were tracking the first inbound wave of 189 aircraft that had been launched from the Japanese carriers 260 miles north of Pearl Harbor at 26 degrees north longitude, 158 degrees west latitude. Surprisingly, Lockard and Elliott did not detect the pair of Mitsubishi A6M "Zero" floatplanes, one each from the cruisers *Tone* and *Chikuma*, sent in advance of the main strike force to reconnoiter Pearl Harbor and the Lahaina Roads anchorage at Maui. *Chikuma's* aircraft sent a report of the number and types of aircraft in Pearl Harbor as well as a weather report back to the strike force's carriers. *Tone's* floatplane could only report that no American Naval vessels were in the deep-water anchorage at Lahaina—where the Japanese preferred to

Colorized photo of a sailor being rescued by a launch with West Virginia (BB-48) and Tennessee in the background (BB-43). Tennessee, obscured by smoke during most of the attack, was only struck by two bombs. The battleship was seriously threatened by fires from Arizona and West Virginia, and did suffer fire damage on the stern. Fire hoses were used to keep floating fires away from the ship, and the engines were run at five knots to push away the flames. When West Virginia settled on the harbor bottom, the ship pinned Tennessee between the forward mooring quay and Ford Island. Tennessee's engines were run up to 10 knots, but the ship could not make any headway. *(U.S. Army Signal Corps)*

Arizona (BB-39) was mortally wounded during the opening minutes of the Pearl Harbor attack. These images show Arizona as the forward magazines explode. *(National Archives/80GK-13512)*

attack, rather than the shallow waters of Pearl Harbor. *Hiei, Kirishima, Tone,* and *Chikuma* each launched a Type 95 reconnaissance floatplane (Nakajima E8N) to patrol around the fleet during the attack.

Two waves of attacking aircraft had been launched, the second following 40 minutes behind the first. As the first wave crossed the Oahu coast, flight leader Lt. Cmdr. Mitsuo Fuchida signaled to his flight that they had achieved complete surprise. At 7:49 A.M., he gave the signal to begin the attack. At 7:53, he announced to the fleet *Tora, Tora, Tora,* confirming the attack's surprise as the fighters descended to begin strafing the airfield at Ford Island and the torpedo bombers lined up on the battleships and cruisers in the harbor.

Achieving Air Superiority

While the torpedo bombers roared in, low over the water, nine dive-bombers focused their attention on aircraft parked in rows in front of Ford Island's Hangar 6. All airfields on Oahu had been alerted to the possibility of sabotage attacks by General Walter Short, who ordered all aircraft parked in rows, wingtip to wingtip, to make the planes easier to guard. Short also ordered that the bullets be removed from each aircraft's machine guns at nightfall.

Ford Island was home to Patrol Wing 2's PBY Catalinas and also served as the overhaul station for all Naval carrier-based aircraft. Thirty-three of the 70 aircraft on Ford Island were destroyed in the opening seconds of the attack by a flight of "Val" dive-bombers. Bombs destroyed Hangar 6 and heavily damaged Hangar 38. From his headquarters on Ford Island, Rear Admiral Patrick N. L. Bellinger sent a message to all Naval commands saying, "Air Raid, Pearl Harbor. This Is No Drill." The message was sent at 7:58 A.M. The worst of the attack was still to come. Around 8:30 A.M., 15 Douglas SBD dive-bombers from VS-6, the scout bombing squadron aboard the carrier *Enterprise* (CV-6), approached Ford Island during the middle of the first Japanese attack wave. Thirteen landed safely at Ford Island; one was lost to the Japanese, and one landed on Kauai.

Simultaneous to the attack on Ford Island, Zero fighters descended upon Kaneohe Naval Air Station, home to 36 Catalina patrol planes, on the eastern side of the island. Three of the base's aircraft were on patrol when the Japanese arrived overhead. The remaining patrol planes were moored in the bay, parked on the tarmac, and under repair in the base's hangars. The first attack lasted nearly 15 minutes, just long enough to set half the aircraft ablaze. When the Zeros departed, squadron personnel went into action, attempting to save the undamaged aircraft and put out those on fire. With the entire base turned out to fight the fires, a second squadron of Zeros roared over the field, strafing the men and aircraft, and scoring a direct bomb hit on Hangar 3 and the four PBYs inside. When the Zeros left for the last time, only six damaged PBYs remained to greet the three that were out on patrol.

Wheeler Field and the Schofield Barracks, located in the center of the island on Leilehua Plain, came under attack at 8:02 A.M., by 25 Aichi D3A Val dive-bombers. Of the more than 150 planes at Wheeler Field that morning, nearly 80 were parked wingtip to wingtip in rows only 20 feet apart. Diving down from 5,000 feet, the Vals bombed Wheeler's hangars and returned for low-level strafing of the ramp and barracks areas. The attack lasted 15 minutes, and then the men began the task of fighting fires and attempting to arm planes for combat. During the lull, four P-40s and a pair of P-36s took off from Wheeler to engage the enemy. The fighters of Lieutenants George S. Welch and Kenneth M. Taylor had been flown to Haleiwa, a dirt strip on the north coast of Oahu untouched by Japanese fighters. Welch and Taylor downed four aircraft each; in all, Army Air Corps pilots shot down 12 aircraft that morning. At 9 A.M., seven Japanese planes returned for a few quick strafing passes en route back to the carriers. At Wheeler, 83 planes were destroyed or heavily damaged.

Wheeler's auxiliary strip, Bellows Field, located on the eastern side of Oahu and south of Kaneohe Bay, saw only one Zero during the first minutes of the attack. This aircraft strafed the tent area and then flew off. At 9 A.M., nine more Zeros turned their attention to Bellows Field, destroying 3of the 20 aircraft parked there.

Two airfields in the vicinity of Pearl Harbor were hard hit. Marine Corps Air Station Ewa Field—west of the entrance to Pearl Harbor, and the Army's Hickam Field on

the eastern side of the harbor were rendered impotent within minutes of the attack. Ewa Field was hit first by six Zeros that approached at 1,000 feet and dived to within 25 feet of the ground to strafe planes and Marines attempting to fight back. Since Ewa was on the way to Pearl Harbor, other Zeros and Vals made a strafing pass at the field either en route to the target, or when returning to the carriers. Marines broke out machine guns from the armory and were able to position one SBD dive-bomber for use as an anti aircraft gun mount. Ewa Marines are credited with downing one Zero during the battle. By the time the attack had ended at 10 A.M., nearly three-quarters of the 48 aircraft on the tarmac were ablaze.

Attacks on Hickam Field were well planned and precise. Home to the 18th Bombardment Squadron's long-range, four-engine B-17 Flying Fortresses and twin-engine B-18 Bolo bombers, these aircraft were perceived as a large threat to the Japanese fleet. The first attack on the field lasted 10 minutes and saw 12 Vals strike the Hawaiian Air Depot. As the machine shops and hangars of the depot exploded, 7 more Vals strafed the flight line. At 8:25 A.M., another flight of Vals scored a direct hit on the airfield's fuel-pumping system, a number of the technical buildings, and the barracks. A third run on the field was made at 9 A.M., when nine aircraft strafed the hangar line and shop area while an additional half-dozen machine-gunned the living quarters, parade ground, and post exchange.

A sailor aboard Solace (AH-5), docked across the harbor, captured the instant of the explosion with a 16mm movie camera. *(National Archives/80GK-13513)*

To increase the dramatic effect of photos from the Pearl Harbor attack, the U.S. Army Signal Corps colorized a number of photos, including this shot of Arizona's forward superstructure and Number Two 14-inch/.45-caliber triple-gun turret. The battleship has settled to the bottom as fuel oil burns on the harbor's surface. Arizona's foremast nearly toppled when the ship's forward magazines exploded, collapsing the forward hull. *(U.S. Army Signal Corps)*

Arriving during the melee, the anticipated flight of B-17s from the 38th and 88th Reconnaissance Squadrons was searching for a place to land after the long flight from California. To increase the Flying Fortress' range, gasoline was loaded instead of ammunition for the bombers' defensive 50-caliber machine guns. Three of the 88th Squadron's bombers were brought into Hickam under fire, two landed at Haleiwa, and Lt. Frank P. Bostrom outran Japanese fighters and was finally able to set his aircraft down on a golf course. The 38th Squadron arrived between attack waves and although one aircraft was damaged in the air, all were able to land safely. Of the 12 B-17s that arrived on the morning of December 7, only 1 was destroyed and 3 were repairable, but heavily damaged.

Although less then two dozen American aircraft were able to sortie during the attack, the Japanese achieved total air superiority in the skies above Oahu. The United States lost 188 aircraft and an additional 151 were heavily damaged, compared to 29 planes lost by the Japanese.

Combined Dive and Torpedo Bomber Attacks

Signalmen on the ships at anchor in the harbor were hoisting the preparatory signal for the 8 A.M. raising of the flag when flights of dive-bombers could be seen approaching Ford Island. In the distance, torpedo planes were flying low as their crews set up attack runs. Twelve planes initiated the torpedo attack, flying into the harbor from the southeast, passing over the fuel tank farm, and heading directly for Battleship Row on the eastern side of Ford Island. Skimming the water at 50 feet, the Nakajima B5N "Kate" bombers dropped torpedoes fitted with wooden boxes around the fins to prevent the missiles from diving deep into the harbor and becoming stuck in the mud. The battleships moored on the outside row—*Arizona* (BB-39), *California* (BB-44), *Nevada* (BB-36), *Oklahoma* (BB-37), and *West Virginia* (BB-48), were struck in the first pass. *Oklahoma* took three more torpedoes on the second pass and began a severe list to port. As the Kates passed overhead, gunners in the rear cockpit strafed the ships.

The third torpedo attack came from the west, over Ford Island, and was launched at the minelayer *Oglala* (CM-4), berthed outside the light cruiser *Helena* (CL-50), both moored at 1010 dock. *Helena* and *Oglala* were berthed at the pier usually reserved for *Pennsylvannia* (BB-38), which, on this day , was in dry dock. The single torpedo passed under *Oglala* and struck *Helena*, flooding one engine and boiler room and shorting the wiring to the main and 5-inch batteries.

Generator power was restored to the turrets which immediately began engaging the low -flying aircraft. Captain R. H. English's crew isolated the flooding and was able to keep the cruiser afloat. The torpedo's concussion split open *Oglala*'s hull plates and the ship began to take on water. Minutes later, a bomb was dropped between the two ships, knocking out power to *Oglala*'s pumps. The minelayer was abandoned, but its crew enlisted the aid of a tug and moved the ship to the pier behind *Helena*. Two hours after the attack, *Oglala* capsized while tied to 1010 dock. Both ships would return to fight another day.

The last torpedo attack of the first wave flew low over the middle loch near Pearl City to launch against the World War I–era battleship, modified into a target ship, *Utah* (AG-16), the light cruisers *Raleigh* (CL-7) and *Detroit* (CL-8), and the seaplane tender *Tangier* (AV-8). Torpedoes missed both *Detroit* and *Tangier*, but the others were not so lucky. *Utah* was moored at F-9, a spot usually reserved for aircraft carriers, and was struck by a pair of torpedoes in rapid succession. By 8:12 A.M., *Utah* rolled over and sank, taking six officers and 52 enlisted men with her. *Detroit*'s crew fought gallantly to keep their cruiser afloat. A single torpedo flooded the Number Two fire room and the forward engine room. Quickly counter-flooding the listing ship, the crew worked to add additional lines to the mooring floats to keep the ship on an even keel. A Kate from the second wave dropped an armor-piercing bomb directly on *Detroit*, but the heavy bomb penetrated straight through the lightly armored ship to explode on the harbor bottom. Also during the second wave, the unscathed *Tangier*'s guns scored direct hits on three aircraft that were seen to crash. Except for *Utah*, the remaining three ships, *Raleigh, Detroit*, and *Tangier,* would return to battle—*Raleigh* present at Tokyo Bay on September 2, 1945, for the Japanese surrender.

While Arizona and West Virginia burn in the background, sailors begin the task of salvaging flyable and repairable aircraft and sweeping up debris on Ford Island. *(U.S. Navy)*

Captured Japanese vertical aerial view of "Battleship Row," beside Ford Island, during the very early part of the horizontal bombing attack. Ships seen are (from left to right): Nevada; Arizona with Vestal moored outboard; Tennessee with West Virginia moored outboard; and Maryland with Oklahoma moored outboard. A bomb has just hit Arizona near the stern, but the ship has not yet received the bomb that detonated her forward magazines. West Virginia and Oklahoma are gushing oil from their many torpedo hits and are listing to port. Oklahoma's port deck edge is already under water. Nevada has also been torpedoed. *(Theodore Hutton Collection, Naval Historical Center, NH 50472)*

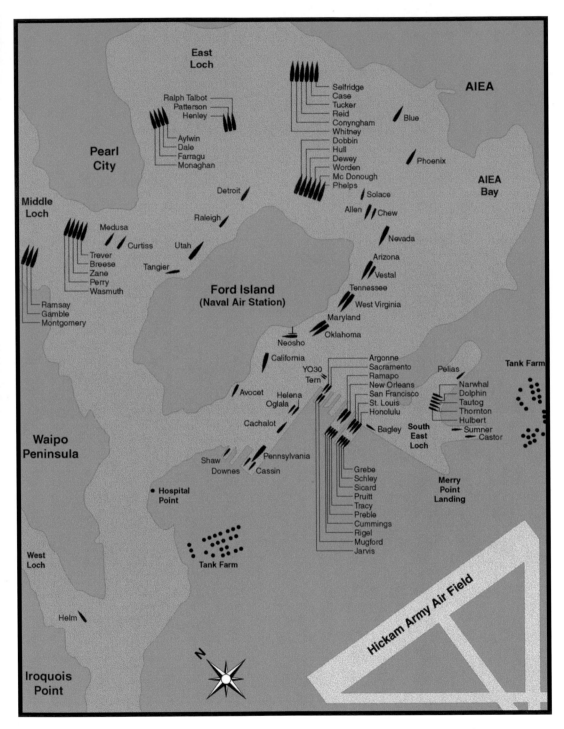

Approximate disposition of ships in Pearl Harbor on the morning of December 7, prior to the Japanese attack.
(Illustration by Gail Felchle)

East
Loch

AIEA

Ralph Talbot
Patterson
Henley

Selfridge
Case
Tucker
Reid
Conyngham
Whitney
Dobbin
Hull
Dewey
Worden
Mc Donough
Phelps

Blue

Aylwin
Dale
Farragu
Monaghan

AIEA
Bay

Pearl
City

Phoenix

Detroit

Solace

Middle
Loch

Medusa

Raleigh

Allen
Chew

Curtiss

Nevada

Utah

Trever
Breese
Zane
Perry
Wasmuth

Tangier

Arizona

Vestal

Ford Island
(Naval Air Station)

Tennessee

Ramsay
Gamble
Montgomery

West Virginia

Maryland

Neosho

Oklahoma

California

Argonne
Sacramento
Ramapo
New Orleans
San Francisco
St. Louis
Honolulu

YO30
Tern

Pelias

Tank Farm

Avocet

Helena
Oglala

Narwhal
Dolphin
Tautog
Thornton
Hulbert
Sumner
Castor

Waipo
Peninsula

Cachalot

Bagley

South
East
Loch

Shaw
Downes

Pennsylvania

Cassin

Grebe
Schley
Sicard
Pruitt
Tracy
Preble
Cummings
Rigel
Mugford
Jarvis

Merry
Point
Landing

Hospital
Point

West
Loch

Tank Farm

Hickam Army Air Field

Iroquois
Point

N

Helm

N

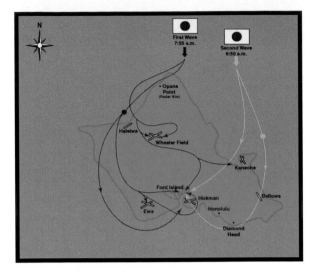

Track chart depicting the approach routes of Japanese aircraft on the morning of December 7. Destroying the island's fighter aircraft on the ground gave the Japanese air superiority, enabling them to attack ships in Pearl Harbor without the threat of American aerial attacks. Only 29 Japanese aircraft were lost during the air raid, 20 of those from the second wave that encountered heavy antiaircraft fire as well as a few American fighters that were able to get airborne. (Illustration by Gail Felchle)

While the first waves of torpedo planes skimmed the harbor, dive-bombers were descending on the fleet. *Arizona*, already reeling from the impact of a torpedo hit under the Number One turret, was struck by a bomb that set the forward 14-inch magazine on fire, which subsequently exploded, destroying the bow section of the battleship. Hundreds of men were killed instantly—including Rear Admiral Isaac C. Kidd, commander of Battleship Division One, and the first flag-rank officer to die in World War II; as well as the ship's

In the foreground, gunners on board Avocet (AVP-4) watch for Japanese aircraft around 10:00 a.m. This shot was taken from atop a building on Ford Island, looking toward the Navy Yard. Nevada is at right, with her bow on fire as Shaw (DD-373) burns in the background. The column of smoke at left comes from the destroyers Cassin (DD-372) and Downes (DD-375), ablaze in Dry Dock Number One. (National Archives/80-G-32445)

During the second Japanese attack wave, bombers scored a direct hit on Shaw (DD-373), igniting her forward magazine. At right is the bow of Nevada. This image was shot from Ford Island, with a dredging line in the foreground. *(National Archives/80GK-16871)*

commander, Captain Franklin Van Valkenburgh. Both were awarded posthumous Medals of Honor.

Another Val dropped a bomb near the *Arizona*'s funnel, a third bomb exploded on the boat deck, and a fourth hit the Number Four turret. Four more bombs struck the superstructure amidships. Lt. Cmdr. Samuel G. Fuqua was the surviving senior officer. He directed the damage control efforts and the removal of the wounded from the ship's decks. Fuqua also gave the order to abandon ship and was one of the last to leave it. Fuqua, too, was awarded the Medal of Honor for his actions. *Arizona* settled upright on the bottom of the harbor, taking 47 officers and 1,056 men with her.

Repair ship *Vestal* (AR-4), moored alongside *Arizona*, was rocked when the battleship exploded, which blew Cmdr. Cassin Young, the ship's captain, over the side. *Vestal* then took two bomb hits while Young was swimming back to the ship. Once on board, Young moved his ship away from the burning battleship and beached it on Aiea Shoal. For his actions, Young was awarded the Medal of Honor.

Tennessee (BB-43) was moored ahead of *Arizona* and inside *West Virginia*. Oil from the *Arizona* was floating on the surface of the harbor, on fire, and threatened both *Tennessee* and *West Virginia*. Pinned between Ford Island and *West Virginia* with the sky obscured by thick black smoke, *Tennessee*'s gunners could not see to shoot at any of the attacking planes. While the crew attempted to fight the fire on

Battleship Row in the waning minutes of the Japanese attack. To the right is West Virginia, sunk, alongside Tennessee. Oklahoma has rolled over alongside Maryland. Crews on Tennessee's stern are using fire hoses to keep the burning oil away from the ship. *(National Archives/80-GK-33035)*

Signal Corps photo of battleship California's crew abandoning ship as oil fires on the harbor's surface reach the wounded ship. (U.S. Army Signal Corps)

the water, the rear of the ship caught fire. High-flying Japanese bombers scored two hits on *Tennessee*, one each on top of Turret Number Two and Turret Number Three. The bombs they dropped were converted 14- or 15-inch, armor-piercing shells. When the attack was over, *Tennessee* was afloat, but salvage crews had to dynamite the forward mooring quay to release the vessel. The battleship rejoined the fleet on December 20.

West Virginia was mortally wounded in the first torpedo pass by three torpedoes that struck below the ship's armor belt and one that impacted the belt. Two more torpedoes are thought to have entered through the first torpedoes' impact holes—when the ship was listing to port more than 20 degrees,— and gutted many parts of the battleship's aft interior. The rudder was blown off the ship and was later found on the bottom of the harbor. High-level bombers dropped two 15-inch shells on *West Virginia*, but neither shell exploded and were later found inside the ship. Fuel oil on fire from *Arizona* entered the ship and added to the conflagration. The fires became so intense that the ship was abandoned; the crew moved to *Tennessee* to help fight fires there. *West Virginia* was refloated and prepared for the voyage to Puget Sound Navy Yard, Bremerton, Washington, for overhaul. *West Virginia* returned to the fleet on July 4, 1944.

Forty minutes after the attack, *Oklahoma* graphically represented the destructive power of Naval aviation. Struck by five and possibly as many as seven torpedoes in the opening salvos of the attack, sailors attempted to isolate the flooding, but it was too late. The ship immediately listed to 30 degrees. As more bombs fell, the weight of the water inside the battleship increased. The crew began to abandon ship toward the starboard side as the ship began to turn. At 8:32 A.M., *Oklahoma*'s list to port became too great and the ship rolled over. Twenty officers and 395 men drowned in the overturned battleship. *Oklahoma* was righted and salvaged, never to return to battle.

Berthed inside *Oklahoma*, and in the same predicament as *Tennessee*, *Maryland* (BB-46) was the most fortunate ship in the harbor. Sheltered by *Oklahoma*, none of the torpedoes launched that morning struck her. Obscured by smoke from *Arizona*, *Tennessee*, and *West Virginia*, most of the Japanese pilots went after more visible prey.

California was moored at F-3, directly across from 1010 dock. Monday, December 8, the ship was slated for an inspection and the manhole covers of 6 hatches into the ship's double bottom had been removed and the nuts of an additional 12 had been loosened. When two torpedoes struck the ship during the first wave, *California* quickly flooded. Ensign Edgar M. Fain ordered counter flooding that prevented the battleship from rolling over. A high-level bomber scored a hit amidships, which started a raging fire. As *California* slowly settled lower in the water, the floating fuel oil fire approached the ship. The fires became so intense that

Nevada attempted to sortie during the attack, but was ordered to beach herself to prevent being attacked and sunk in the Pearl Harbor channel. The tug Hoga (YT-146) can be seen off the port bow helping to fight fires, while the channel marker buoy is hard against the battleship's starboard side. *(U.S. Army Signal Corps)*

at 10:15, Captain J. W. Bunkley, *California's* commanding officer, ordered the ship abandoned. When the fires moved away, the order was rescinded. Three days later, *California* settled to the bottom of the harbor, listing five and one-half degrees to port. *California* was raised on March 25, 1942, and then dry-docked and repaired at Pearl Harbor. On June 7 she sailed east under her own power to Bremerton for overhaul, rejoining the fleet on January 31, 1944.

Tanker *Neosho* (AO-23), moored at the gasoline wharf, berth F-4, had just finished unloading aviation fuel to tanks on Ford Island when the Japanese appeared overhead. As the fires spread around *California* and threatened the tanker, *Neosho* slipped her lines and backed away from Ford Island, seeking safer refuge and opening up an escape route for *Maryland*.

Tied up at berth F-8 behind *Arizona* and *Vestal, Nevada* had steam in its boilers when the attack began. A torpedo hit the ship around 8:10 A.M., as bombers in the rear of the Japanese formation sought undamaged targets. A four-to five-degree list to port was addressed by counterflooding and making the ship watertight—known as Condition Zed. Burning fuel oil from *Arizona* began to engulf the water around *Nevada* when the senior officer present, Lt. Cmdr. J. F. Thomas, ordered the ship

moved to a safer location. Steaming down the channel past *Arizona* and *Oklahoma* at approximately 9 A.M., five dive-bombers pounced on *Nevada* in an attempt to sink it, blocking the channel. One bomb hit the ship, passed through the side, and exploded in the harbor; two bombs struck the forecastle; another bomb exploded in the gasoline tank; and the fifth bomb pierced the deck near the Number One turret. Seven minutes later, more bombs rained down on the ship, one striking the port gun director platform, and another demolishing the crew's galley.

Realizing that his ship may indeed block the channel if sunk, Thomas ran the battleship into the mud off Hospital Point. Tugs arrived and nursed the ship across the channel where she sat with her stern aground and bow afloat. Four months after the attack, *Nevada* went in the Pearl Harbor Navy Yard for repair. On April 22, 1942, the ship departed for overhaul at Bremerton.

The second wave of attacks saw 15 dive-bombers attack ships in the yard and dry dock area including the battleship *Pennsylvannia* (BB-38), and the destroyers *Cassin* (DD-372) and *Downes* (DD-375). *Pennsylvannia* was struck by a bomb that penetrated the main decks, amidships, causing a fire. Two officers and 16 men were killed in the blast.

27

Oglala on her side at 1010 dock, having flooded and rolled over. A torpedo had been fired at Oglala, but passed under the minelayer, striking light cruiser Helena. Concussion from the torpedo's explosion buckled Oglala's hull plates and the crew was unable to isolate the flooding. The ship was later raised and returned to the fleet on February 28, 1944. (U.S. Navy)

Immediately the dry dock was ordered flooded to within a foot of flotation in case the Japanese burst open the dock. Forward in the dry dock off the battleship's port bow was *Cassin*, and *Downes* off the starboard side. Around 8:50 A.M., 10 to 15 bombers approached the dock area. Destroyer *Shaw* (DD-373) in floating dry dock Number Two took a bomb to its forward magazine that promptly exploded, blowing off the ship's bow. *Shaw* was a total loss. *Cassin* and *Downes* suffered a number of bomb hits that ignited magazines and stored torpedoes, and fires on one ship fed the other. *Cassin* rolled over to starboard, pinning *Downes*.

Seaplane Tender *Curtiss* (AV-4) was the victim of a Val's dive-bombing attack. One small bomb detonated on the main deck, taking the lives of 21 men and wounding another 58. Immediately exacting revenge upon the Japanese, *Curtiss'* gunners scored direct hits on a Val that was pulling out of a dive. Killing the pilot, the plane flew out of control and crashed into *Curtiss'* forward, starboard crane. The Val burned on the deck, destroying the ship's wiring, pipes, and steam lines. *Curtiss* was returned to the fleet on May 28, 1942.

Just as the high-altitude bombers completed their mission at 9:15 A.M., 27 Vals returned to strafe the harbor. Thirty minutes later, at 9:45 A.M., it was all over. Watching the Japanese aircraft fly north to rendezvous with the carriers, many stared at the utter destruction wrought during the one-hour, 45-minute attack. Looking past the loss of 2,280 military personnel killed and 1,109 wounded, only *Arizona*, *Oklahoma*, and *Utah* would not return to the fleet. One hundred and 88 hard-to-replace aircraft were also destroyed in the attack. In the face of these losses, the Japanese left much of Pearl Harbor's infrastructure intact: the fuel tank storage farms were ignored; the submarine base went unscathed; only 3 of the 30 destroyers present were knocked out of action; the Navy yard—hub of the rebuilding effort, also went undamaged; and to the eventual death of many Japanese soldiers, sailors, and airmen, none of the carriers were sunk.

Submarine Operations

On the night of December 6, five midget submarines were launched from specially modified I-boat fleet submarines 50- to 100 miles off Pearl Harbor. Tasked with attacking the fleet in the harbor during the air raid and sinking any ships that attempted to sortie after the attack, all of the midget subs' two-man crews were prepared to give their lives for the Emperor. Destroyer *Ward* made that fact a reality before the air raid began. It is believed that a Navy PBY dropped depth charges on what it thought was a midget sub, but the kill went unconfirmed. At 8:37 A.M., *Curtiss* and *Tangier* were firing on a midget sub in the channel on the northwestern side of Ford Island. *Monaghan* watched as the sub flooded its tanks to submerge as the destroyer attempted to ram it. Two depth charges were dropped and the sub was never heard from again.

Twenty minutes after the air raid had ended, the light cruiser *St. Louis* (CL-49) had sortied from the harbor. Near the

entrance, two torpedo wakes were spotted, headed for the cruiser. *St. Louis* changed course and the missiles exploded on a reef near shore. At about that moment, the midget sub, now lighter by two torpedoes, broke the surface. The cruiser's gunners opened fire, striking the sub, which sank immediately.

The last midget sub was commanded by Ensign Kazuo Sakamaki and had been launched from *I-24*. Sakamaki began to have gyro compass troubles and was unable to enter the harbor, no matter how many times he tried. Sakamaki eventually ran down the batteries' charge and was stopped dead in the water. He drifted most of December 7 and eventually ran aground near Bellows Field the following morning. Although Sakamaki was able to swim to shore, his crewman drowned, and he was captured to become America's first prisoner of war in the conflict.

such a long-distance invasion brought. Having achieved the two main goals of the mission, Adm. Nagumo began recovering aircraft at 10:30 A.M. With all but 29 aircraft aboard at 1:30 P.M., the Japanese task force retired toward Kure. En route, carriers *Hiryu* and *Soryu*, cruisers *Tone* and *Chikuma*, and destroyers *Tanakaze* and *Urakaze* split off to participate in attacks on Wake Island.

American Carriers Spared

Fortuitously, none of the Pacific Fleet's carriers were at Pearl Harbor on the morning of December 7. *Saratoga* (CV-3) was more than 2,000 miles away at San Diego preparing to return to Hawaiian waters. On November 28, *Enterprise* and Task Force 8 (CV-6, three cruisers, and nine destroyers) under the command of Adm. William "Bull" Halsey, left Pearl Harbor, transporting Marine Fighter Squadron VMF-211 to Wake Island. When the attack occurred, the carrier was less than 200 miles from port. After refueling and resupplying, *Enterprise* sortied from the harbor on December 8 to patrol against a possible second Japanese attack. On December 10, SBDs from *Enterprise's* air wing sank *I-70* north of the Hawaiian Islands.

The Pacific Fleet's last carrier, *Lexington* (CV-2) was part of Task Force 12 (CV-2, three cruisers, and five destroyers). Adm. J. H. Newton had been dispatched to Midway Island with 25 scout bombers for the Marine Corps. At the time of the attack, Task Force 12 was still 460 miles from Midway. Also out at sea during the attack was Adm. Wilson Brown and Task Force 3, centered around the cruiser *Indianapolis* (CA-35), accompanied by five destroyer mine sweepers. Task Force 3 was at Johnston Island to test a new type of landing craft. Immediately after the attack, Task Force 3 was recalled and joined Task Force 12 with Adm. Brown assuming command.

No Saving Face

In Washington, one hour after the first bombs found their targets in Pearl Harbor, Admiral Nomura and Saburo Kurusu arrived and presented Japan's reply to the American note of November 26. Secretary Hull, who knew that Pearl Harbor had been attacked before the Admiral did, was outraged and lambasted Nomura. "In all my 50 years of public service I have never seen a document that was more crowded with infamous falsehoods and distortions—infamous

The Fleet Retires

Japanese naval air power had quickly achieved air superiority over Oahu, and its aircraft dealt a crippling blow to the U.S. Pacific Fleet. The Imperial Navy decided against invading the Hawaiian Islands due to the logistical problems

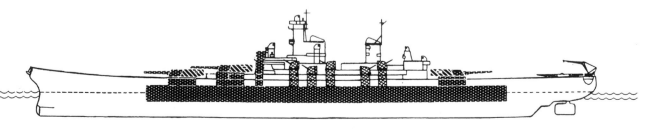

Oklahoma resting on the harbor bottom, inverted, the day after the Japanese attack. Maryland is on the right, and California's masts can be seen in the distance. A barge is tied up to Oklahoma as the rescue effort gets under way to free men trapped in the overturned hull. (National Archives/80-GK-32453)

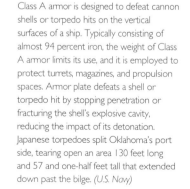

Class A armor is designed to defeat cannon shells or torpedo hits on the vertical surfaces of a ship. Typically consisting of almost 94 percent iron, the weight of Class A armor limits its use, and it is employed to protect turrets, magazines, and propulsion spaces. Armor plate defeats a shell or torpedo hit by stopping penetration or fracturing the shell's explosive cavity, reducing the impact of its detonation. Japanese torpedoes split Oklahoma's port side, tearing open an area 130 feet long and 57 and one-half feet tall that extended down past the bilge. (U.S. Navy)

On Memorial Day, May 31, 1942, sailors place wreaths on the graves of fellow servicemen killed in the line of duty at Naval Air Station Kaneohe, Oahu. These men were buried on December 8, 1941, following the Japanese attack on the air station. (National Archives/ 80-GK-13328)

falsehoods and distortions on a scale so huge that I never imagined, until today, that any government on this planet was capable of uttering them."

December 7 was the day Japan served notice to America that it was pursuing its "Greater East Asia Co-Prosperity Sphere"—first by drawing blood, then through diplomatic channels. For America, the Second World War had officially begun. The following day, President Roosevelt declared war on the Japanese.

Simultaneous Attacks

The battleships, cruisers, and destroyers were still smoldering when Japanese troops assaulted the beaches at Kota Bharu, Malaya—supported by air power based in French Indochina. Japan's 15th and 25th Armies stormed ashore at Singora and Patani, Thailand, on the Malay Peninsula. Hong Kong and Shanghai were taken by force. From French Indochina, troops crossed into Thailand, headed for Bangkok. In the Philippines, Batan Island, 125 miles north of Luzon, was captured to become an advanced air base for the coming attacks on Manila. Midway was shelled, and Guam bombarded.

On December 10, Guam fell. That same day the British battleship HMS *Prince of Wales* and battle cruiser HMS *Repulse* were sunk off Kuantan, Malaya, as the Japanese drove toward Singapore. Having secured Guam, Wake Island (an atoll consisting of Wake Island, Peale Island, and Wilkes Island) was slated for invasion next. Guam and Wake stand between Hawaii and the U.S. mainland, and Japanese bases

there would prevent any American reinforcements. Wake was "softenedup" on December 8 and 9 during two days of pre invasion bombing. At 5 A.M., on the morning of December 11, a few more than 500 U.S. Marines, a couple of 5-inch cannons, and four Grumman F4F Wildcat fighters of VMF-211 repulsed an attempted landing on the island by elements of the Imperial Navy's Fourth Fleet. This attack force included 450 assault troops supported by a light cruiser and six destroyers.

Wake's respite lasted 12 days. In the interim period, the island was bombed on a daily basis. At daylight, Japanese troops stormed ashore. Fierce hand-to-hand combat by superior numbers of Japanese troops helped establish a number of beachheads. Planes from the carriers *Hiryu* and *Soryu* supported the attack, and the American garrison surrendered at 6:30 A.M.

On December 16 the Japanese navy landed troops on Borneo at Miri and Seira to capture the oil fields and refineries there. By the end of the month, troops were ashore at Legaspi, Davao, Lingayen, Lamon Bay, and Jolo, as the Japanese moved to take control of the Philippines.

The Pacific was beginning to look like a Japanese lake. To make matters worse, Germany and Italy—partners in the Tripartite Pact, declared war on the United States on December 11. America was now fighting a war on two fronts. The world was truly in flames.

Merchant Ships Under Siege

Moments after the attack on Pearl Harbor, a freighter carrying lumber on charter to the U.S. Army was attacked by gunfire 1,290 miles southeast of San Francisco at 34° N, 145° W—halfway to Honolulu. The 2,140-ton S.S. *Cynthia Olson*, built in 1919 and owned by Oliver J. Olson and Co. of San Francisco, was shelled and subsequently sunk by the Imperial Japanese Navy (IJN) submarine *I-26*. None of *Cynthia Olson*'s 31 crew members were rescued. *I-26*'s commander, Minoru Yokota, would later achieve success by torpedoing and heavily damaging the carrier *Saratoga* during the naval battle of the Eastern Solomons on August 31, 1942.

In the 11 days since the start of the war, five Japanese "I-boats" would claim six merchant vessels in Hawaiian waters. *I-172*, under Commander Togami, would sink two vessels—the 632-ton schooner *Royal T. Frank* on December 7, and the 5,113-ton freighter *Prusa* on December 19. Fourteen of *Prusa*'s crew were rescued on December 27 by the Coast Guard Cutter *Tiger*. Eleven other survivors sailed their lifeboat 2,700 miles until rescued by a Fijian vessel. *I-10* sank the 4,473-ton freighter *Donerail* 300 miles south of the islands, and on December 14 the Norwegian ship *Hoegh Merchant* was sunk by *I-4*, Commander Nakagawa, within sight of Oahu. *Hoegh Merchant*'s entire crew of 35 plus five passengers survived.

The Matson Navigation Company—whose liners *Lurline*, *Matsonia*, *Mariposa*, and *Monterey* would play a vital role transporting troops during the war—suffered heavy losses during the first two weeks of fighting. Eventually, the steamship company would lose 15 freighters from its fleet during World War II, all but one to enemy action. Between December 10 and 17, three of the company's freighters were sent to the bottom. The *Mauna Ala*, en route to Honolulu when the Japanese struck, was recalled to Portland, Oregon. During the evening of December 10, the ship was attempting to locate the mouth of the Columbia River. The West Coast was blackedout, no navigation lights were available to aid the ship, and *Mauna Ala* grounded on Clatsop Spit, 700 feet from the shore. All 35 crew members were rescued by the Coast Guard motor lifeboat *Triumph*. Soon after, the waves broke the ship's back—she was a total loss.

Matson's 5,645-ton steam freighter S.S. *Lahaina* was carrying 745 tons of molasses and 300 tons of scrap iron from Ahukini, Kauai, to San Francisco when the war broke out. Ordered by the U.S. Navy to sail to the nearest port, Captain Hans O. Matthiesen turned the freighter around for Kauai. Having nearly reached Kauai, Matthiesen was ordered to return to the West Coast. Fearing the worst, Captain Matthiesen ordered the lifeboats stocked and ship's upper surfaces to be painted a dull gray. While work was progressing on the afternoon of December 11, *I-9* surfaced and fired a warning shot across *Lahaina*'s bow to stop the ship. Another shot destroyed the port lifeboat. Under fire and unable to defend themselves, 34 of the crew boarded the only lifeboat left, on the ship's starboard side—designed to carry 17 passengers—and cast off from the ship. After eight shells had struck the ship and it began to sink by the stern, *I-9* sailed away. *Lahaina* continued to burn through the night, and when daylight came the crew saw that the

ship's ladder and engineer's house were still intact. Returning to the ship, Matthiesen and a couple of crewmen retrieved blankets, a few dozen eggs, biscuits, butter, and 10 gallons of water. Around 10 A.M., *Lahaina* rolled over and slid beneath the waves. Matthiesen began steering for Maui, estimated to be more than 700 miles to the southwest. After nine days at sea and four deaths along the way, the remaining 30 crew members came ashore at Sprecklesville Beach, Kahului, Maui.

On December 17 at 6:40 P.M., while *Lahaina*'s castaways were sailing toward Maui, the Matson Line's S.S. *Manini* was struck by a torpedo from Commander Noriki Inoue's *I-175* approximately 180 miles south of Hawaii at 17°45' N, 157°03' E. *Manini* went under in less than seven minutes. The crew got off in two lifeboats that quickly became separated in the heavy seas. After drifting for nine days, and 10 hours, the first lifeboat was recovered by the U.S. destroyer *Allen (DD-66)*, 25 miles south of Kauai. The second lifeboat was recovered on December 28 by the destroyer *Patterson (DD-392)*.

Strategic Decisions: Allies Meet at the Arcadia Conference

Britain had been at war with the Axis powers for more than two years when the United States was drawn into the conflict by Japan. On December 11, 1941, both Germany and Italy declared war on the United States. Now faced with war on two fronts, the United States called a meeting with its strongest ally. To determine the prosecution of the war, President Roosevelt and American military officers met with Prime Minister Winston Churchill and the British Chiefs of Staff Committee in Washington, D.C., from December 21, 1941, through January 14, 1942. The three-and-a-half-week conference, code-named ARCADIA, declared a "Germany first" strategy, while a defensive posture would be adopted in the war against Japan.

On December 20, 1941, the Socony-Vacuum Company's S.S. Emidio, a 429-foot-long, 6,912-ton tanker, was en route from Seattle to San Francisco. Sailing off Blunt's Reef—nine miles north of Mendocino, the tanker was shelled by Cmdr. Kozo Nishino's I-17. After the seventh shell struck, Emidio's captain ordered all hands to abandon ship. Five of the ship's 36-man crew perished. Japanese subs were now patrolling off the U.S. West Coast. *(Los Angeles Maritime Museum Photo Archives)*

A visible sign of war on the West Coast beached itself on December 24, 1941. The forward half of torpedoed General Petroleum tanker Emidio drifted 60 miles in California's coastal waters until grounding on Steamboat Rock, outside the entrance to Crescent City Harbor. Emidio's stranded hull, down by the stern, was a shocking sight to the American public already reeling from the Japanese attack on Pearl Harbor. *(San Francisco Maritime National Historic Park/Richard Childs Photographic Collection)*

In the fight against Germany, the Army Air Forces would team up with the British Royal Air Force to bomb the Nazis on the European continent around the clock. German Field Marshall Erwin Rommel's Afrika Korps would be driven from Africa when the U.S. Army invaded the continent later in 1942, and Europe would see Allied troops one year later.

For the Pacific, the decision was made to sacrifice the Philippines, maintain open air and sea lanes to Australia, and make a stand at the Malay Barrier (Burma and the Malay Peninsula). The Americans would battle the Japanese alone until the British and its Allies were relieved of the German threat.

From the Arcadia conference came the American "Joint Chiefs of Staff," the counterpart of the British Chiefs of Staff Committee. The Joint Chiefs of Staff consistedof: President Roosevelt's military advisor, Adm. William D. Leahy, who served as the Chief of Staff to the Commander in Chief of the Army and Navy; Gen. George C. Marshall, who became Chief of Staff of the Army; Adm. Ernest J. King—Chief of Naval Operations and Commander in Chief of the U.S. Fleet; and Gen. Henry H. "Hap" Arnold, who served as Deputy Army Chief of Staff for Air as well as Chief of the Army Air Corps.

Prosecution of the war and the implementation of the president's strategic directives would be handled by the Joint Chiefs.

Attacks On the West Coast

While the Japanese fleet sailed east for safer waters after its surprise attack on Pearl Harbor, 10 long-range I-boats took up patrol stations off the U.S. West Coast. Assigned to locate and sink the absent American carriers or any warships en route to reinforce Pearl Harbor, the I-boat captains were not about to pass up any target that presented itself. *I-23,* commanded by Genichi Shibata, was first to attack on December 20, 1941. Shibata brought the war to the West Coast at 2:15 P.M. (PWT – Pacific War Time), when he attacked Richfield Oil Company's 6,771-ton tanker *Agwiworld* sailing less than 20 miles off the coast near Cypress Point—on the southern side of Monterey Bay, California. *I-23's* first shell from its deck gun screamed through the ship's rigging without doing damage. Having only two small pistols to defend itself, *Agwiworld's* captain, Frederick B. Goncalves, turned the tanker and attempted to ram *I-23.* As the two ships attempted to outmaneuver each other, the sub continued to fire its deck gun. Seven shots chased *Agwiworld* as she plowed across Monterey Bay to the safety of Santa Cruz harbor, arriving unharmed.

While *Agwiworld* was under fire, another tanker, 200 miles to the north, was falling victim to a Japanese sub's cannon fire. The Socony-Vacuum Company's *Emidio,* a 429-foot-long, 6,912-ton tanker, was being stalked by Commander Kozo Nishino's *I-17.* Sailing off Blunt's Reef—nine miles north of Mendocino, en route from Seattle to San Francisco—*Emidio's* crew sighted *I-17* one-quarter mile off the stern. They quickly radioed an S.O.S. distress call.

Captain C. A. Farrow recounted *I-17*'s pursuit in a *San Francisco Chronicle* report on December 23, 1941: "As soon as we sighted the submarine, we put on full speed and dumped ballast, but we had no chance to escape and we were rapidly overtaken. The submarine was making about 20 knots. I tried to get behind her, but the sub reversed her course and kept after us." *I-17* began shelling *Emidio*, and after the seventh shell struck, Captain Farrow ordered all hands to abandon ship.

"It may have been 10 or 15 minutes after our S.O.S. that two big U.S. bombing planes came roaring overhead from the coast. To us in the lifeboats that was a mighty welcome sight.

"The sub submerged. One of the two planes, circling where the sub had gone down, dropped a depth charge. But later, as the planes were still circling, the periscope of the sub came slowly to the surface 200 yards away and, while still partially submerged, fired a torpedo. We saw the torpedoe's trail as it headed for the tanker. There was a loud explosion as it struck. Back came the planes as the sub sank out of sight again. One of the planes dropped another depth charge. We didn't see her again. We rowed 14 hours through the rain and night. We could finally see the Blunt's Reef lightship and we made for that." *Emidio*'s 31 survivors were rescued from the lightship by the Coast Guard Cutter *Shawnee* and returned to the mainland on December 21.

Two of *Emidio*'s crew of 36 died during the initial attack, 5 were wounded, and 3 subsequently drowned while awaiting rescue. Commander Nishino believed his torpedo had delivered the *coup de grace*, and when the bombers arrived he wasn't about to wait around to confirm the sinking. Down by the stern and its decks awash, *Emidio* drifted north with the tide for 60 miles, before eventually stranding on Steamboat Rock near the entrance to the harbor at Crescent City.

Forty-eight hours later, on December 22, Commander Shogo Narahara in *I-19* pursued the 10,763-ton Standard Oil tanker S.S. *H.M. Storey*. *I-19* fired three torpedoes at the tanker near Point Arguello (275 miles south of San Francisco and 45 miles north of Santa Barbara). *H.M. Storey* began laying a smoke screen and zigzagging to avoid the torpedoes. The attack was seen by witnesses on shore, who reported that shortly after *I-19* submerged, a Navy patrol bomber arrived to drop depth charges. *H.M. Storey* continued her voyage to San Francisco unharmed.

In the early-morning hours of December 23, the 440-foot, 8,272-ton Union Oil tanker S.S. *Montebello,* en route from Avila, California, to Vancouver, Canada, with 12,000 tons of gasoline, was struck by a torpedo under the bridge on the port side at 5:45 A.M., near central California's Piedras Blancas Lighthouse (35°30' N, 121°51' W). The ship went dead in the water and, as the crew abandoned ship, *I-21*'s commander, Hiroji Matsumura, ordered the *Montebello* shelled. Forty-five minutes later, *Montebello* slid beneath the Pacific. Olaf Eckstrom, *Montebello*'s captain, described the scene after the torpedo struck in the December 24 *San Francisco Chronicle,* "While the crewmen were trying to free the lifeboats, the submarine fired eight or ten shells at us. We got four boats away. Thirty of the men went in the first three and I went with the others in the fourth boat. I went over the side about 6 A.M., and at 6:30 I saw the ship go down. She stood up on her bow and slid under." *I-21* machine-gunned the lifeboats, but somehow none of the crew were injured.

A few hours later in the same vicinity, *I-21* shadowed and attacked the 994-ton tanker *Idaho*, but the vessel escaped without damage.

Farther up the California coast near Cape Mendocino, *I-17* shelled the 7,033-ton Richfield Oil Company tanker S.S. *Larry Doheny*. The tanker escaped without damage. December 23 was the *Larry Doheny*'s lucky day, for 10 months later the tanker would meet up with *I-25* on October 5, 1942, and the results would be far different. Sailing from

Another victim of the Japanese I-boats in American coastal waters was the 440-foot, 8,272-ton Union Oil tanker S.S. Montebello, en route from Avila, California, to Vancouver, Canada, on December 23, with 12,000 tons of gasoline. Near Central California's Piedras Blancas Lighthouse Montebello was struck by a torpedo from I-21. The tanker was shelled and finally sunk. Although the Japanese machine-gunned the life boats, all of the tanker's crew were rescued unharmed. *(Los Angeles Maritime Museum Photo Archives)*

WAR UPON THE AXIS IS DECLARED

To the Congress of the United States:

Yesterday, December 7, 1941—a date which will live in infamy—the United States of America was suddenly and deliberately attacked by naval and air forces of the Empire of Japan.

The United States was at peace with that Nation and, at the solicitation of Japan, was still in conversation with its Government and its Emperor looking toward the maintenance of peace in the Pacific. Indeed, one hour after Japanese air squadrons had commenced bombing in Oahu, the Japanese Ambassador to the United States and his colleague delivered to the Secretary of State a formal reply to a recent American message. While this reply stated that it seemed useless to continue the existing diplomatic negotiations, it contained no threat or hint of war or armed attack.

It will be recorded that the distance of Hawaii from Japan makes it obvious that the attack was deliberately planned many days or even weeks ago. During the intervening time the Japanese Government had deliberately sought to deceive the United States by false statements and expressions of hope for continued peace.

The attack yesterday on the Hawaiian islands has caused severe damage to American naval and military forces. Very many American lives have been lost. In addition American ships have been reported torpedoed on the high seas between San Francisco and Honolulu.

> Yesterday the Japanese Government also launched an attack against Malaya.
> Last night Japanese forces attacked Hong Kong.
> Last night Japanese forces attacked Guam.
> Last night Japanese forces attacked the Philippine Islands.
> Last night the Japanese attacked Wake Island.
> Last night the Japanese attacked Midway Island.

Japan has, therefore, undertaken a surprise offensive extending throughout the Pacific area. The facts of yesterday speak for themselves. The people of the United States have already formed their opinions and well understand the implications to the very life and safety of our Nation.

As Commander in Chief of the Army and Navy I have directed that all measures be taken for our defense.

Always will we remember the character of the onslaught against us.
No matter how long it may take us to overcome this premeditated invasion, the American people in their righteous might will win through to absolute victory.

I believe I interpret the will of the Congress and of the people when I assert that we will not only defend ourselves to the uttermost but will make very certain that this form of treachery shall never endanger us again.

Hostilities exist. There is no blinking at the fact that our people, our territory, and our interests are in grave danger.

With confidence in our armed forces—with the unbounded determination of our people—we will gain the inevitable triumph—so help us God.

I ask that the Congress declare that since the unprovoked and dastardly attack by Japan on Sunday, December seventh, a state of war has existed between the United States and the Japanese Empire.

—Franklin D. Roosevelt
The White House, December 8, 1941

Long Beach, California, to Portland, Oregon, carrying 66,000 barrels of fuel oil, *I-25* sent a torpedo into *Larry Doheny*'s port side under the number two tank at 10:07 P.M. (Pacific War Time). Two of the ship's crew and four of the Armed Guard complement perished in the attack. Thirty-six survivors were rescued by the seaplane tender *Coos Bay* (APV-25). *Larry Doheny* slid beneath the waves the following morning.

Christmas Eve saw Commander Shogo Narahara's *I-19* torpedo the 409-foot-long, 5,696-ton freighter S.S. *Absaroka* near San Pedro, California. Dozens witnessed the attack—some claiming that the sub used a "false fishing boat superstructure" to sneak close to the coast. Of the two torpedoes fired, one struck *Absaroka* near the stern. Immediately the ship began taking on water, listing to the stern. The crew abandoned ship, but reboarded when salvage tugs arrived. Buoyed by its cargo of lumber, the steamer was towed into San Pedro where it was repaired. One sailor died in the attack. That same day, near Monterey Bay, the 1,289-ton schooner *Dorothy Philips* was attacked by gunfire from *I-23*. Although taking on water, *Dorothy Philips* was able to reach port safely.

Shortly before Christmas, all of the Japanese submarines patrolling the West Coast were ordered back to Kwajalein for

supplies. En route to refuel, on December 28, *I-25* shelled the tanker *Connecticut* at the mouth of the Columbia River, near the border between Washington and Oregon, but the ship escaped.

As the I-boats sailed westward, anti-Japanese hysteria gripped the West Coast. Field artillery pieces were positioned near the beaches, and Coast Guard patrols were increased, while pursuit and bomber aircraft flew over coastal areas during daylight hours. A *New York Times* wire story reported that "Jap Subs May Be Refueling In Mexico." Guatemala and Brazil were rumored to be "honeycombed with Axis airbases."

While the Japanese submarines were refueling in the Central Pacific, things were quiet on the West Coast. New Year's Eve came and went, and so did the month of January 1942.

Cannon Shells Rain Down on the Mainland

By mid-February, numerous sightings of submarines were reported off the coast of Southern California. These sightings, many near Goleta, just north of Santa Barbara, California, were credible—some seen by U.S. Navy officers. After being reported to Naval Headquarters at San Diego, they were dismissed as whale sightings. Complacent that the threat of Japanese attacks had diminished, the Army

transferred its two cannons from Goleta to Griffith Park, 120 miles inland near Los Angeles. On February 22, the Coast Guard discontinued its patrols of the Santa Barbara Channel. The theory was, that upon an alert, the cannons could be moved back into place within a matter of hours.

Washington's Birthday, 1942, was to be celebrated on February 23, with President Franklin D. Roosevelt slated to address the nation by radio at 7 P.M. (PWT). Shortly after Roosevelt began to speak, submarine *1-17* surfaced off the coast north of Goleta, at Ellwood. The deck gun of *1-17* began to fire at the oil derricks on the hill behind the beach at 7:07. Firing at a leisurely pace, the sub lobbed 15 rounds onto the beach over a 30-minute period. One direct hit was scored on an oil well owned by the Bankline Oil Co., causing minor damage to the pumping unit and the derrick itself.

Concerned citizens jammed phone lines inquiring about the shelling. Local authorities dismissed it as Army coastal defense target practice. One aircraft spotter was able to get a call through to headquarters at Los Angeles, but fighter and bomber aircraft that were expected to counter attack the submarine never came. Soldiers on the beach were unable to fire back at *I-17* because their cannons were sitting idle at Griffith Park.

The February 23, 1942, attack on Ellwood, California, was the first time a foreign power had attacked, albeit ineffectively, the continental United States since the War of 1812. Sixty days after the attack on Pearl Harbor, America's wheels of mobilization were just beginning to turn. The question on the public's mind was, "When are we going to strike back?"

Upon their triumphant return to Japan after patrolling in American waters, I-17's officers were decorated for their actions. From left, Torpedo Officer Lt. Nubukiyo Nambu, Cmdr. Kozo Nishino, and an unidentified officer, stand on I-17's foredeck after returning to Japan. In addition to shelling the American mainland, I-17 sunk the 6,912-ton S.S. Emidio and damaged the S.S. Larry Doheny and S.S. William H. Berg. *(Harvey Beigel Collection)*

I-17, similar in configuration to I-15, surfaced off the California coast on February 23, 1942, and began shelling the oil derricks at Elwood. For 30 minutes the sub lobbed shells at the oil field, scoring a direct hit on a derrick owned by the Bankline Oil Co. I-17's bombardment was the first attack on the continental United States since the War of 1812. *(Harvey Beigel Collection)*

1942: REBUILD, REARM, COUNTERATTACK

The Imperial Japanese Army and Navy spent December 1941 reinforcing its newly acquired territories while a stunned American military surveyed its precarious position in the Pacific. To protect the vital shipping lanes between the U.S. West Coast, Hawaii, and Australia from harassment by the Japanese, the U.S. Navy dispatched the Second Marine Brigade to secure Pago Pago, American Samoa. Sailing from San Diego on January 6, 1942, aboard the Matson Liners *Lurline*, *Monterey*, and *Matsonia*—in company with attack cargo ship *Jupiter* (AK-43), and the ammunition-hauling *Lassen* (AE-3)— the convoy was escorted across the Pacific by Adm. Frank J. Fletcher's Task Force (TF) 17 with aircraft carrier *Yorktown* (CV-5),transferred from the Atlantic Fleet on December 16.

January 11 was not a good day for U.S. forces. During the Marines' trans-Pacific voyage, a Japanese submarine shelled Pago Pago, adding to the fears that the island was ripe for an invasion. Later that same day, the Japanese declared war on the Netherlands and landed troops at Tarakan, Borneo. The day's *coup de grace* was delivered by *I-6* approximately 500 miles southwest of Oahu when one of the sub's torpedoes struck *Saratoga* (CV-3), killing six sailors and flooding three fire rooms. The carrier, en route to join *Enterprise* near Pago Pago, was able to limp back to Oahu for temporary repairs. Subsequently, *Saratoga* sailed to Bremerton for further repairs and updating of the carrier's antiaircraft armament, leaving only three carriers in the Pacific Fleet to defend against Japanese advances. *Saratoga* returned to the Pacific six months later, on June 6, just days after the Battle of Midway.

Near Samoa, TF-6, built around Adm. Halsey's *Enterprise*, joined Adm. Fletcher and *Yorktown*. Both task forces were supporting the Marines' landing in Samoa when, on January 23, the Japanese landed at Rabaul on New Britain Island in the Bismarck Archipelago. Rapidly overwhelming the Australian troops defending the harbor area, the Japanese settled in for a long stay. Naval and air forces from Rabaul used the harbor to attack shipping traveling between the United States and Australia, and served as a jumping-off point for attacks on New Guinea and the Solomon Islands.

Having safely delivered the Marines to Samoa, TF-6 and -17 sailed for a joint attack of the Marshall Islands on February 1. *Enterprise* focused its strength on the seaplane bases at Wotje, Maloelap, and Kwajalein, while *Yorktown* struck Jaluit, and in the Gilbert Islands, Mili, and Makin. Under the light of a full moon, *Enterprise*'s air group began launching at 4:43 A.M. Arriving over the north end of Kwajalein Atoll at sunrise, Roi airfield was covered with low-lying clouds and *Enterprise*'s SBD dive-bombers circled while the weather improved. Droning overhead, the SBDs alerted Roi's defenders to their presence, and when they did attack, they were met with fierce resistance. Four of the dive-bombers were shot down as they attacked, including Lt. Cmdr. H. L. Hopping, the squadron's commander.

Forty-four miles to the south, SBDs and Douglas TBD torpedo bombers mauled the harbor at Kwajalein Island, sinking *Bordeaux Maru*, a 6,500-ton cargo ship as well as a sub chaser. Ships damaged in the attack include *Tokiwa*, a 9,240-ton minelayer, *I-23* and sub tender *Yasukuni Maru*, oiler *Toa Maru*, tanker *Hoyo Maru*, army transport *Shinhei Maru*, as well as the light cruiser *Katori*. SBDs from *Yorktown* attacked the *Nagata Maru* at Makin and heavily damaged cargo ship *Kanto Maru* at Jaluit.

As aircraft from the task force delivered its deadly cargo, ships from the task force sank the gunboat *Toyotsu Maru* as well as auxiliary submarine chaser *No. 10 Shonan Maru*. American cruisers and destroyers shelled *Wotje* and *Maloelap*, inflicting light damage. TF-11 around *Lexington* covered the attacking ship's withdrawal. The toll on U.S. ships was relatively light: *Enterprise* was lightly damaged by a "Betty" bomber that grazed the port side of the ship while attempting to crash into the carrier; cruiser *Chester* (CA-27) was struck by a bomb that exploded on her main deck, killing eight and wounding another 38.

Although the damage to the Japanese was relatively light, to the American people stateside, Adm. Halsey emerged as the hero—one so desperately needed for the demoralized folks back home.

Submarines built at Manitowoc Shipyards, Manitowoc, Wisconsin, were side-launched due to space limitations within the channel fronting the shipyard. Peto (SS-265) began its Navy career with a big splash on April 30, 1942, into the Manitowoc River. Peto was the first Manitowoc-built sub, and went on to sink seven Japanese ships for 29,139 tons during World War II. The Navy held the sub in its inventory until August 1, 1960, when the boat was stricken. Peto was subsequently sold for $35,686 to a Dallas, Texas, firm that scraped the warrior. *(Harry F. Burns/Wisconsin Maritime Museum, 68-1-25)*

S.S. Lurline of the Matson Navigation Line displaced 26,141 tons and, in peacetime, catered to the needs of 459 first-class and 242 cabin-class passengers. Operated by the U.S. Maritime Commission and crewed by Matson employees during the war, the ship was fitted to carry 3,851 troops. Lurline was escorted in coastal waters and then sent across the Pacific unescorted due to the liner's 22-knot cruising speed—too fast for any submarine except one directly in its path. *(Matson Navigation)*

Bora Bora in the Society Islands was selected as a naval fuel station for ships transferred from the Atlantic en route to Australia, New Zealand, and Samoa. Teauanvi Harbor, with the town of Vaitape in the left center, became a bustling port. The light cruiser is believed to be Trenton (CL-11) with destroyer Sampson (DD-394) riding at anchor. *(National Archives/80GK-1117)*

Adm. Chester W. Nimitz assumed command of the Pacific Fleet on December 31, 1941, on board the submarine Grayling (SS-209) at Pearl Harbor. Adm. Husband E. Kimmel was relieved by Adm. William S. Pye on December 17, 10 days after the Pearl Harbor attack. Pye served temporarily until Nimitz assumed command. Nimitz served as commander of the Pacific Fleet until the end of the war. *(National Archives/80GK-5973)*

Roll of the Kettledrums

The realities of war were driven home to those Americans living on the East Coast in January 1942. Two weeks after the attack on Pearl Harbor, the German *Kriegsmarine* granted Adm. Karl Donitz, commander of U-boats (*Befehlshaber der Unterseeboote*—BdU), permission to launch strikes against shipping in U.S. waters. Known as Operation *Paukenschlag* (Roll of the Kettledrums), six Type IX U-boats were dispatched—*U-502* departed December 18, and aborted the mission on December 22; *U-125* sailed on December 18; *U-123* departed on December 23; *U-66* on December 25; plus *U-109* and *U-130* , which both sailed on December 27 from the U-boat base at Lorient, France, on the Bay of Biscay.

Paukenschlag was the opening salvo in Hitler's attempt to destroy war materiel from America destined for Britain and the European front. Arriving off the coast between Newfoundland and Cape Hatteras, North Carolina, in the early days of January, the five U-boats took up station and, following orders, waited through many tempting targets until their prey had arrived. Tasked with sinking ships over 10,000 tons, *U-123*'s Kapitänleutnant Reinhard Hardegen struck first, sinking the 9,076 –gross-registered-ton (grt) steam freighter *Cyclops*, 300 miles east of Cape Cod, in a torpedo attack.

▲ Saratoga (CV-3) at NAS Ford Island, Pearl Harbor, in the early days of 1942. The carrier was torpedoed by submarine I-6 approximately 500 miles southwest of Oahu on January 11. Saratoga limped back to Pearl Harbor and, after repairs, sailed to Bremerton, Washington, to have its antiaircraft armament updated. The carrier returned to the Pacific fleet on June 6, just a few days after the Battle of Midway. *(National Archives/80GK-456)*

In the early months of 1942, a mariner's biggest fear was not the cape's unpredictable seas, but the German submarines sailing its waters. Hardegen (*U-123*), Richard Zapp (*U-66*), and Ernst Kals (*U-130*), commanding the long-range Type IX boats, were able to exploit the Cape Hatteras bottleneck and attack the large number of ships passing through the area. The majority were oil-laden tankers traveling from the Gulf ports of Galveston and New Orleans, and from the Caribbean oil depots up the East Coast. On January 19, Zapp fired torpedoes at, and sank, the passenger liner *Lady Hawkins*. Positioning the Canadian ship between the nighttime shore and *U-66*'s bow, Zapp fired two torpedoes at the silhouetted liner. Unable to send a distress signal, only three lifeboats were launched before the ship went under. It took five days before the surviving 100 passengers and crew, out of 300 on board, were rescued. Zapp sank another four ships, for 33,456 gross tons, before returning east for Lorient.

In addition to the five Type IX boats in U.S. waters, an additional 10 shorter-range Type VII submarines sortied from Brest, France (*U-84, U-86, U-203*); Kiel, Germany (*U-87, U-135, U-333, U-701, U-754*); and St. Nazaire, France (*U-552*), searching for targets in the Western Atlantic and waters off Newfoundland.

To drive home their presence, unmolested by the U.S. Navy and Coast Guard, the German submarines patrolled within sight of American shores. For ships sailing from the Gulf of Mexico and up the East Coast to ports in Massachusetts, New Jersey, and New York, a bottleneck was formed by Cape Hatteras, protruding out into the Atlantic. The waters off the cape can be treacherous because the warm, northerly Gulf Stream current collides with water flowing south from the colder Arctic regions, causing freak storms, huge waves, and shifting shoals.

Hardegen continued to maul shipping in the Cape Hatteras area as well. Within hours of the *Lady Hawkins*, sinking, *U-123* torpedoed and sank two ships and damaged a third. The 5,269-grt. *City of Atlanta* was *U-123*'s first victim in the Hatteras area. One torpedo struck amidships, and within 10 minutes the steamer had capsized. Of the 46 on board, only an officer and two seamen survived. The next unfortunate ship was the 3,779-grt. steamer *Ciltvaira*. A torpedo struck the small ship, and the crew abandoned the burning vessel. Certain his prey was going down, Hardegen turned his attentions to *Malay*, an 8,206-grt. tanker. Attacking with his deck gun, *U-123*'s gunners fired 10 rounds—half hitting the tanker, before the sub's port diesel broke down. *Malay* quickly outdistanced the sub while fighting fires and received assistance from the freighter *Scania*.

◄ Lt. Edward H. "Butch" O'Hare of Fighter Squadron Three (VF-3, on board Lexington) shot down five Mitsubishi G4M "Betty" bombers and damaged a sixth during an aborted raid on Rabaul, New Britain, February 16, 1942. O'Hare was awarded the Medal of Honor for his actions, and Chicago's O'Hare Airport is named in the aviator's honor. *(National Archives/80GK-13380)*

Once the fires were under control, *Malay* turned toward Hampton Roads, Virginia. Pursuing the wounded *Malay* on one engine, *U-123* was able to send a torpedo into a ballasted compartment on the starboard side. *U-123* was out of torpedoes, and turned for home. Suffering severe damage, *Malay* was able to make Hampton Roads, where she was repaired.

U-130 was the last to depart American waters on February 25. The German subs that sailed for the Western Atlantic and U.S. waters in January sank 71 ships for 400,966 gross tons; the February boats destroyed 57 ships for 344,494 gross tons—a total of 169 ships. Nearly one million tons of shipping were lost in the first quarter of 1942. As each ship went to the bottom, it took with it valuable cargoes of oil or other war material, and highly trained seamen.

Adm. Donitz continued to send two dozen or more U-boats to the profitable Western Atlantic/U.S. East Coast area for months, each group as successful as the last. Commander of the Eastern Sea Frontier Adm. Adolphus Andrews organized "bucket brigade" convoys, where four or five merchant vessels were escorted by one or two small (less than 100 feet in length) armed ships. Eventually, Andrews was able to get a commitment of resources from Fleet Adm. Ernest J. King, and a coastal convoy system was finally instituted, which eventually reduced the number of ships sunk within sight of American shores.

During the nine-month period from December 1941 through August 1942, BdU sent 184 U-boats to waters off the U.S. East Coast, Gulf of Mexico, Caribbean, and Canada, where the *Unterseebootes* sank 609 ships of 3,122,456 grt. The U-boat menace would never be fully controlled, nor would they ever sink as many ships in such a concentrated area over such a short time period. American and Allied antisubmarine warfare techniques and technologies—such as airborne surface search radar— improved faster and killed U-boats quicker than the Germans could counter such measures and build new boats to replace losses. In late 1943, the Allies turned the tide against the U-boats, but the battle had a long, costly course to sail, and German submarines in American waters were a constant threat until the war's end.

Indonesia and the Philippines Fall

Japan's southward expansion continued in the opening months of 1942. The Imperial Army was consolidating its positions in Malaya, Borneo, and Sumatra. On the night of January 23–24, the Japanese landed at oil-rich Balikpapan, Borneo. American destroyers sank five transports during the landing, but the action was not enough to slow the numerically superior enemy.

To interdict Allied reinforcements and supplies moving south of Java, the Japanese invaded Bali and captured the airfield on February 19. Bali's strategic location gave the Japanese air superiority over Lombok Strait—a bottleneck through which all north-south shipping traffic passing from the Indian Ocean to the Java Sea must pass. Twenty-four hours later, Japanese aircraft carriers *Akagi, Kaga, Hiryu,* and *Soryu* launched 189 aircraft for a raid against the coastal town of Darwin, Australia. The port and surrounding airfields received heavy damage from bombing and strafing attacks. In addition, five ships were damaged, and the destroyer *Peary* (DD-226) was sunk.

Rear Admiral Karel Doorman of the Royal Netherlands Navy, commander of the ABDA (American, British, Dutch, and Australian) forces, launched a counter attack against the retiring Bali invasion force. In what became known as the Battle of Badoeng Strait, Doorman's three cruisers and six destroyers sortied from Surabaya to engage Japanese ships retiring from Bali. Expending hundreds of shells and dozens of torpedoes, Doorman's force had little impact upon the Japanese, but heavily damaged destroyers *Michisio* and *Ushio*. The Dutch destroyer *Piet Hien* was sunk and Dutch cruisers *Java* and *Tromp* were heavily damaged by Japanese naval gun fire. Retiring to Surabaya, the ABDA ships began to repair the damage.

The following morning, February 20, the Japanese used paratroopers to secure the airfield at Koepang, Timor. This operation was only the second time the Japanese used paratroopers in battle (paratroopers were previously used to capture Palembang, Sumatra, on February 14, 1942). Koepang, only 500 miles from the airfields and port facilities at Darwin, was now within fighter range of the Japanese.

American TF11, under Adm. Brown with carrier *Lexington* serving as flagship, sortied to attack Rabaul, New Britain, on February 16. One day's sailing from the planned attack point, the task force was spotted by enemy flying boats. *Lexington's* position was radioed to Rabaul, and the Japanese dispatched land-based bombers to sink the carrier. Two waves of nine, twin-engine, Mitsubishi G4M Betty bombers arrived over the fleet at around 5 P.M., and concentrated their attacks on *Lexington*. Lt. Edward H. "Butch" O'Hare of Fighter Squadron Three (VF-3), flying Grumman F3F-3 Bureau No. 4031, destroyed five of the Bettys, heavily damaged a sixth, and scattered the remainder of the flight. (Upon O'Hare's return stateside, he was awarded the Medal of Honor by President Roosevelt on April 21.) Twelve other Bettys were shot down by *Lexington's* combat air patrol or ship's antiaircraft fire. The defenders alerted, Adm. Brown elected to cancel the raid and retired to the south.

Japan's hold on Indonesia was completed with the fall of Java. But before the Japanese could consider the matter closed, they had to deal with the remaining ABDA forces in the area. On February 22, the U.S. Navy dispatched the aircraft depot ship/tender *Langley* (AV-3—America's first aircraft carrier) from Freemantle, Australia, to Tjilatjap, Java, with a load of 32 Curtiss P-40 fighters to be delivered to the island's defenders. In the early-morning hours of February 27,

On April 18, 1942, airmen of the U.S. Army Air Forces led by Lt. Col. James H. "Jimmy" Doolittle took the war to the heart of the Japanese Empire with a surprise raid on military targets at Tokyo, Yokohama, Yokosuka, Nagoya, and Kobe. The attack was the result of close Army Air Force and U.S. Navy cooperation where 16 B-25 medium bombers were embarked aboard the carrier Hornet (CV-8) and transported within striking distance of the Japanese coastline. One of the task force's escorting destroyers patrols near the horizon. (U.S. Air Force via McClellan Aviation Museum)

Langley was joined by destroyers *Edsall* (DD-219) and *Whipple* (DD-217) for the last leg of the journey to Tjilatjap. Approximately 75 miles short of its destination, nine Japanese bombers attacked *Langley* in threes—the first two groups missing the target. The third wave scored five direct hits on *Langley*, causing the aircraft on deck to catch fire and the ship to lose its steering. The tender immediately took on a 10-degree list to port. Sixteen men died in the Japanese attack. Water began flooding compartment after compartment and at 1:32 P.M., unable to make headway, the order to abandon ship was given. Without air cover, *Langley*'s escorts were forced to withdraw. Before heading south, *Edsall* and *Whipple* sent nine 4-inch shells and two torpedoes into *Langley*.

In a valiant effort against a vastly superior force, Adm. Doorman sortied his force on the afternoon of February 27, against the Japanese invasion fleet headed for Java. Doorman's fleet consisted of the cruisers USS *Houston*, HMS *Exeter*, HMAS *Perth*, HMNS *De Ruyer* and *Java*, supported by nine destroyers, four American ships of World War I vintage (*Alden* DD-211, *John D. Edwards* DD-216, *John D. Ford* DD-228, and *Paul Jones* DD-230), three British ships (*Electra, Encounter,* and *Jupiter*), and two

Dutch ships (*Kortenaer* and *Witte de With*). Doorman's armada sailed directly into battle against three substantial columns of Japanese ships, screening 41 transports of the Java invasion force.

Steaming parallel to the Allied ships, the Imperial Japanese Navy's Destroyer Squadron 2 (light cruiser *Jintsu*, destroyers *Amatsukaze, Hatsukaze, Tokitsukaze,* and *Yukikaze*) was sighted six miles off Doorman's starboard bow. Heavy cruisers *Haguro* and *Nachi*, screened to port by destroyers *Kawakaze, Sazanami, Yamakaze,* and *Ushio,* were advancing from the north. These destroyers would fall into Destroyer Squadron 2's column for the forthcoming battle. Destroyer Squadron 4 (light cruiser *Naka*, destroyers *Asagumo, Harukaze, Minegumo, Murasame, Samidare,* and *Yudachi*) paralleled *Haguro* and *Nachi*'s southward track, two miles to the west.

Between 4:03 P.M. and 4:16 P.M., Destroyer Squadron 4 fired three separate salvos of torpedoes at Doorman's ships without results. At 4:38, *Exeter* took a shell hit from *Nachi* that began a severe fire. Two minutes later, a Japanese "long lance" 24-inch torpedo struck and rapidly sank *Kortenaer*. Doorman's ships turned south, but the column was in a

state of disarray and was having trouble communicating between the Dutch-speaking and English-speaking ships. The southward turn allowed the Allied column to regroup—the four cruisers screened by the American destroyers, and crippled *Exeter* screened by the three British and one remaining Dutch destroyers. In the ensuing 35 minutes, the Japanese launched more than 30 torpedoes at the Allied column, but all were outmaneuvered and none struck their targets.

Exeter, reduced to five knots, and its escorting destroyers made a prime target for the Japanese. Destroyer Squadron 2 sent a full spread of torpedoes toward *Exeter* and its escorts—none of which found their target. Destroyer *Electra* took *Asagumo* under fire, damaging the Japanese destroyer enough that it had to withdraw from the battle. *Asagumo* had scored two well-placed hits on *Electra*, and at 5:46 P.M., the British destroyer sank.

Adm. Doorman sailed north in pursuit of the transports, but again ran into *Nachi, Haguro, Jintsu,* and their escorting destroyers. Trading shot volleys, neither side was hit, but Doorman was prevented from approaching the transports. While maneuvering to regroup, at approximately 7 P.M.,

destroyer *Jupiter* struck a mine and sank. Soon after, Doorman dispatched the four American destroyers to Surabaya for fuel and to rearm with torpedoes, leaving only the four remaining cruisers, *De Ruyter, Perth, Houston*, and *Java,* to battle the Japanese. Once refueled, the American destroyers were ordered to sail for Australia and were out of the battle.

At 10:33 P.M., sailing in the opposite direction some 14,000 yards apart, Doorman's cruisers approached *Haguro* and *Nachi*. For four minutes the cruisers traded shots. Then *Haguro* and *Nachi* sent a spread of 12 torpedoes toward the ABDA cruisers. One torpedo found *De Ruyter*'s aft magazine, which exploded, rapidly sank, and took Doorman and 344 others with it. *Java* was struck and sunk by a torpedo four minutes later. *Houston* and *Perth* were ordered to retire to Batavia to fight again another day.

When the sun broke over the horizon on March 1, the Battle of Java Sea was near the end and the Battle of Sunda Straight was about to begin. *Exeter*, crippled the previous afternoon, accompanied by destroyers *Encounter* and *Pope*, had refueled and made repairs at Surabaja during the night. The plan was to sail north and then turn west after passing

Sailors gather to watch flight crews arm their B-25s on the deck of Hornet. Fifty-caliber machine-gun ammunition is being brought on deck through the elevator in the top right, while belted bullets are removed from shipping crates and loaded into turret ammo cans on deck. *(U.S. Air Force via McClellan Aviation Museum)*

One of the Doolittle Raiders thunders down Hornet's pitching deck headed for targets in Japan. Pilots had to lift their 31,000-pound Mitchell bombers off the carrier's deck in less than 750 feet. Each aircraft carried 1,141 gallons of gasoline and was expected to fly from the carrier, attack targets in Japan, and continue on to land at air bases in China. Of the 16 planes, 1 headed for Russia, another ditched off the coast of Ningpo, China, 3 crashed-landed, and the crews of the remaining 11 aircraft bailed out when their fuel was exhausted. (U.S. Air Force via McClellan Aviation Museum)

Adm. William F. "Bull" Halsey Jr., a Naval Academy graduate, Class of 1904, trained as an aviator and earned his wings of gold in 1935. Before World War II, he served in such aviation-related duties as captain of Saratoga, commanding officer of Naval Air Station Pensacola, Florida, and Commander Aircraft Battle Force (June 1940). Halsey commanded Task Force 16 in April 1942 and was responsible for delivering the Army Air Force "Doolittle Raiders" to within striking distance of the Japanese home islands. (National Archives/80GK-3051)

Bawean Island, proceed west passing Jakarta, and exit the Java Sea through the Sunda Strait that evening. Once through the strait, the ships would head for the British port of Colombo, Ceylon.

Exeter and its accompanying destroyers were spotted by Japanese aerial reconnaissance aircraft as soon as the ships left the harbor at Surabaja around 9 A.M. The ships sailed into the crossfire of cannon shells and torpedoes and by 11:30, Exeter was on the bottom. Encounter, riddled by cannon shells, went under five minutes later, followed by Pope a few minutes after noon.

The last two remaining ABDA ships in the Java Sea, cruisers Houston and Perth, were steaming for Tjilatjap, which could only be reached by passing through the Sunda Strait. Spotting the transports off-loading troops at Bantam Bay, Houston and Perth turned to port and took the unarmed Japanese ships under fire. Cruisers Mikuma, Mogami, and Natori, and nine destroyers, came to the transports' aid. Houston and Perth dodged a spread of torpedoes fired from destroyer Fubuki. When the cruisers and destroyers converged upon the two Allied cruisers, the melee began. Cannon shells rained down as torpedoes crisscrossed the sea. Houston and Perth put up a gallant fight, but with two torpedo and

numerous shell hits, Perth went under at 11:42 P.M. With three torpedoes in her side, Houston went to the bottom an hour later. ABDA's naval presence in Java had been eliminated, and the Dutch formally surrendered on March 8.

Continuing their southward expansion, the Japanese invaded Lae and Salamaua, New Guinea, on March 8, and the following day Java surrendered. The Allies did not let the landings go unchallenged and dispatched Australian Air Force Hudson bombers to harass the Japanese fleet lying off Lae and Salamaua in Huon Gulf.

In a prelude of what was to come at the Battle of the Coral Sea, carriers Enterprise and Lexington launched a combined 90 aircraft to attack ships in Huon Gulf on March 10. Both carriers were on the south side of the Papuan Peninsula when the Japanese landed on the north side in the Huon area. Enterprise and Lexington's aircraft flew across the peninsula, over the 7,000-foot-high Owen Stanley Mountain Range, to take the Japanese by surprise. Three ships (Kongo Maru, an armed merchant cruiser; minelayer Ten'yo Maru; and transport Yokohama Maru) were sunk and another nine ships were heavily damaged, including the light cruiser Yubari and five destroyers. The loss of three ships and nine damaged did not stop Japanese ground troops from taking Finschhafen on the Huon Peninsula.

The Japanese now controlled Indonesia and were establishing a foothold on Papua New Guinea. Allied sea and air lanes from Australia to the Philippines had been effectively severed.

The Japanese army's advance across the Philippines was also a crossroads in American command. In Washington, Gen. George C. Marshall was faced with deciding whether Gen. Douglas MacArthur should remain on Luzon to the bitter end, move to Mindanao and fight with partisans, or be evacuated to Australia where MacArthur could assume command of the U.S. Army forces in the Far East. Over MacArthur's objections, President Roosevelt ordered the general to Australia. MacArthur would be transported from Manila south to Mindanao's Del Monte Airfield for the flight to Australia.

On the evening of March 12, MacArthur, his wife, son, and the child's nurse boarded *PT-41* under the command of Lt. John D. Bulkeley. Seventeen of MacArthur's staff officers followed in *PT-32, PT-34,* and *PT-35.* The boats began the journey at 9:15 P.M. local time, easing through the harbor and navigating the mine-field defenses before turning south toward Mindanao.

Traveling through the night, one of the patrol boats became separated. When it came upon the other three boats it mistook them for Japanese patrol boats and jettisoned the extra fuel lashed to the deck in preparation for combat. Realizing their mistake, the passengers were transferred to the remaining three boats that had enough fuel to make the entire journey. The group stopped at the Cuyo Islands to rest during daylight hours and to avoid Japanese air and sea patrols. The following evening, the remaining three boats sailed into the Mindanao Sea and headed for Magajalar Bay to land their human cargo.

When MacArthur arrived at Del Monte Field, he found that only one of the four B-17s requested had landed safely. MacArthur did not consider this aircraft flight worthy and he requested three more B-17s to be sent from Australia. Two aircraft landed on the night of March 16. During the night, the planes were refueled and serviced, and the general's party departed at 9 A.M. the following morning. With MacArthur out of the Philippines, Lt. Gen. Jonathan M. Wainwright assumed command.

Japan's quest for domination of the Pacific reached a major milestone when the last American defenders of the Philippines, entrenched on Corregidor Island at the mouth of Manila Bay, surrendered. After the Japanese had conquered Luzon and taken the Bataan Peninsula, they were able to constantly bombard Corregidor, located only two miles into the bay, with artillery and daily attacks from both high- and low-level bombers. On May 5, two battalions of the Japanese 61st Infantry began the assault on Corregidor against fierce American opposition. On May 6, Gen. Wainwright made arrangements to surrender the fortified islands of Manila Bay.

Target Tokyo: America Strikes Back

The U.S. Army Air Force (AAF) asked for volunteers from the 34th, 37th, and 95th Bombardment Squadrons (17th Bombardment Group) and the 89th Reconnaissance Squadron to fly a secret mission—destination unknown. The flyers were led by Lt. Col. James H. Doolittle; the crews were not hand-picked, each man was willing to risk his life for his country. The task was to fly a medium bomber 2,400 miles with a 2,000-pound bomb load. The job fell to the AAF because the Navy did not have a carrier-based bomber capable of carrying a bomb load to such an extreme range.

For the mission, they would fly the North American Aviation B-25 "Mitchell" bomber. At Eglin Field, Florida's overhaul depot, the bomber's lower, remotely sighted, twin .50-caliber machine gun turret was removed to save weight, and two wooden machine-gun barrels were added to the rear fuselage to give the appearance of tail guns. Additional fuel cells were installed in the plane, and on the mission, crews could count on an extra 50 gallons stored inside the aircraft in five-gallon cans. For the mission, each bomber would have 1,141 gallons on board.

The crews began specialized training on March 1. Navy Lt. Henry F. Miller taught the AAF pilots how to lift their heavily laden, 31,000-pound B-25s off a runway in less than 750 feet. The air crews also underwent rigorous low-level bombing practice, usually dropping their ordnance from 1,500 feet. On March 24, 22 aircraft left Eglin on a cross-country flight to the Sacramento Air Depot, California. Final engine, electrical, and armament checks were performed at Sacramento, then the group departed for Alameda Naval Air Station, 95 miles to the southwest.

During the morning of April 1, 16 of the aircraft were hoisted onto the deck of the carrier *Hornet* (CV-8) under the command of Capt. Marc A. Mitscher. The following day, *Hornet*—its flight deck crowded with B-25s as well as 71 Army officers and soldiers—the cruisers *Vincennes* (CA-44) and *Nashville* (CL-43), destroyers *Balch* (DD-363), *Benham* (DD-397), *Ellet* (DD-398), and *Fanning* (DD-385), as well as the fleet oiler *Cimarron* (AO-22), sailed west past San Francisco and out into the Pacific. Halfway into the Pacific, the sailors and airmen were told that their target was Tokyo.

Battered by storms and heavy seas, the *Hornet* group rendezvoused with the *Enterprise* group that included cruisers *Northampton* (CA-26), and *Salt Lake City* (CA-25), destroyers *Grayson, Gwin, Meredith,* and *Monssen,* and the oiler *Sabine,* to form Task Force 16 under the command of Adm. William "Bull" Halsey. After refueling on April 17, the destroyers and oiler took up station while both the carriers and cruisers steamed toward Japan at flank speed.

The plan was to launch the bombers at night from a point 500 miles off the coast of Honshu. The first aircraft, flown by Col. Doolittle, was to depart three hours ahead of the main group and drop incendiary bombs to light the

target area. From each aircraft's individual target, the planes would fly another 1,100 miles across the Inland Sea to airfields in China.

Unfortunately, things did not go according to plan. While more than 700 miles from the coast, on April 18, two picket boats were detected by radar at 2:10 A.M. The task force changed course, and at dawn launched scout planes. Less than 50 miles from TF-16, another picket boat was spotted, but this patrol boat had also seen Halsey's armada and radioed a warning of the ship's approach. At 6:44 another picket boat was spotted and taken under fire by *Nashville*. Although short of the planned launch point, Adm. Halsey knew the B-25s would have to be launched, and the longer his ships loitered in Japanese waters, the greater the chance one or all would be attacked and sunk. At 7:25 A.M., still 670 miles from Tokyo, Doolittle's heavily loaded B-25 thundered down the pitching deck and clawed its way into the stormy sky. Within an hour, all 16 were airborne and headed for Japan.

Thirteen of the planes bombed industrial targets in and around Tokyo; one bomber damaged the carrier *Ryuho* dry docked at Yokosuka Naval Base. Only the crew attacking Nagoya encountered any resistance, and by 12:45 P.M. all 16 of the B-25s were headed for China. Running low on fuel, one aircraft, piloted by Lt. Edwark

▲ Antiaircraft gunners on board Yorktown bravely fought off six "Val" dive-bombers on the afternoon of June 4 during the Battle of Midway. The gunners destroyed one aircraft in the air, but its bomb continued the aircraft's trajectory and struck behind the Number Two elevator on the carrier's starboard side. Two more bombs did extensive damage, but the carrier was able to make way three hours later. Yorktown was further damaged by two torpedoes from I-168 that led to the carrier's sinking the following morning. *(National Archives/80GK-5790)*

◄ Yorktown SBDs and TBDs struck the Japanese invasion force at Tulagi, Solomon Islands, on May 4, 1942, sinking the destroyer Kikusuki, seen undergoing salvage, the minesweeper Tama Maru, and the auxiliary minesweepers Wa 1 and Wa 2. Another destroyer, a minelayer, transport, and cargo ship were damaged in this attack, the opening salvo of the Battle of the Coral Sea. *(National Archives/80GK-6108)*

An aviation ordnanceman checks the ammo feed for a Douglas SBD's twin .30-caliber defensive guns. During the Battle of Midway, the low- and slow-flying TBD torpedo bombers diverted the attention of Zeros flying combat air patrol and the intense antiaircraft fire when attacking the Japanese carriers. SBD dive-bombers from Yorktown and Enterprise arrived simultaneously as the torpedo bombers struck, and made their attacks unmolested. Soryu, Akagi, and Kaga were virtually destroyed in the morning attacks, and Hiryu was wrecked that afternoon by American dive-bombers. (National Archives/80GK-13776)

York, diverted to Vladivostok where the crew and aircraft were interned. One aircraft ditched off the coast of Ningpo, China, three others crash-landed, and the crews of the remaining 11 aircraft bailed out when their fuel was exhausted. Of the 80 intrepid aviators, four men were drowned, one perished when his 'chute failed to open, Lt. Robert J. Meder died while in captivity, and Lt. Dean E. Hallmark, Lt. William G. Farrow, and Sgt. Harold A. Spatz were executed on October 15 by the Japanese for the attack.

Task Force 16 quickly retired to the south and joined the destroyers and oiler for the trip back to Pearl Harbor. *Enterprise* aircraft attacked 16 Japanese patrol ships, heavily damaging most and sinking *No. 1 Iwate*

Maru and *No. 21 Nanshin Maru,* which was scuttled the following day.

In terms of targets destroyed or damaged, the Doolittle Raid only inflicted minor damage on a number of industrial targets. What the raid did do was rally a demoralized American public, showing them that the Japanese homeland could be attacked and Pearl Harbor would be avenged. In Japan, the raid shocked military leaders, who held back hundreds of men, ships, and aircraft to defend the home islands against a repeat American attack that would not come for another two years. The Japanese assumed that the raid had staged through or was launched from Midway and, in late May, the Imperial Japanese Navy sortied to destroy the island.

Coral Sea: Baptism By Fire

While preparing for the Midway operation, the Japanese planned to execute Operation "MO" (under the command of Vice Adm. Shigeyoshi Inouye) to capture the natural resources of Nauru and the Ocean Islands (halfway between Rabaul and the Gilbert Islands), the island of Tulagi in the Solomons, and Port Moresby, New Guinea. Port Moresby would give the Japanese a port and airfield complex within striking distance of Northern Australia as well as air superiority over a majority of the Coral Sea. In addition, forcing the Allies out of Port Moresby would remove the threat of air attacks against the Japanese stronghold at Rabaul, New Britain.

In what became known as the Battle of the Coral Sea, a Japanese invasion force, including carriers *Shokaku* and *Zuikaku*, departed Truk Island on April 30 en route to Port Moresby. The force first secured Tulagi, Solomon Islands, on May 3, for use as a future seaplane base. The invasion armada then continued on to capture Nauru and the Ocean Islands. The following morning, aircraft from *Yorktown* (together with *Lexington*-formed Task Force 17), retaliated against the Japanese naval force at Tulagi, sinking destroyer Kikuzuki and damaging *Yuzuki*, plus the minelayer *Okinoshima*. In a second strike around noon, two patrol boats were sunk and the transport *Tama Maru* was heavily damaged, sinking on May 6. Planes from *Yorktown* struck Tulagi a third time late in the afternoon, finding the area devoid of shipping targets.

Earlier that same day, May 6, in the Philippines, the last bastions of resistance in Manila Bay, the islands of Corregidor and Fort Drum, surrendered. America had been driven out of the Philippines, and Lt. Gen. Jonathan M. Wainwright and the last vestiges of his army surrendered.

Although the Americans faced a numerically superior Japanese naval force at this stage of the war, U.S. Navy cryptanalysts were close to breaking the Imperial Navy's code and were able to infer its intent. Thus, the U.S. Navy believed the Japanese were planning to attack Port Moresby, and it was only a matter of pinpointing the exact hour.

Attacks on Tulagi by carrier aircraft alerted the Japanese to the presence of one or more American flattops in the Coral Sea area. The Japanese expected to face resistance from Allied ships, and had planned to catch them in the Coral Sea, far from land-based air cover. The lack of Japanese carriers in the waters around Tulagi told American naval planners that the enemy flattops were still at sea with the Port Moresby invasion force. Frustrated that the invasion ships had departed Tulagi, the Americans began an intensive search of the surrounding sea by long-range air patrol and submarine reconnaissance. The Japanese had weighed anchor and sailed to the Shortland Islands to refuel and regroup before steaming south to Port Moresby.

While the Allied and Japanese carrier task forces searched for one another, the Port Moresby invasion force left Rabaul on May 4 intending to sail through Jomard Pass in the Louisiades—off the southeastern tip of New Guinea. Here it would rendezvous with Vice Adm. Takeo Takagi's Carrier Striking Force (*Zuikaku*, *Shokaku*, six destroyers, and the oiler *Toho Maru*), and the Distant Covering Force led by Adm. Goto (light carrier *Shoho*, heavy cruisers *Aoba*, *Furutaka*, *Kako*, *Kinugasa*, and destroyer *Sazanami*). At 10:30 A.M., on May 6, Adm. Goto's force was sighted by a flight of Port Moresby based B-17s south of Bougainville, and subsequently attacked without causing any damage. Around 1:00 P.M., the invasion force was sighted by Allied planes. Believing that the American carrier planes were at the far limit of their range, Takagi continued with the "MO" operation. By midnight, his ships had reached the Louisiades Islands and would prepare to launch scouts at first light.

Shortly after dawn, Japanese scout planes discovered the American oiler *Neosho* (AO-23) and destroyer *Sims* (DD-409) en route to the next refueling point. They were also trailing *Yorktown* and reporting its position on an hourly basis. Mistakenly, *Neosho* was reported to the Japanese fleet as a carrier and *Sims* as a cruiser. Hearing this news, Adm. Takagi first sent 15 horizontal bombers after the pair at 9:30 A.M. This strike failed to cause any damage, and an additional 10 horizontal bombers attacked *Sims* an hour later. Again, both ships remained afloat, relatively unscathed. Takagi finally sent three dozen Val dive-bombers to destroy the two American ships. *Neosho* was hit by seven bombs and one aircraft that crashed onto her deck and was left a blazing wreck, albeit still afloat. *Sims* received most of the dive-bomber's attention; three 500-pound bombs struck the ship and she began to go down by the stern. Only 16 men from *Sims* survived. *Neosho* remained afloat until May 11, when both her crew and those from *Sims* were rescued by the destroyer *Henley* (DD-391). *Henley* finished what the Japanese had started.

The horizontal-and dive-bombers that sent *Neosho* and *Sims* to the bottom were from *Zuikaku* and *Shokaku*; neither carrier's presence was known to Task Force 17. American scout aircraft did locate Adm. Goto's Distant Covering Force at around 8:45 A.M., and proceeded to attack the column. Focusing their efforts on *Shoho*, 13 bombs and seven torpedoes found their mark. Only four aircraft were lost in the attack. *Shoho* went under at 10:35 A.M., with a loss of more than 525 men. The Allies had sunk a Japanese carrier in—what was to become the first of many.

Fully aware of the American carriers and their location, Adm. Inouye ordered the Port Moresby attack transports to remain north and east of the Louisiades Islands until the threat from the flattops could be neutralized. Task Force 17 took precautions of its own. Unable to locate *Shokaku* or *Zuikaku*, but aware of their presence in the area through radio traffic, Task Force 17 began steaming to intercept the Port Moresby attack transports when they entered the Coral Sea. Weather began to worsen as the day wore on. Near sunset, a flight of 27 Japanese bombers and torpedo planes were intercepted by combat air patrol (CAP) fighters from *Yorktown* and *Lexington*. Nine Japanese planes were shot down at a cost of three F4F Wildcats. By the time the melee ended, it was dark and most of the aircraft on both sides were short on fuel. Many of the Japanese planes entered the American carrier's landing circles, only to be shot down. *Yorktown*'s radar showed the Japanese planes entering a landing circle about 100 miles to the north. The Allies now had a rough idea of where their search for *Shokaku* and *Zuikaku* would begin.

When dawn arrived, Task Force 17 was in the clear. The band of low clouds and showers that had prevented Task Force 17 from being spotted by the Japanese the previous afternoon, had now moved north. At 6:25 A.M 18 scouts from *Lexington* were launched to find *Shokaku* and *Zuikaku*. An hour later, the Japanese carriers and their escorting ships were spotted. Immediately both *Yorktown* and *Lexington* launched an 82-plane strike. *Yorktown*'s aircraft arrived first to discover the Japanese carriers operating approximately eight miles apart. This day the weather favored the enemy. *Zuikaku* slipped into a rainsquall as the American airplanes approached, while *Shokaku* turned into the wind to launch additional Zero fighters for protection.

Overhead, *Yorktown*'s dive-bombers orbited to enable the slower Douglas TBD "Devastator" torpedo bombers to find the target and attack. Lacking experience in delivering aerial torpedoes in combat, most of the TBD pilots released too early or, if they did score a hit, the torpedoes failed to explode. Once the TBDs were clear of the targets, dive-bombers descended upon *Shokaku*, scoring one hit forward on the flight deck and another near the aft end of the ship. Only one dive-bomber from *Lexington* scored a hit. *Shokaku* was heavily damaged with more than 100 men killed during the attacks. Adm. Takagi dispatched *Shokaku* for repairs, and the carrier would return to fight again another day.

Simultaneous to the American aircraft launches, *Shokaku* and *Zuikaku* dispatched 69 aircraft toward the estimated position of *Yorktown* and *Lexington*. American combat air patrol was reinforced as the Japanese aircraft approached minutes before 11 A.M. *Lexington* was attacked by torpedo planes, first from the port bow, and then from starboard, making evasive maneuvering to avoid torpedoes almost impossible. Eleven torpedoes missed before one found its mark near the port bow, quickly followed by a second striking opposite the bridge on the port side as well. Two dive-bombers scored direct hits while others struck the water near the ship, buckling the hull. *Yorktown* maneuvered to avoid eight torpedoes, and then came under a rain of bombs from Val dive-bombers. One hit scored: an 800-pound bomb struck the flight deck near the carrier's "island." The bomb bored down to the fourth deck before exploding, killing more than 50 men instantly. The U.S.

Navy lost 33 aircraft in the engagement, while 43 Japanese did not return to their carriers.

When the attack was over, *Lexington* was listing, on fire, and three of her boiler rooms were flooded. The list was countered by shifting fuel oil, and aircraft were brought aboard beginning around 11:45 A.M. A little more than an hour later, a huge explosion rocked *Lexington*. Fuel vapors had seeped into a generator room, and were ignited by electrical equipment. The first explosion set off a chain of smaller blasts, but the ship continued to make 25 knots headed into the wind to recover aircraft from the morning's raid. Shortly before 3 P.M., a second giant explosion tore through the fire and engine rooms, quickly spreading throughout the ship. The destroyer *Morris* (DD-417) came alongside to offer firefighting assistance and take off all unnecessary personnel and any wounded. *Morris* took aboard more than 500 men.

At 4:30 P.M., the boilers were secured and the crew prepared to go over the side. At seven minutes after five o'clock, the order was given to abandon *Lexington*, her crew was taken aboard *Anderson* (DD-411), *Hammann* (DD-412), and *Morris*. Close to 8 P.M., destroyer *Phelps* (DD-360) sent torpedoes into *Lexington*'s side and the once mighty carrier slid beneath the Coral Sea.

The U.S. Navy could ill afford the loss of *Lexington*, but the firsthand tactical training U.S. Naval aviators gained during the Battle of Coral Sea would pay handsome dividends less than one month later in the waters surrounding Midway Atoll.

The Japanese lost the light carrier *Shoho,* and the Port Moresby invasion force was turned around to regroup at Truk lagoon. *Shokaku* was heavily damaged, and the air group aboard *Zuikaku* was decimated; neither carrier would be available for the upcoming operation at Midway. Adm. Inouye reset the invasion date for July 3. Thus, the first naval engagement where neither ship saw the other had ended, and the first battle between aircraft carriers saw one ship on each side sunk.

At this point in the war, the Japanese had numerical superiority in aircraft carriers over the United States and its Allies, but the Battle of the Coral Sea cost the Imperial Navy dozens of highly trained pilots. A war of attrition of naval aviators had begun.

Pivotal Point in the Pacific: The Battle of Midway

Steaming into Pearl Harbor after the successful Doolittle Raid, Adm. Halsey's carriers were ordered to resupply and immediately depart for the Coral Sea to assist *Lexington* and *Yorktown*. *Enterprise* and *Hornet* were unable to cross the South Pacific in time, and arrived in the area near the New Hebrides on May 11, after the battle had ended. Halsey's carriers operated in the region for five days until being ordered back to Pearl Harbor. Something big was brewing and the Pacific Fleet's carriers were being readied for major action.

A Higgins-built motor patrol boat gets under way in the Aleutians. The Japanese struck Dutch Harbor, Unalaska Island, and invaded Attu and Kiska with the intent of drawing American carriers into battle. Seaplane bases in the Aleutians would have given the Japanese a way to patrol the northern Pacific Ocean to prevent another Doolittle Raid–type attack on the home islands. (National Archives/80GK-8143)

Japanese Adm. Isoroko Yamamoto was educated in the United States and had seen America firsthand. He knew the vastness of both American industrial and natural resources, and this knowledge led him to believe that war with the United States had to be won within the first 6 months to ensure Japan's victory. If the war lasted more than 18 months, Yamamoto believed American industrial might would overwhelm the Japanese. Yamamoto planned to destroy the U.S. Pacific Fleet in one single stroke by capturing Midway Island—from which an invasion of Hawaii and increased strikes on the U.S. West Coast were possible, and engaging the Americans in a decisive naval battle. A diversionary assault on the Aleutian Islands would serve to occupy American forces on the U.S. West Coast. Once the Japanese had secured the atoll, American carriers were expected to sortie from the

safety of Pearl Harbor to counterattack. The Imperial Japanese Navy would then ambush the American ships as they neared the island. With the Pacific Fleet eliminated, Japan could negotiate peace with the Western powers that would recognize the Greater East Asia Co-prosperity Sphere.

Midway Atoll is, as its name implies, halfway between the U.S. West Coast and Manila or Tokyo. An outlying island of the Hawaiian chain, the atoll is circular, six miles in diameter, and encircled by a barrier reef that is 5 feet high in a number of places. Two major islands—Eastern Island (328 acres) and Sand Island (850 acres), are the largest land masses. The runway was located on Eastern, while the seaplane hangars were situated on Sand.

The fact that the Americans knew the Japanese were planning an operation in the north central Pacific was a

President Adams (AP-38) at Noumea, New Caledonia, on August 4, 1942, prior to the invasion of Guadalcanal. The attack transport delivered the 3rd Battalion, 2nd Marine Division to beaches at Guadalcanal and Tulagi, subsequently evacuating the wounded to hospital facilities in Samoa. President Adams began a six-month-long shuttle service between Samoa and Guadalcanal carrying the wounded to the rear area and delivering food, supplies, and equipment to the men on the front lines. *(National Archives/80GK-556)*

direct result of communications intelligence. The U.S. Navy was unable to reconnoiter Japanese harbors to determine the disposition of its fleets, thus pulling information from the airways and triangulating on a ship's radio traffic was the service's only option.

Having broken the Japanese Naval Code JN-25, the Navy was able to extract two types of information from the airways: Traffic Intelligence (TI), giving a message's address (ship or commanding officer's information), and its location through triangulation; or Decryption Intelligence (DI) where the text of a message is decoded or conclusions are deduced from the information.

During the first week of May, DI showed that eight of the IJN's carriers were being readied for a major engagement. They would face all the carriers of Nimitz's Pacific Fleet—*Yorktown, Enterprise,* and *Hornet.* Through DI, the Navy was able to deduce that the Japanese were headed for a target only designated as "AF." Cryptanalysts knew that Oahu was coded AH, Port Moresby was RZP, Rabaul was R, and Saipan was PS.

Through a crafty trick, the Navy instructed the commanding officer of the naval base at Midway to send a

clear text message to Pearl Harbor stating that the water distillation plant was out of service. As hoped, the Japanese heard the message and included a note that "AF is short of water" in an intelligence report that was decoded by the U.S. Navy. Based upon this information, Adm. Nimitz began reinforcing Midway with PBY patrol planes and Army Air Force B-17 long-range bombers, and dispatched submarines to scout west of the island.

Another message decoded days later gave the invasion's sailing date from Saipan. Using this information, it was determined that the attack would take place on or shortly after June 1. On May 25, another message was decoded, giving the entire Japanese battle plan as well as the date of the attack: June 4. On May 28, the Japanese switched to a new code system and the Navy was once again in the dark—but they knew everything they needed to ambush the Japanese.

Adm. Halsey, suffering from the skin ailment shingles, was asked by Adm. Nimitz to name his successor before he was sent stateside for medical attention. Rear Adm. Raymond A. Spruance, who had commanded the cruiser forces under Halsey, was selected. Spruance was placed in command of Task Force 16 (*Enterprise* and *Hornet*) and departed Pearl

Harbor for the waters north of Midway on May 28. On May 30, Task Force 17, under the command of Rear Adm. Frank J. Fletcher (*Yorktown*), sortied as well. Both task forces positioned themselves 350 miles north of Midway on June 2 with Fletcher in overall command. In addition to surface ships, Rear Adm. Robert H. English was in command of 25 submarines patrolling in Midway waters. Counting scout planes aboard the task force's cruisers, the Navy had 235 aircraft at its disposal, supplemented by 115 Army Air Force, Navy, and Marine Corps planes stationed at Midway.

French Frigate Shoals, located 500 miles northwest of Oahu, was used as a staging base for Japanese reconnaissance of Pearl Harbor in March. A pair of Kawanishi H8K "Emily" flying boats from the Yokohama Naval Air Corps flew from Wotje Atoll, Marshall Islands, to French Frigate Shoals where they refueled. After flying to Oahu on the night of March 3–4, they found the island covered by a cloud layer, and dropped their bombs harmlessly.

In an effort to deny the Japanese use of French Frigate Shoals as a staging base to reconnoiter Pearl Harbor prior to the Midway operation, Adm. Nimitz had the area mined, and stationed minelayer *Preble* (DM-20) at the atoll. In addition, various small combatant ships were positioned at the numerous small, outlying islands or reefs between Kauai and French Frigate Shoals to prevent a flying boat/submarine rendezvous closer to Oahu.

Prior to the Midway operation, destroyer-seaplane tender *Thornton* (AVD-11) relieved *Preble*. This action was fortuitous, as the Japanese had planned to repeat their operation of March 3–4, and had dispatched three submarines laden with fuel to supply another flight over Pearl Harbor (*I-122* to Lisianski Island southeast of Midway, and *I-121* and *I-123* to French Frigate Shoals). Denying the Japanese the opportunity to determine if the U.S. carriers were still in Pearl Harbor gave the Americans a tremendous advantage. The Japanese proceeded to set their trap for the American carriers while sailing directly into Nimitz's ambush.

Admiral Yamamoto had gathered 200 ships for the Midway operation, and separated them into five groups. The Advanced Expeditionary Force consisted of 16 submarines. The Main Body was based around three battleships including the *Yamato* and the light carrier *Hosho* under Adm. Yamamoto. The Carrier Striking Force included *Akagi, Kaga, Hiryu,* and *Soryu* plus battleships *Haruna* and *Kirishima* under Adm. Chuichi Nagumo. The Midway Occupation Force included the battleships *Kongo* and *Hiei* under Adm. Nobutake Kondo. The Northern Force for the diversionary raid on the Aleutians included the battleships *Ise, Hyuga, Fuso,* and *Yamashiro* plus carriers *Ryujo* and *Junyo*.

On June 3 at 9:04 A.M., a PBY patrol bomber spotted two ships from Yamamoto's invasion task force 470 miles southwest of Midway. Nine B-17Es from the 431st Bomb Squadron led by Lt. Col. Walter C. Sweeny attacked the transport column headed by the light cruiser *Jintsu* and screened by destroyers; none of the B-17s scored any hits.

At around 1 A.M., June 4, four PBYs located the same transport column using airborne search radar and attacked, this time scoring a single torpedo hit on the tanker *Akebono Maru* and strafing the remaining ships. *Akebono Maru* was able to repair the torpedo damage while under way and maintained its position within the ship column.

At 5:45 A.M., a PBY patrolling northwest of the island spotted a large formation of Japanese planes headed for the atoll and reported, "Many enemy planes heading Midway bearing 320 degrees, distance 150 (miles from Midway)." This sighting was confirmed by radar on the atoll. Minutes later, the enemy's carriers were spotted by another PBY that reported, "Two carriers and battleships bearing 320 degrees, distance 180, course 135, speed 25." Four torpedo-carrying B-26 Marauders, six newly arrived Grumman TBF "Avenger" torpedo bombers, and Marine Air Group Twenty-Two's (MAG-22) fighters and dive-bombers immediately took off from Midway for the carriers. Fourteen B-17s en route to attack the transport group were also diverted to the same target.

On board the American carriers, the PBY's warning report was plotted, putting the Japanese fleet 200 miles to the southwest. While *Yorktown* recovered the morning's search planes, *Enterprise* and *Hornet* steamed southwest to close the distance between the fleets.

Fighters from MAG-22 met the onrushing Japanese attackers and quickly shot down eight Nakajima B5N Kate bombers. After diving through the Kates, the Marine's F4F "Wildcat" and Brewster F2A "Buffalo" fighters climbed to engage the escorting fighters. Japanese A6M Zero fighters downed 15 Marine flyers in the ensuing aerial battle. When the dogfight was over, 33 Kates and 36 Aichi D3A Val dive-bombers were still winging their way toward the atoll.

Midway's hangars, fuel transfer lines, and an electrical power–generating plant were destroyed and most of the shore installations were strafed. American antiaircraft gunners on the beaches downed four more Japanese aircraft by the time the attack was over. Lt. Tomonaga from *Hiryu*, who was leading the flight, radioed back to his carrier that due to the losses suffered at the hands of the Marine pilots, a second strike would be necessary to neutralize the defenders on Midway. Tomonaga's request for an additional raid had grave consequences for the Japanese fleet later in the morning.

At 7:05 A.M., the Marauders and TBFs descended to wave-top height to deliver their torpedoes against *Akagi*. They were met by a hail of antiaircraft fire—half of the B-26s and four of the TBFs were downed during the attack. None of the torpedoes found their targets. The B-17s dropped their bombs, scoring several near-misses, but no direct hits.

When the Japanese strike aircraft bound for Midway were launched, Adm. Nagumo held back 93 aircraft. The reserve bombers were moved on deck and armed with torpedoes to deal with any American surface ships that might attempt to challenge the Japanese fleet. After hearing Tomonaga's request for a second attack on Midway and being attacked by land-based B-17s, B-26s, and TBFs, Adm. Nagumo ordered the reserve aircraft cleared from the decks of his carriers to recover the first wave of attackers and to rearm the torpedo planes with bombs.

At 7:28 A.M., a scout plane from the cruiser *Tone* reported seeing 10 American ships 240 miles from Midway. Adm. Nagumo instructed his carrier commanders to discontinue the switch from torpedoes to bombs, and then radioed the *Tone* scout to clarify the types of ships it had seen. At 8:09 A.M., the scout reported seeing five cruisers and five destroyers. Eleven minutes later, the scout reported the presence of a single aircraft carrier. While communicating with the scout plane at 7:55 A.M., Adm. Nagumo's ships were under attack from Midway-based dive-bombers. None scored any bomb hits, but their presence added to the tension on the flag bridge. While bombs rained down on the Japanese fleet, submarine *Nautilis* (SS-168) came up to periscope depth at 8:25 A.M., and fired one torpedo, missing a battleship.

Enterprise and *Hornet* began launching planes at 7:02 A.M. Having seen the *Tone* scout halfway through the aircraft launch, it was determined to continue with the strike even though the element of surprise had been lost. Adm. Spruance launched every aircraft, except those held back for combat air patrol over the carriers, to ensure a numerical advantage over the Japanese. *Enterprise* and *Hornet* put up 29 TBD torpedo bombers and 67 SBD dive-bombers, which were accompanied to the target by 18 F4F fighters. By 9 A.M., *Yorktown* had launched 17 SBDs, two dozen TBDs, and six F4Fs. Unlike the Coral Sea battle, weather around Midway was clear, a light breeze was blowing, and some scattered clouds sailed through the sky.

Although *Yorktown*'s aircraft were launched an hour later than those of *Enterprise* and *Hornet*, planes from all three carriers arrived over the Japanese fleet simultaneously. The torpedo bombers were first to attack, drawing off the Japanese fighter cover. Those planes that escaped the Zeros were finished off by antiaircraft fire from the fleet. Ensign George Gay from *Hornet* was the only survivor from his squadron of 15 TBDs, all planes having been shot down. Zeros attacked the torpedo bombers on the way in, pulled up when the planes came within range of the ship's guns, and then swooped down to attack those aircraft that made it through the fleet's fire.

Japanese fighters and antiaircraft fire from the fleet decimated the slow-flying TBD torpedo bombers, but failed to anticipate the arrival of the American dive-bombers high over-head. During the torpedo attacks, the Japanese were busy refueling and rearming aircraft. Bombs were on the hangar decks, torpedoes were being moved back to the magazines, and fuel hoses were dispensing the volatile liquid when the dive-bombers approached.

Robert M. Elder, then a lieutenant (junior grade) and later captain, was flying SBDs with *Yorktown*'s VB-3. "It was an awesome sight that morning when we spotted the Japanese carriers," Elder said. "We saw three of the carriers (*Akagi, Kaga,* and *Soryu*) as *Hiryu* had gone under a cloud bank. We started our dives from 17,000 feet and released our single 1,000-pound bomb at 1,800 feet. Our standard-release altitude is 2,500 feet, but when we were going for keeps, we took it down to where we were damn sure we were gonna have a hit."

Yorktown's dive-bombers concentrated on *Soryu* while *Enterprise*'s planes wrecked *Akagi* and *Kaga.* When the dive-bombers began their descent, nearly 40 aircraft were on *Akagi*'s deck in various states of being fueled or armed. One bomb missed *Akagi*'s port bow by about 30 feet, a second split the aircraft elevator amidships, and a third went through the flight deck on the port side near the stern. The second and third bombs penetrated to the hangar deck and exploded, which in turn caused secondary ignition of bombs and torpedoes being moved to and from aircraft. *Akagi* was abandoned by 5 P.M. that afternoon, and was sent to the bottom by torpedoes and gunfire from destroyers *Arashi, Hagikaze,* and *Nowake; Kaga* was struck by four bombs and a single torpedo from an American sub that did not detonate. Secondary explosions finished the ship off, and by 7:30 P.M. *Kaga* was also on the bottom of the Pacific.

"I was about the tail-end Charlie in our squadron and had a good look at the battle as it transpired. I saw all three of those carriers hit—boom, boom, boom. Almost simultaneously—within one minute at the most," Elder, who was credited with a hit on *Soryu*, said. "Those decks were loaded with aircraft fueling and ordnance was all over the place. When the first bomb hit *Soryu*, the explosion went about 6,000 feet in the air. That was an awesome sight. It just decimated it. The internal explosions were ripping it apart. She was gone after the first bomb hit, really. You could see the aircraft starting to take off down the deck and being blown over the side." After the dive-bombers retired, submarine *Nautilus* positioned herself to administer the *coup de grace.* Three torpedoes were fired and seen to explode, setting the ship on fire. Later that evening, *Soryu*'s aviation gasoline storage tanks exploded, ripping the carrier in two.

The battle to this point seemed one-sided—three Japanese carriers on their way to the bottom of the Pacific, but the day was only half over and the IJN had yet to strike.

At noon, *Yorktown*'s radar detected three dozen aircraft 40 miles away, coming fast. SBDs from the morning strikes orbiting to land were waved off and told to assist the CAP with repelling the on-coming Japanese. Eighteen Val dive-bombers escorted by 18 Zero fighters, were met head-on by *Yorktown*'s F4F CAP fighters. Nine

Vals were knocked down by the fighters and two more were blasted out of the sky by cruisers *Astoria* and *Portland*. But six dive-bombers made it through the fighters and the ship's antiaircraft barrage to attack *Yorktown*. Just as antiaircraft gunners exploded one of the Vals, its bomb was released, striking behind the Number Two elevator on the starboard side. The bomb exploded upon contact with the flight deck, killing a number of men and starting severe fires on the hangar deck below. A second bomb exploded in the ship's smokestack, damaging the boilers. Only the Number One Boiler was able to produce steam and *Yorktown's* speed dropped from 30.5 knots down to 6—virtually dead in the water. A third bomb penetrated to the fourth deck, exploding in a rag storage area adjoining the forward gasoline storage compartment and ammunition magazines, starting a fire. The magazines were flooded to prevent explosion and the

gasoline storage area had been filled with CO_2 to prevent ignition when the ship went to battle stations, thus limiting the damage from the third bomb.

Three hours later, bomb damage to *Yorktown's* boilers had been repaired to enable the ship to make 20 knots. Just minutes before 4 P.M., a group of Japanese aircraft was detected on radar at a distance of 33 miles. Between 10 and 15 miles from the carrier, CAP Wildcats intercepted the torpedo planes, quickly shooting down three. Antiaircraft fire from *Yorktown* and her screening ships accounted for a few more but, at 4:20 P.M., a torpedo struck the carrier's port side, followed quickly by a second torpedo. The rudder was jammed 15 degrees to port, all power—both steam and electric were lost, and the carrier began to list to port. When the list reached 26 degrees, Capt. Elliot Buckmaster gave the order to abandon ship.

At 8:00 p.m., on August 7, the day the Marines landed on Guadalcanal, Lt. Cmdr. Henry G. Munson, skipper of the S-38, surfaced to see seven Japanese cruisers and a destroyer pass within yards of his submarine en route to attack American transports at Lunga Roads. The cruisers passed so close they tossed the submarine about in their wakes. Unfortunately, S-38 was too close to fire torpedoes, but did send a position report. This conning tower photo of Marlin (SS-205) shows the cramped quarters in the submarine. At the periscope is Lt. Cmdr. John C. Nichols, who went on to command Silversides (SS-236). Wartime censors have blacked out the deep-depth gauge located between the heads of the two sailors controlling the sub's buoyancy. *(National Archives/80GK-16013)*

Submarine lookout in the periscope shears ready to raise his binoculars at the sight of an approaching ship or aircraft. An entire crew's fate depended upon the alertness of its lookouts. *(National Archives/80GK-13793)*

The following morning, June 5, Buckmaster, 29 officers, and 141 men returned to *Yorktown* in an effort to salvage the ship. A towline was secured to oceangoing tug *Vireo* (AT-144), and at 1:08 P.M., *Yorktown* began inching forward. *Vireo* pulled through the night, but her charge was beyond the tug's towing capacity.

On June 6, destroyer *Hammann* (DD-412) pulled alongside to offer power and pumping facilities to the salvage crew. *Yorktown's* list was reduced by filling the starboard oil tanks with seawater and pumping a number of below-decks compartments dry. While salvage work progressed, *I-168* fired four torpedoes at the trio of ships. *Hammann* was hit by one torpedo that split the destroyer in two, sinking in a matter of minutes. As the destroyer went down, its depth charges exploded, killing many men in the water. *Yorktown* took two torpedoes below the turn in the keel and was mortally wounded. The fourth torpedo passed harmlessly behind the carrier. *Yorktown* remained afloat, but with night coming, *Vireo* evacuated the salvage crew and those wounded on board. As the destroyers hunted for *I-168*, the decision was made to re-attempt a tow in the morning.

The following morning, June 7, at 5:30 A.M., before salvage work could begin again, *Yorktown's* list to port noticeably increased. At 7:01 A.M., the carrier rolled onto her port side and slid beneath the waves.

The U.S. Navy lost two ships during the Battle of Midway and, although *Yorktown* was damaged by aircraft, the sinkings were claimed by a single submarine two days after the battle had ended.

On the afternoon of June 4, the U.S. Navy still had one Japanese carrier to deal with. When *Yorktown* was damaged during the battle, the carrier's air groups dispersed to *Enterprise* and *Hornet*. Lt. Elder's VB-3 was operating from *Enterprise*. At 3:30 P.M., *Enterprise* launched 14 of its own SBDs plus 10 guests from the *Yorktown*. Elder described the attack: "We took off and went straight to the *Hiryu*, and she was all alone. We knew by then where she was as there was no way for her to escape the area.

"*Hiryu* was ready for us. Planes were on deck and planes were in the air. She had every single fighter that was left at that point of the operation on board. There were Zeros in the air like flies. It can never be denied that those Japanese facing us were as good a group of fighter pilots that ever existed; that group had between eight and nine years flying together in Manchuria prior to World War II. As we approached, they came in—just rolling and firing. They were just deadly, and boy, they just pounced us. We were shot up, and lost two of our aircraft," Elder said.

In spite of the fierce Japanese resistance, four American bombs struck *Hiryu*, including one dropped by Edler, who was awarded the Navy Cross for his actions on June 4. Ablaze, *Hiryu* floated during the night while her crew attempted to extinguish the fires. At 3:15 A.M., June 5, the carrier was ordered abandoned. Two hours later, destroyers *Kazegumo* and *Yugumo* launched torpedoes to scuttle *Hiryu*.

The Japanese believed that Midway would be the decisive naval engagement where the U.S. carriers would be lured from the safety of Pearl Harbor and destroyed. Instead, through the ability to read and interpret Japanese Naval signals intelligence, the American Navy was able to spring a trap that destroyed four aircraft carriers (*Akagi, Hiryu, Kago,* and *Soryu*), the cruiser *Mikuma*, 253 aircraft, and more than 3,500 men. The loss of the carriers and trained pilots was a loss Japan would never recover from. On the American side, the U.S. Navy lost a carrier and a destroyer, 150 aircraft, and 307 men.

Diversionary Attack in the Aleutians

The Aleutian Islands extend more than 1,000 miles south from the Alaskan Peninsula into the Bering Sea, separating the sea from the Pacific Ocean. Weather in the outer islands of the chain is not conducive to sustained land-based aircraft operations. However, from a strategic standpoint, once Japan had captured the islands, seaplane bases could be established to patrol the western approaches to Midway and the vast Northern Pacific. The Japanese only planned to capture Adak, Attu, and Kiska Islands, all west of 170 degrees latitude, to establish the bases needed for defense of Midway and the home islands. Seaplane patrols in this area would prevent a repeat of the Doolittle Raid, which was a total surprise to Japan's military leaders.

On June 3, aircraft from the carriers *Ryujo* and *Junyo* struck the military complex at Dutch Harbor on Unalaska Island. The Dutch Harbor complex was under construction, but included an Army airfield, barracks, radio station, hospital, and the *Northwestern*—a beached barracks ship located at Fort Mears, while the Navy's port facilities were comprised of a seaplane base, wharf area with tender *Gillis* (AVD-12), destroyer *Talbot* (DD-114), plus submarine *S-27* at anchor, and an oil tank farm.

The strike was timed one day before the Midway operation in an attempt to divert forces from the U.S. West Coast north to the Aleutians rather than to support operations in the Pacific. Poor weather conditions prevented all but six fighters and 13 bombers, all from *Ryujo*, from attacking Dutch Harbor. The tank farm, hospital, and barracks area were bombed and a couple of PBYs were strafed. Ships in the harbor put up fierce antiaircraft fire, knocking down one dive-bomber.

On June 4, the carriers attempted to strike Adak and Atka, but were thwarted by weather—both thick cloud cover and rough sea conditions. Retracing the 450 miles to Dutch Harbor, the Japanese fleet sent two floatplanes to reconnoiter the weather over Unalaska Island. Finding conditions right, *Ryujo* and *Junyo* launched a combined 32-aircraft strike that wrecked *Northwestern* and completed the destruction of the

Crewing a submarine was a dangerous business. Fifty-two U.S. subs never returned to port. Taken from the periscope shears, this stern view of a submarine cruising on the surface shows a good portion of its wake stretching to the horizon. Patrolling aircraft can see a wake from a greater range than a submarine's lookouts can spot an attacker. And when it came to submarines, many pilots and ships' captains attacked first and asked questions later. *(National Archives/80GK-16021)*

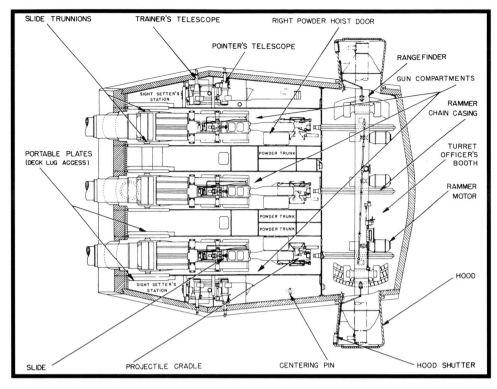

SLIDE TRUNNIONS TRAINER'S TELESCOPE RIGHT POWDER HOIST DOOR

POINTER'S TELESCOPE RANGEFINDER

GUN COMPARTMENTS

SIGHT SETTER'S STATION

RAMMER CHAIN CASING

PORTABLE PLATES (DECK LUG ACCESS)

TURRET OFFICER'S BOOTH

POWDER TRUNK

RAMMER MOTOR

POWDER TRUNK
POWDER TRUNK

SIGHT SETTER'S STATION

HOOD

SLIDE PROJECTILE CRADLE CENTERING PIN HOOD SHUTTER

Plan view of a typical turret housing three large-caliber cannons. Entry to the turret was through a hatch from the ship's main- or weather-deck into the turret officer's booth. The booth contained the range finder, computers, and the firing and communication circuits. To supply a battleship's 16-inch/.50-caliber cannons, power was hoisted from the powder handling room six decks below up to the gun house. Shells came from the projectile rooms typically located five decks below. (U.S. Navy)

port fueling facilities while killing a number of U.S. servicemen. After the attack, *Junyo's* aircraft rendezvoused over Umnak Island where eight Curtiss P-40s of the 11th Fighter Squadron were waiting. The P-40s came from a newly constructed field at Otter Point on Umnak. Three Val dive-bombers and a Zero fighter were destroyed before the engagement broke off.

While the carriers were engaged in attacking Dutch Harbor, the Midway operation had become a total disaster and Adm. Yamamoto recalled the carriers and put the invasion of the Aleutians on hold. Hours later, when it was determined that Midway was a lost cause, Yamamoto turned the invasion force around, and the occupation of Attu and Kiska proceeded.

Adak's relatively close proximity to the airfield at Otter Point made the island a poor target and the invasion troops were shifted to the attack on Attu. More than 1,200 men of the Hokaido Army Detachment were put ashore on Attu at Holtz Bay by the *Magane Maru* and *Kinugasa Maru* on the morning of June 7. The island's population of 26 adults and 15 children was subdued and the transports discharged their cargo during the next three days.

Simultaneous to the Attu landings, Kiska was invaded. The transport *Hakusan Maru* disembarked 550 members of the Maizuru Special Naval Landing Force and *Tamagawa Maru* delivered its cargo of 700 construction troops and their equipment.

The Japanese were entrenched on American soil and, with the Midway operation over, expected the American carriers to be deployed into Aleutian waters. Adm. Yamamoto dispatched a pair of battleships, four cruisers, and the carriers *Zuiho* and *Zuikaku* to reinforce the Aleutian invaders and deal a death blow to any American carriers that would sortie to repel the Japanese. The Imperial Navy never got the chance as *Enterprise* and *Hornet* had retired to Pearl Harbor after the Battle of Midway.

After establishing an air base on Adak in September, the U.S. Navy and Army Air Corps began an air and sea blockade of Attu and Kiska. On May 12, 1943, the Americans landed on Attu and after 15 days of heavy fighting were able to retake the island. Kiska was bypassed and the Japanese were unable to supply the garrison there. Faced with losing 5,100 men, two cruisers and 10 destroyers evacuated the garrison on July 29, 1943. The U.S. Navy constantly bombarded the island while the Army Air Corps bombed known Japanese positions on Kiska in preparation for the final assault on the island. On August 15, 1943, more than 34,000 U.S. and Canadian troops invaded the island, only to find it unoccupied.

The Solomons: On the Offensive in the Pacific

If the Battle of Midway was the location where the U.S. Navy stopped the Japanese fleet, Guadalcanal Island was the place where the offensive war in the Pacific began. Securing Guadalcanal in the Solomons chain guaranteed that New Caledonia, Fiji, Samoa, and Port Moresby would become beyond the reach of any planned Japanese invasion, and the seaplanes from America to Australia would remain unmolested. From an offensive standpoint, an airfield on Guadalcanal would enable America and its Allies to strike into the Bismarck Archipelago and eventually northward to the Philippines while securing the flank for operations in New Guinea.

The only thing standing in the way of executing an offensive strategy using Guadalcanal was the island's Japanese construction force and its supporting troops. The Japanese had arrived from Tulagi in late June and began to build an airfield complex on the coastal plane at Lunga Point. By early August, most of the air base's infrastructure—hangars, shops, radio stations, and power-generating plants, were complete, and a 3,600-foot runway was almost ready for operations. Once the strip at Lunga Point was finished, the Japanese would have an airfield that could provide land-based aircraft to cover a future invasion of Port Moresby.

To eliminate the threat of an airfield on Guadalcanal, the island would have to be taken. On August 7, Vice Adm. Robert L. Ghormley, commander South Pacific Force, launched Operation Watchtower to capture Tulagi and Guadalcanal. This was the first amphibious landing by U.S. forces since June 10, 1898, when the Marines landed at Guantánamo Bay, Cuba, during the Spanish-American War.

On July 26, the invasion force of 75 ships rendezvoused 400 miles south of Fiji before setting sail for the Solomon Islands.

The morning of August 7 dawned clear with high clouds—the perfect weather for air operations and to send wave after wave of landing craft to Guadalcanal and Tulagi's beaches. Fifteen transport ships had dispatched more than 11,000 Marines to a point east of Lunga Point by the end of the day. The Japanese garrison was completely taken by surprise and resistance was light. By 5 P.M. on August 8, the airstrip was under Marine control and the estimated 2,000 Japanese had fled into the hills. The Japanese at Tulagi were quickly overwhelmed and the U.S. Navy and Marines spent the night ever vigilant for counterattacks.

Minutes after the Marines landed on the beaches on August 7, Japanese Vice Adm. Gunichi Mikawa ordered five heavy cruisers that had just departed Kavieng to sail to Rabaul. Here the cruiser *Chokai* entered Rabaul with destroyer *Yumagi* to take Adm. Mikawa aboard, while the remaining cruisers headed to Cape St. George for a rendezvous. *Chokai* and *Yumagi* sortied in the company of light cruisers *Tenryu* and *Yubari* and met up with heavy cruisers *Aoba*, *Furataka*, *Kinugasa*, and *Kako*. The flotilla steamed past Cape St. George on New Ireland, Green Island, Bougainville, and into "The Slot"—a rectangular body of water bordered by Choiseul Island on the north; New Georgia on the west; Santa Isabel on the east; and Florida, Savo, and Guadalcanal on the southern end. At 8 P.M., the cruiser force passed so close to U.S. submarine *S-38* that the ships' wakes tossed the little undersea craft about. *S-38* was too close to fire torpedoes, but sent a report giving the ship's approximate speed and heading.

The following morning, August 8, at around 6:30 A.M., Adm. Mikawa sent five floatplane scouts to reconnoiter the landing area at Guadalcanal and Tulagi. At 10:30 A.M., a Royal Australian Air Force (RAAF) Hudson spotted the cruiser force and attempted to trail but was driven off by intense antiaircraft fire. When the scouts returned at noon, Adm. Mikawa was told that a battleship, half a dozen cruisers, nearly 20 destroyers, and another two dozen transports were in the area. The admiral was spoiling for a fight and increased speed to 24 knots in an attempt to catch the ships at anchor during darkness. The Battle of Savo Island was under way.

While en route to Savo Island, Adm. Mikawa dispatched six troop ships from Rabaul to reinforce the men on Guadalcanal. Steaming south, the troop ships and their escorting destroyers also crossed paths with submarine *S-38* near Cape St. George around 8 P.M. The sub's skipper, Lt. Cmdr. Henry G. Munson, fired two torpedoes that hit the 5,600-ton transport *Meiyo Maru*. When the troop ship sank, 14 officers and 328 men went with her to the bottom. With the loss of *Meiyo Maru*, Adm. Mikawa recalled the remaining five transports to Rabaul to await further reinforcements and a more opportune time to land troops.

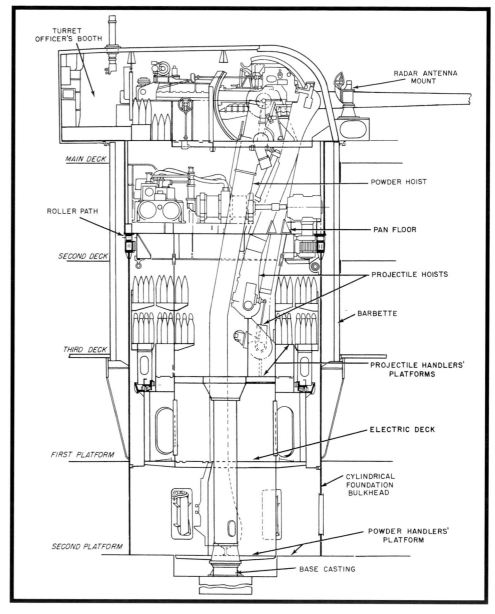

Rear Adm. Richmond Kelly Turner, in charge of the amphibious force, was supported by aircraft from Adm. Fletcher's *Wasp* (CV-7), *Enterprise*, and *Saratoga*. Unloading of supplies for the Marines was behind schedule, but Fletcher, nervous after having lost *Lexington* in the Coral Sea and *Yorktown* at Midway, decided to retire the air support force rather than risk the loss of a carrier to a marauding Japanese torpedo plane or submarine. With the carriers gone by 6 P.M., August 8, Adm. Turner had to rely on B-17 and Hudson bombers under the command of Gen. Douglas MacArthur or PBYs under Adm. John S. McCain to scout for a Japanese retaliatory strike. As luck would have it, B-17s patrolling near Choiseul missed spotting Adm. Mikawa's force due to bad weather.

Section view of a 6-inch/.47-caliber, dual-purpose gun turret. The 6-inch/.47-caliber triple-gun turret was the main armament of the Cleveland class of cruisers. Twenty-seven were built, including its namesake CL-55 Cleveland, which was launched November 1, 1941, by New York Shipbuilding of Camden, New Jersey. Sent straight into the war in the Pacific, Cleveland faced four Japanese cruisers on the night of November 1 at Empress Augusta Bay, Solomon Islands. Fire from Cleveland's guns helped send cruiser Sendai to the bottom. *(U.S. Navy)*

An SBD receives a thorough check-up topside before battle. At the port of Casablanca, SBDs quickly silenced the French battleship Jean Bart's four 15-inch guns before the dreadnought could fire at the approaching American invasion fleet. Douglas' SBD is regarded as the best U.S.-built dive-bomber of World War II. *(National Archives/80GK-14168)*

In anticipation of Adm. Mikawa's arrival, the defending cruisers and destroyers under the command of Royal Navy Rear Adm. V. A. C. Crutchley, took up night-patrolling positions. To defend the anchorage off Lunga Point, the defending force was split into three groups. The Southern Force, which patrolled between Guadalcanal's Cape Esperance and Savo Island, consisted of the Royal Navy cruisers *Australia* and *Canberra*, the U.S. cruiser *Chicago* (CA-29), and destroyers *Bagley* (DD-386) and *Patterson* (DD-392). The Northern Force, which patrolled Savo and Florida Island, consisted of the cruisers *Astoria* (CA-34), *Quincy* (CA-39), and *Vincennes* (CA-44) plus the destroyers *Helm* (DD-388), and Wilson. The Eastern Force, to protect the approaches through Sealark and Lengo channels, consisted of cruiser *San Juan* (CL-54) and HMAS *Hobart* with destroyers *Monssen* (DD-436) and *Buchannan* (DD-484). In addition to the three cruiser groups, destroyers *Ralph Talbot* (DD-390) and *Blue* (DD-387)—both fitted with surface search radar— were stationed north and west of Savo Island to provide early warning of any ships approaching down "The Slot." *Ralph Talbot* and *Blue's* radar had a range of only 10 miles, and peaks of nearby islands could shelter approaching vessels in the radar return's clutter. At 8:30 P.M., Adm. Crutchley was summoned to Adm. Turner's command ship *McCawley* (AP-10). This action took *Australia* out of the Southern Force's patrol line.

The night of August 8–9 was hot and humid with low, overcast clouds and, at 11:30 P.M., a heavy tropical rain enveloped the area. Minutes before 1:00 A.M., Adm. Mikawa's force steamed astern of *Blue* at 24 knots as the destroyer was on its outbound patrol leg sailing away from Guadalcanal. The Japanese cruisers went unnoticed.

Sailing through the Savo Strait, *Chokai* led the cruisers past destroyer *Jarvis* (DD-393), which had been heavily damaged during an air raid at noon on August 8. The destroyer's antiaircraft gunners hit a Kate, and as the bomber disintegrated its torpedo struck *Jarvis*, ripping a 50-foot gash in the hull. After being towed to Lunga Roads and making repairs, *Jarvis* sailed to Tulagi under her own power. Considered seaworthy, the destroyer left Tulagi at midnight en route to Sydney, Australia, for repairs. Passing behind the Japanese cruisers, they fired a spread of torpedoes at the destroyer, but none found their target.

Having passed *Jarvis*, *Ralph Talbot*, and *Blue* undetected, Japanese lookouts quickly spotted *Chicago* and *Canberra* of the Southern Force. At 1:38 A.M., torpedoes from Vice Adm. Mikawa's ships splashed into the Savo Strait, headed for *Bagley*, *Canberra*, and *Chicago*. As the torpedoes raced to find their targets, destroyer *Patterson* spotted the Japanese ships and radioed, "Warning, Warning: Strange Ships Entering Harbor!" Seconds later, floatplanes from the Japanese cruisers dropped parachute flares above Lunga Roads, illuminating the transports and silhouetting *Canberra* and *Chicago*. As the bright light flashed across the night sky, startling sailors on the American ships, Vice Adm. Mikawa ordered his force to open fire.

Canberra took two torpedoes in the starboard side, followed by shells that killed her captain and the gunnery officer. The cruiser was able to fire two torpedoes and a few shells from her main batteries before coming to a dead stop and listing to starboard. Destroyers *Bagley* and *Patterson* fired torpedoes at the Japanese column without effect. *Patterson* took a shell near the Number Four gun turret, starting fires, yet *Bagley* was by passed by the Japanese gunners. *Chicago* dodged two torpedoes, but a third struck the bow while her gunners groped for targets in the darkness. Seventeen torpedoes had been fired at the Southern Force and three found their mark, effectively eliminating those ships from the rest of the battle.

Traveling at 26 knots, the Japanese ships quickly left the Southern Force behind. *Chokai* and attending cruisers then began a left turn to skirt Savo Island, approaching the Northern Force from the rear. The maneuver did not go well, and the Japanese cruisers split into three columns—*Chokai* by itself; *Aoba, Kinugasa, Kako,* and *Furataka* (in steaming order); and *Tenryu* and *Tatsuta* closest to Savo Island. At 1:48 A.M., *Chokai* unleashed a spread of torpedoes at the Northern Force. On board *Astoria,* last in the Northern Force column, another set of parachute flares dropped by the Japanese floatplanes over the transports caused the ship to go to General Quarters. Moments later, shells from *Chokai* landed short and *Astoria* returned fire. *Chokai's* fifth volley of 8-inch shells had the proper range and impacted *Astoria* amidships. Severe fires were started, making the cruiser a beacon for Japanese gunners who relentlessly pounded the cruiser.

Quincy was caught in *Aoba's* searchlight and shells quickly rained down on the American ship. All five of the cruiser's SOC-3 floatplanes were destroyed, the aviation gasoline illuminating *Quincy's* decks for the Japanese gunners. Shells landed on *Quincy* from bow to stern, killing Captain Samuel Moore and almost everyone else on the bridge. Within an hour, *Quincy* was on the bottom, adding to the tally of ships that would earn this body of water the nickname "Iron Bottom Sound."

The leading cruiser in the Northern Force column was *Vincennes,* and like *Quincy* before her, was caught in the searchlights of the Japanese cruisers. *Kako's* second salvo fired at *Vincennes* struck the bridge, aircraft, and hangar, and severed power to the turrets while cutting the communication lines. Even without power, *Vincennes* was able to fire her batteries, hitting *Kinugasa.* Then the torpedoes came—two, maybe three 24-inch Long Lance torpedoes struck the cruiser's port side. Then shellfire came from starboard. *Vincennes* was caught between two of the three Japanese cruiser columns, burning brightly. At 2:15 A.M., the Japanese ceased fire. Fifteen minutes later the order to abandon ship was given, and shortly before 3 A.M., *Vincennes* rolled over and sank.

Ralph Talbot, the picket destroyer that missed detecting the oncoming Japanese cruisers, was mauled as they passed Savo Island retiring from action. *Yubari, Furutaka,* and *Tenryu* sighted the American destroyer at 2:15 A.M., and began firing. *Ralph Talbot* was able to fire a number of 5-inch shells as well as four torpedoes before taking on a 20 degree list. Then providence intervened and a squall line crossed between the destroyer and the Japanese cruisers.

Vice Adm. Mikawa decided to retire from the battle, unable to attack the Lunga Roads anchorage and escape before daylight. He believed American carriers were lurking nearby, which had air superiority above the Guadalcanal area during daylight hours.

At 3:25 A.M., *Blue* spotted *Jarvis* limping its way toward Sydney. *Blue* made contact with the destroyer but the *Jarvis* declined assistance. Shortly after dawn, *Jarvis* was sighted streaming oil approximately 40 miles from Guadalcanal by a scout plane from *Saratoga.*

When the sun rose over Savo Island, *Vincennes* and *Quincy* were on the bottom and it was only a matter of time for *Canberra* and *Astoria.* Destroyer *Patterson* came alongside *Canberra* in the early-morning hours and attempted to aid the damage-control process. Unable to salvage the cruiser in time to withdraw as part of the amphibious force, *Canberra* was ordered scuttled at 8 A.M. *Astoria's* sailors fought to keep the ship afloat. The ship was abandoned at 4:45 A.M., but the crew returned in a valiant effort to save her. Around 11:00 A.M., one of the ship's magazines exploded and by 12:15 P.M., *Astoria* was also on the bottom.

Armorers load Grumman TBF-1s in preparation for battle in North Africa. Sangamon (CVE-26) and Suwannee (CVE-27) each had nine TBFs that could deliver up to 1,600 pounds of torpedoes or bombs. The TBF quickly replaced the aging Douglas TBD Devastator as the U.S. Navy's primary carrier-based torpedo bomber. *(National Archives/80GK-15239)*

THE MEDAL OF HONOR

Lt. Cmdr. John D. Bulkeley was one of only 57 U.S. Navy personnel to be awarded the Medal of Honor during World War II. Bulkeley was recognized for his leadership of Motor Torpedo Boat Squadron Three from December 7, 1941, to April 10, 1942. Bulkeley's squadron fought the Japanese during the dark opening days of the war against Japan in the Philippines. Gen. Douglas MacArthur was evacuated from Manila on board Bulkeley's PT-41.
(National Archives/80GK-13927)

The Medal of Honor is given to active duty U.S. service-members for conspicuous gallantry, and is America's oldest, continuously awarded honor. President Abraham Lincoln signed Public Resolution 82 establishing the U.S. Navy's Medal of Valor on December 21, 1861, "to be bestowed upon such petty officers, seamen, landsmen, and Marines as shall most distinguish themselves by their gallantry and other seaman-like qualities during the present war." In recognition of Army soldiers who distinguished themselves on the battlefield, Lincoln signed a resolution providing the Army Medal of Honor for "such noncommissioned officers and privates as shall most distinguish themselves by their gallantry in action, and other soldier-like qualities, during the present insurrection." In 1863, Congress combined the two services' medals into one, and adapted the name Medal of Honor. In 1942, the medal's qualification criteria was changed, and the award was subsequently given for combat bravery only.

During World War II, 440 servicemen received the Medal of Honor, 250 of which were posthumously awarded. The Medal of Honor was awarded to 301 soldiers, 57 sailors, 81 Marines, and one Coast Guardsman. Representative of those selected to receive America's highest honor, John D. Bulkeley, pictured above, distinguished himself while commander of Motor Torpedo Boat Squadron Three operating in the Philippines from December 7, 1941, to April 10, 1942. His Medal of Honor citation reads, in part: "The remarkable achievement of Lt. Cmdr. Bulkeley's command in damaging or destroying a notable number of Japanese enemy planes, surface combatant and merchant ships, and in dispersing landing parties and land-based enemy forces during the four months and eight days of operation without benefit of repairs, overhaul, or maintenance facilities for his squadron, is believed to be without precedent in this type of warfare.

"His dynamic forcefulness and daring in offensive action, his brilliantly planned and skillfully executed attacks, supplemented by a unique resourcefulness and ingenuity, characterize him as an outstanding leader of men and a gallant and intrepid seaman. These qualities, coupled with a complete disregard for his own personal safety, reflect great credit upon him and the Naval Service."

Of the millions of men and women who have defended America and its Allies, only 3,407 men and one woman have received the Medal of Honor since its inception, and 19 of those have received two medals, each for a separate battle.

Vice Adm. Mikawa's ships had fired 61 torpedoes, 1,020 8-inch and 885 4.7-inch shells to sink four heavy cruisers and heavily damage another cruiser and two destroyers. In the engagement, the Allies lost 1,023 men killed and 709 wounded. Only *Kako* was lost when, on the return voyage to Kavieng, Lt. Cmdr. John R. Moore in *S-44* fired four torpedoes that sent the Japanese cruiser to the bottom.

Guadalcanal would not come cheaply for the U.S. Navy afloat, the Marines ashore, or the Army's flyers in the skies above. Before the year was out, five additional large-scale naval engagements took place (Battle of the Eastern Solomons, August 8–9; the Battle of Cape Esperance, October 11–12; the Battle of Santa Cruz, October 25–26; the Battle of Guadalcanal, November 12–15, and the Battle of Tassafaronga, November 30). In the engagements, the Allies lost the carrier *Hornet*, the cruisers *Atlanta, Helena, Juneau,* and *Northampton,* plus eight destroyers. On the Japanese side of the loss column, battleships *Kirishima* and *Hiei,* aircraft carrier *Ryujo,* cruisers *Furutaka* and *Kinugasa,* plus six destroyers, and seven *Marus* were all sunk by the Allies.

For the remainder of the year, the Japanese primarily employed aircraft to harass the Allies, and it would be more than a year before the sea around Guadalcanal could be considered in Allied hands.

Operation Torch: Allies Invade North Africa

American strategic planners of the Joint Chiefs of Staff had envisioned a strike at the heart of Germany as the quickest way to end the war. Gen. George C. Marshall proposed a cross-channel invasion in 1942, with Allied forces holding parts of France until a follow-up push across the continent in 1943, then crossing the Rhine River and into the heart of Germany in early 1944. The idea looked great on paper, but in reality there were no troops to accomplish the mission. For a cross-channel invasion to occur in 1942, the manpower would have to come primarily from England. But the British did not have enough troops for the operation as they were committed to fighting the Germans at home, in North Africa, and were fighting the Japanese in India and Burma.

The British Combined Chiefs of Staff agreed to an invasion of Morocco and Algeria on July 24, 1942, with a number of conditions, one of which was to plan and prepare for the attack without committing to the operation until mid-September. Two days later, with procrastination political suicide for both President Roosevelt and Prime Minister Winston Churchill, the American leader committed the Allies to the operation.

An invasion of North Africa would give the Allies a second front in the battle with German General Erwin Rommel's Afrika Korps, control over the mouth of the Mediterranean Sea, and new air and naval bases to fight the anti submarine war in the Atlantic. Plans called for a three-pronged attack, securing French Morocco as well as the coastal areas of Algeria, and then an overland march into Tunisia to fight the Afrika Korps.

The invasion was set for the morning of November 8. Two of the three invasion fleets sailed from England for Algerian landing zones in the Mediterranean, the Center Naval Task Force bound for Oran with 39,000 troops, and the Eastern Naval Task Force to Algiers with 33,000 men. The third, the Western Naval Task Force (Task Force 34) under Rear Adm. H. Kent Hewitt, embarked 35,000 troops under the command of Gen. George S. Patton at Hampton Roads, Norfolk, Virginia, on October 23. Task Force 34 included the battleships *Massachusetts* (BB-54), *New York* (BB-34), and *Texas* (BB-35), the cruisers *Augusta* (CL-31), *Brooklyn* (CL-40), *Cleveland* (CL-55), *Philadelphia* (CL-41), *Savannah* (CL-42), *Tuscaloosa* (CA-37), and *Wichita* (CA-45), plus 38 destroyers, 31 transports, five oilers, and other support ships. The operation's aircraft carriers sortied from Bermuda and joined the task force in the mid-Atlantic. Air cover was provided by carriers *Ranger* (CV-4), *Sangamon* (CVE-26), *Santee* (CVE-29), and *Suwannee* (CVE-27). *Chenango* (CVE-28) sailed with a deck-load of 77 P-40s from the 33rd Fighter Group that would provide post-invasion air support for Army ground units.

The Eastern Naval Task Force landed the 34th U.S. Infantry Division (consisting of regiments of the 9th Infantry and 1st Armored Divisions—10,000 men) and the 78th British Infantry Division (23,000 men) at Algiers. Resistance ended that night, but German bombers continued to harass the task force for the next week, damaging the transport *Leedstown* to the point where the ship was abandoned and later sunk.

Chenango (CVE-28) sailed to North Africa with a deckload of Curtiss P-40s belonging to the 33rd Fighter Group. Once the Port Lyautey Airfield was secured, Chenango catapulted the fighters to support Army troops in the march across North Africa to Tunisia. Seventy-seven P-40s were launched by CVE-28, of which two were lost at sea and 17 were damaged in landing accidents. *(National Archives/80GK-874)*

The Center Naval Task Force landed the U.S. 1st Infantry Division and elements of the 1st Armored Division on the east and west sides of Oran, Algeria. In a two-pincer attack, the troops took Oran the following day. Ships off shore suffered greatly in the combined German and Italian submarine attacks as well as bombing from Axis aircraft. Ten transports, the British Destroyer *Martin*, and antiaircraft ship *Tynwald* were all sent to the bottom. In exchange, *U-259, U-331, U-595, U-605,* and *U-660* were all sunk by Allied forces in the area.

The Western Naval Task Force sailed across the Atlantic, split into three assault forces, and landed troops at Casablanca, Sadi, and Mehdia, French Morocco, on November 8. The main thrust, at Casablanca, saw troops go ashore at Fedhala, approximately 18 miles north of the city. While the landing craft steered toward shore, cruiser *Brooklyn* began shelling the coastal defense guns at "the Sherki." One gun and the battery director were put out of action as American troops went ashore. Fighting was limited as the French were retreating toward Casablanca and reinforcing their position on the outskirts of town. By late afternoon, more than 7,750 troops were ashore, heading for an assault on Casablanca.

Defending the port of Casablanca was the El Hank coastal battery, four 8-inch cannons, backed up by the French battleship *Jean Bart*'s four 15-inch guns. Attacked at first light by American SBD dive-bombers, *Jean Bart* was silenced for the day while El Hank was only out of the battle for a short time. During a lull in the battle, around 8:15 A.M., seven French destroyers sortied from Casablanca harbor to attack American transports and landing craft.

▲ SBD gunners were given the opportunity to practice their craft firing the plane's twin .30-caliber machine guns from the deck during the long transatlantic crossing prior to the invasion of North Africa. The national insignia of planes participating in the invasion were given yellow surrounds to increase the speed of aircraft recognition. This was done to aid the thousands of American antiaircraft gunners who had never been in combat prior to Operation Torch. *(National Archives/80GK-15976)*

◀ Escort carrier Sangamon (CVE-29) under way in calm seas near Bermuda headed for North African waters. Two officers stroll among the SBD-3 dive-bombers parked to port and to starboard the carrier's complement of F4F-4 fighters. Sangamon carried nine Grumman TBF Avenger torpedo bombers, nine Douglas SBDs, and 30 Grumman F4F Wildcats into battle. *(National Archives/80GK-15250)*

Destroyer *Ludlow* (DD-438) was under fire from the French ships and had taken a 6-inch shell in the forward hull when *Augusta* and *Brooklyn* engaged the attackers. The rapid, accurate fire of the American cruisers and destroyers sent French destroyers *Fougueux* and *Boulonnais* to the bottom and heavily damaged light cruiser *Primauguet* and destroyers *Brestois* and *Frondeur*—all three were later sunk by U.S. Navy dive-bombers. The only American setback was the wounding of 14 men aboard *Wichita*, which was struck by a shell from El Hank.

Safi, to the south of Casablanca, was a small man-made harbor, deep enough to accommodate the 27.2-foot draft of *Lakehurst* (APV-3), a tank transport ship. *Lakehurst's* cargo of Sherman tanks was to unload at Safi and battle their way to Casablanca, forming the southern pincer in the attack on the city. To secure the harbor, destroyers *Bernadou* (DD-153) and *Cole* (DD-155) made a daring night attack on Safi Harbor. Each destroyer steamed into the harbor under fire and landed assault troops of the 47th Infantry. The battle raged most of the day with *New York* and *Philadelphia* bombarding the coastal defense *Batterie Railleuse* north of town. Aircraft from *Santee* maintained air superiority over the invasion area and destroyed most of the aircraft at the nearby Marrakech airfield before the French planes could take off. By midday the port of Safi was secured, and *Lakehurst* was docked and unloading tanks, gasoline, and ammunition by 3 P.M.

To outflank the defenders of Casablanca, landings were made 80 miles north at Mehdia. Situated at the mouth of the Sebou River, the town and invasion areas were protected by the Kasba fortress. U.S. troops had to secure Mehdia and the fortress before moving north to capture their prime objective, the airfield at Port Lyautey. The guns from Kasba put out a tremendous volume of shellfire and, in spite of constant pounding from the cruiser *Savannah*, were not silenced until November 10 when Army ground troops captured the fortress. In an attempt to bypass the Kasba and advance toward the Port Lyautey airfield, the World War I–vintage destroyer *Dallas* (DD-199) embarked a 75-man U.S. Army Raider battalion.

On the morning of November 10, the raiders cut the net blocking the river mouth and *Dallas* steamed up the Sebou under intense fire. Guided by French river pilot Rene Malavergne (who was later awarded the Navy Cross—the first such foreign national so awarded), *Dallas* was steered around numerous sunken ships and other obstacles, over shallow sand and mud bars, to eventually land the raiders within striking distance of the airfield. Joining elements of the Army's 2nd Armored Division, the airfield at Port Lyautey was captured, and the P-40s from *Chenango* began landing around 10:30 A.M.

Later that morning, just 15 minutes before Gen. Patton's troops were to assault Casablanca, French Adm. F. C. Michelier offered a truce. Orchestrated by American Army Gen. Mark Clark, Robert Murphy of the American Foreign Service, and Admiral J. L. F. Darlan, the French agreed to cease fire and cooperate with the Allies. Now the march to Tunisia could begin.

Although the French had ceased hostilities, the Axis were not going to let the invasion of French Morocco go unchallenged. German U-boats were dispatched to the area to attack Allied shipping, and after sunset on November 11, *U-173* let her presence be known. The U-boat slipped through the destroyer screen and around a defensive minefield to sink the 9,359-ton transport *Joseph Hewes*. The sub also torpedoed the oiler *Winooski* and destroyer *Hambleton* (DD-455), but neither hit was fatal. *Hambleton* was hit on the portside, amidships, and began listing to port.

Once the Harbor at Casablanca was secured, *Hambleton* was towed in, the ship cut in half, and a section of hull 40 feet long was removed and the ship rejoined. The destroyer returned to Boston in the company of an ocean-going tug for permanent repairs. (*Hambleton* later went on to a distinguished career in the Atlantic, participating in the sinking of *U-616*, and in the Pacific.) Four nights later, *U-173* sent a torpedo into the starboard side of attack transport *Electra* between Safi and Casablanca. The ship was beached at Casablanca, and four months later returned to the United States for overhaul and repair.

Having sunk one ship and heavily damaged three others, *U-173* continued its search for targets of opportunity in French Moroccan waters on the night of November 16. The sub was depth charged by destroyers *Quick* (DD-490), *Swanson* (DD-443), and *Woolsey* (DD-437) off Casablanca Harbor, with a loss of all 57 on board.

U-130 joined the fray on November 12, sending nearly 35,000 tons of U.S. transports and their cargoes to the bottom. *Edward Rutledge* (AP-52), 9,360 tons, was the first ship to sink, taking 15 men with her. *Hugh L. Scott* (AP-43), 12,479 tons, was hit by a torpedo and burst into flames. Eight officers and 51 men perished in the attack. *U-130's* final victim was the transport *Tasker H. Bliss* (AP-42), 12,568 tons, hit by a torpedo that caused severe fires. The transport burned through the night and sank at 2:30 A.M. the following morning. *U-130* made good its post attack escape and continued its fight against Allied shipping into the spring of 1943.

The capture of bases in northern Africa enabled the Allies to control the Straits of Gibraltar, increase air patrols into the Atlantic, and pursue the Germans into Tunisia. Rommel's Afrika Korps put up a gallant fight to the end and surrendered on May 13, 1943. Operation Torch gave the Allies valuable experience in amphibious operations. The lessons learned in north Africa would later be applied in the invasions of Anzio, Iwo Jima, Normandy, and Okinawa.

Manitowoc-built boats were tested in the Great Lakes, then barged by dry dock down the Mississippi River to be launched in the Gulf of Mexico. Raton (SS-270) enters dry dock at Lockport, Illinois, July 29, 1943, for the journey downriver. To clear low-lying bridges, the sub's periscope shears have been removed. Between November 1943 and May 1945, Raton accounted for 13 Japanese vessels of 44,178 tons. (*Wisconsin Maritime Museum, P68-1-44*)

SHORT-LIVED USS LAFAYETTE

Lafayette (ex-French liner Normandie) on her side in New York Harbor. When this late-spring 1943 photo was taken, the entire superstructure of the liner had been cut away and pumping operations were under way. *(National Archives/80GK-3874)*

Once the pride of the French shipping line Compagnie General Transatlantique, S.S. Normandie was launched from the Penhoë Shipyards at St. Nazaire on October 29, 1932. Normandie had an overall length of 1,029 feet, displaced 83,423 tons, and was one of the largest ships plying the transatlantic route in the late 1930s. The French liner competed for passengers with the ships of Britain's Cunard-White Star Line, including the 80,774-ton Queen Mary and 83,673-ton Queen Elizabeth. World renowned for its beautiful art deco interior furnishings, luxurious accommodations, and 29-knot cruising speed, Normandie could accommodate 848 first-class passengers, 670 in second, and 54 third-class passengers. It took 1,345 officers and crew to run the ship.

Normandie was interned by the United States in New York Harbor when France capitulated to Nazi Germany in June 1940. On December 12, 1941, the liner was seized and subsequently transferred to the U.S. Navy for use as a troopship. Renamed U.S.S. Lafayette (AP-53), the Todd Shipyards subsidiary Robins Dry Dock and Repair Co. began the ship's conversion from luxury liner to troopship configuration.

On February 9, 1942, at approximately 2:30 p.m., workers were stripping out the ship's interior when a spark from a welder's torch caught a pile of mattresses on fire. The fire quickly spread while workers tried to extinguish the blaze. Fireboats came alongside and began pouring water into the burning ship as smoke from the blaze settled across the New York skyline. As darkness approached, the liner began to list to port from the weight of the water poured in to fight the fire. At 2:25 a.m., on the morning of February 10, Lafayette rolled to port, coming to rest on the harbor bottom.

A tremendous salvage effort, one rivaling operations in Pearl Harbor at the time, was began to right and re-float the liner. After cutting off the ship's superstructure, Lafayette was righted on August 7, 1943. The ship was subsequently dry docked, reclassified as an aircraft and personnel transport (APV-4), and surveyed. Deemed too heavily damaged to be economically returned to the fleet, the hull was stored for the duration of the war. On October 11, 1945, Lafayette was stricken from the Navy's inventory and sold for scrap to Lipsett, Inc., of New York City on October 3, 1946.

Huge crowds watched as the 1,029-foot-long Lafayette was tugged down New York Harbor to dry dock in October 1943. Deemed uneconomical to repair, the hull was stored until after the war and sold for scrap. *(National Archives/80GK-3864)*

After righting the ship on August 7, 1943, Lafayette rests at its berth prior to being dry docked. Note that the name Normandie can clearly be seen on the starboard bow behind the anchor. *(National Archives/80GK-3873)*

The Japanese were still heavily entrenched on the northern coast of New Guinea during the opening days of 1943. On January 19, eight transports escorted by two cruisers and five destroyers landed 9,400 Japanese troops at Wewak, 300 miles up the coast from Finschhafen. The garrison was re supplied on February 19, and during the next few months the Japanese constructed an airfield complex with four runways at Wewak.

Gen. MacArthur had made progress routing the Japanese from the northeastern coast of New Guinea, evicting the Japanese from the Buna-Gona area. The brutal fighting involving American and Australian troops lasted nearly 60 days. In addition to fighting the Japanese, the Allies had to defend themselves from malaria and dengue fever. This battle cost the Americans 787 killed and 2,172 wounded, while the Australians lost 2,165 killed and 3,533 wounded. In addition, U.S. forces evacuated 7,920 men suffering various jungle ailments.

In March, the Australians were engaging Japanese troops around Wau, New Guinea, near the Huon Gulf. Believing that additional troops were needed to evict the Australians from Wau, the Japanese planned to reinforce the 3,500-man garrison at Lae with nearly 7,000 troops from the 18th Army. At midnight, February 28, eight transports and eight destroyers, commanded by Rear Adm. Masatomi Kimura, left Rabaul's Simpson Harbor with 6,912 men bound for Lae. The load of men, rations, ammunition, fuel, and equipment had been equally distributed between the transports to prevent a single ship's loss from aborting the entire mission. Sailing through a storm, the group went undiscovered by Allied search planes as it sailed the length of New Britain's northern coast.

A B-24 "Liberator" from the 321st Bomb Squadron, 90th Bomb Group, spotted Adm. Kimura's ships escorting the transports at 4 P.M. on March 1. In what became the opening action of the Battle of the Bismarck Sea, the B-24 transmitted the convoy's position, speed, and course, and monitored its progress until 9:30 P.M. The following morning, at 8:25 A.M., a Liberator from the 320th Bomb Squadron relocated the ships. Two dozen American heavy bombers attacked Adm. Kimura's ships, dropping bombs from 5,000 feet.

Kyokusei Maru, a 5,493-ton transport carrying 1,203 men as well as a pair of 150-mm artillery pieces, was sunk, and *Teiyo Maru* (6,870 tons) and *Nojima* (8,125 tons) suffered bomb damage. Destroyers *Asagumo* and *Yukikaze* rescued more than 900 men from the sinking *Kyokusei Maru* and, racing ahead landed the survivors at Lae, before returning to guard the transports. During the night of March 2–3, an Australian PBY monitored the ship's speed and course.

Having sailed within reach of Allied land-based medium bombers on the morning of March 3, the Japanese convoy was given an air escort of forty A6M Zero fighters. The ships were located at 8:30 A.M., and, at 10:00 A.M., all hell broke loose when bombers of the American Fifth Air Force approached the convoy. A flight of B-17 bombers escorted by 16 P-38 "Lightning" fighters approached from 5,000 feet, while Douglas A-20 and North American B-25 medium bombers came in at wave-top height to skip bomb the ships. Twin-engine Royal Australian Air Force Beaufighters added to the conflagration by strafing the ships. Simultaneously, the Japanese airfields around Lae were attacked by Allied fighters to prevent any further aircraft from joining the fight.

When the Fifth Air Force and its Australian counterparts had retired for the day, four destroyers were capable of making way, two were dead in the water, and one transport remained afloat. Destroyers *Asagumo, Shikinami, Uranami,* and *Yukikaze* picked up as many survivors from the water as they could before fleeing north to the safety of Simpson Harbor.

By nightfall, the job of finishing off the Japanese convoy had fallen to the PT-boats of the U.S. Navy's Lt. Cmdr. Barry K. Atkins from Tufi, New Guinea. Ten boats set out, but two had to return to base after striking objects in the water. When the boats arrived in the waters off Lae, transport *Oigawa Maru* (6,494 tons) had been abandoned and was on fire. Still afloat, *PT-143* and *PT-150* each fired a single torpedo, sinking the ship. The following morning, March 4, destroyer *Arashio* was located by a B-17 that scored a direct hit, sinking the destroyer, and the other destroyer was sunk by skip-bombing B-25s.

A PT-boat gun crew practices antiaircraft firing with the boat's single afterdeck 20-mm cannon. Photos of PT-boat crews in action against the enemy are extremely rare as most of their operations were conducted at night. Mellville, Rhode Island's school boats and trainee crews offered the best opportunity to photograph the PTs in action. *(National Archives/80GK-13626)*

▲ At the Battle of the Bismarck Sea, PT-boats were called in to mop up after the Japanese had been mauled by U.S. Army Air Force and Royal Australian Air Force aircraft. PT-143 and PT-150 participated in the sinking of transport Oigawa Maru (6,494 tons). This study of PT-333 was shot off New York on August 20, 1943. *(National Archives/80GK-3914)*

▶ PT-314 patrols the coast near the PT-boat school at Mellville, Rhode Island, in July 1943. Fitted with a 20 mm cannon on the stern, two twin .50-caliber machine gun mounts, two torpedoes, and six depth charges, the PTs played a vital role in the Mediterranean and Pacific theaters. *(National Archives/80GK-13597)*

upper right ▶▶

The crew of a Higgins-built PT-boat prepares to launch a Mk-XIII torpedo at Miami sub chaser training school. Note the exhaust trail from the engine and turning prop. *(National Archives/80GK-6659)*

lower right ▶▶

On board Missouri (BB-63) Seaman Second Class Charles J. Hanson works on a 40-mm gun mount. His tattoos commemorate Vincennes (CA-44) and its crew, of which Hanson was a member. Vincennes escorted the Doolittle Raid, participated in the Battle of Midway, and was lost on August 9, 1942, during the Battle of Savo Island. *(National Archives/80GK-4510)*

The loss of destroyers and transports in Huon Gulf was the last attempt to supply the New Guinea garrisons by large surface ships. Allied air superiority forced the Japanese to supply its troops on New Guinea by submarine or small barges sailing at night.

Yamamoto's "I" Operation

In what was to become the last air major offensive in the Solomons, Adm. Yamamoto launched the "I" Operation on April 1. Aircraft from the carriers *Hiyo, Junyo, Zuikaku,* and *Zuiho* bolstered the land-based aircraft at Rabaul. Combined, the "I" Operation had 182 fighters, 92 dive-bombers, 72 twin-engine bombers, and nearly two dozen torpedo planes. In preparation for the operation, aircraft from Rabaul were staged at Buka, Ballale, and Kahili airfields. The air assault was broken into two phases: first, an aggressive attack on the ships anchored at Lunga Roads off Guadalcanal and Tulagi Harbor; and second, on April 11, an air assault of the airfields and harbor of Port Moresby, New Guinea.

The April 7 attack saw 67 Val dive-bombers and 110 A6M Zero fighters maul the Allied ships. Tanker *Kanawha* (AO-1), which had just departed Tulagi Harbor, was struck by five bombs. The crew returned to the ship to extinguish the fire and with the assistance of tug *Rail* (AT-139) beached the oiler. In spite of the crew's brave efforts, the ship slid off the beach and sank in deep water during the night. The Val dive-bombers next struck the New Zealand Navy destroyer

Up-close deck view of a Fletcher-class destroyer at sea detailing the ship's torpedo tubes, Number Three 5-inch/.38-caliber gun, and twin 40-mm mount. The overall solid-blue scheme was known as Measure 21 camouflage. *(National Archives/80GK-6067)*

▶ Convoys along the U.S. East Coast, Gulf of Mexico, and in the Caribbean were often escorted by Navy airships. The ability to slowly glide over a convoy's merchant ships while scouting for enemy submarines made the blimp a formidable weapon in the war against the U-boat. Seventy-seven lighter-than-air craft crewmembers were lost during World War II. It is estimated that more than 88,000 ships were escorted by Navy airships. *(National Archives/80GK-13894)*

Moa, which was hit by two bombs and sank within a matter of minutes. Destroyer *Aaron Ward* (DD-483) was escorting *LST-449* past Guadalcanal's Togoma Point when six Vals attacked. One bomb hit and four near-misses severely damaged the destroyer's hull. It was believed the destroyer could be salvaged and was taken in tow by *Ortolan* (ASR-5) and *Vireo* (AT-144), but the destroyer sank that night only three miles from Tulagi Harbor.

After the one-day attack on Guadalcanal, Yamamoto's attentions turned to New Guinea. On April 11, 94 Vals and Zeros attacked shipping in Oro Bay. One transport was sunk, another damaged to the point where it had to be run up on the beach to prevent its sinking, and an Australian navy minesweeper was also hit. The following morning, 131 fighters and 43 twin-engine bombers attacked Port Moresby. The attack was unsuccessful, failing to hit any of the ships at anchor and only damaging a few planes on the airfields surrounding Port Moresby. On April 14, Milne Bay was struck by 188 Japanese planes. The Dutch transport *Van Heemskerk*, carrying a load of gasoline in drums and ammunition, was hit in one of its holds, which ignited. The ship was a total loss.

Adm. Yamamoto believed the claims of his aviators and cancelled the "I" Operation after the attacks on Milne Bay. Two days later, while visiting airfields in the northern Solomon Islands, Yamamoto and his staff were flying from

American shipbuilders were able to construct more ships than the Axis could destroy. The backbone of Allied supply convoys was the Liberty EC-2, a British design built in American yards using the assembly-line process. The dry cargo ship in the foreground of this Atlantic convoy is a Liberty, and a tanker is off its port bow. Most convoys shepherded 40 to 50 ships and, in spite of the armed escort ships, more than 200 Liberty Ships were sunk by the enemy. *(National Archives/80GK-14031)*

Clearing the decks of New York (BB-34) near Iceland. The turret behind the sailors contains 16-inch/.45-caliber cannons. New York escorted convoys to Iceland and Scotland at the height of the U-boat war. *(National Archives/80GK-13596)*

Rabaul to Kahili in a pair of G4M Betty bombers. A flight of 16 P-38s led by Maj. John W. Mitchell intercepted the Betty bombers at 9:35 A.M. while on approach to Kahili. Capt. Thomas G. Lanphier shot down one Betty, and Lt. Rex T. Barber downed the other. Yamamoto, the architect of Japan's attack on Pearl Harbor, and most of his staff were killed in a matter of minutes. Yamamoto was succeeded by Adm. Mineichi Koga.

Battle of the Atlantic

The months stretching from September through November 1942, saw German U-boats patrolling and sinking ships within sight of many East Coast cities. In December, the U-boats shifted their attentions back to covoys carrying war materiel to England and the Soviet Union. In the first three months of 1943, U-boats enjoyed tremendous success—176 U-boat patrols in the North Atlantic sank 128 ships for 779,727 tons. For the U.S. Navy, the U-boat menace was both a public relations nightmare and bonanza at the same time. As horrifying as the losses were, each one encouraged American shipyard workers to build more ships, and build them faster. In the 12 months ending in December 1943, U.S. shipyards built 1,949 ships of more than 13 million tons.

President Roosevelt and Prime Minister Churchill agreed at the Casablanca Conference, which concluded on January 23, that the Allies would fight a "Germany First" war, delaying an all-out assault against Japan until the Nazis had been defeated. In addition, the Allies would demand unconditional surrender terms from the Axis aggressors, and war production priority would be given to antisubmarine weapons. One week after the Casablanca Conference ended, Grossadmiral Karl Dönitz succeeded Grossadmiral Erich Raeder as commander in chief of the German Navy (similar to a U.S. Navy Fleet Admiral).

The conference's agreement to increase production of antisubmarine weapons included new ships. Not only were destroyers (DD) and destroyer escorts (DE) being built in large numbers, but cargo ships were being converted into escort aircraft carriers (CVE). Known as "baby flattops," these smaller ships could carry fewer aircraft, but would work in concert with destroyers and destroyer escorts to give U-boats a one-two punch.

Oftentimes carrier-based aircraft would locate a submarine, mark its location for the destroyers, and then the surface ships would steam in and make the kill. In addition, the successful British-led effort to crack the German naval code gave the escort carrier and destroyer hunter/killer groups an excellent point to begin an antisubmarine search. The deciphered intercepts were known as *Enigma*, a closely guarded secret in the American and British high commands.

When the U-boats were able to employ "wolf-pack" tactics, their success was only limited by the aggressiveness of a convoy's escorts. The success of the U-boats was

demonstrated during the first 20 of March, a time when the weather in the North Atlantic is at its worst. Foul weather causes many ships to fall behind the convoy's protective screen, becoming stragglers—a favorite and easy target for the U-boats. The submarines would shadow the stragglers, and when the weather receded to the point where a successful attack could be made, the U-boats would deal them a deathblow.

Convoy HX-229 (HX—Halifax to the United Kingdom) and Slow Convoy 122 (SC-122) fell victim to both the weather and U-boat wolf-pack tactics in mid-March. SC-122, consisting of 50 transports and nine escorts, sailed on March 8, followed three days later by Convoy HX-229 of five escort ships herding 40 merchant ships. An additional 39 merchant ships and six small escort vessels followed in HX-229A, which departed New York on March 9. SC-122 encountered fierce weather with gale-force winds on March 15. One merchant ship, *Selfoss*, diverted to Iceland and the Canadian trawler *Campobello* sprang a hull leak that required

the ship to be abandoned. *Campobello* was scuttled by a depth charge from the corvette *Godetia*.

As the three convoys steamed eastward across the North Atlantic, they had no idea that two wolf packs were waiting for them. U-boat groups *Dränger* (Harrier), consisting of 11 subs, *Raubgraf* (Robber Baron), 11 subs, and the 18 of group *Stürmer* (Daredevil) were ordered south to intercept the Allied ships. *U-91* (Heinz Walkerling, commander) located HX-229 on March 15. *U-653* (Gerhard Feiler) located additional elements of HX-229 on the same day in a position farther east than that reported by *U-91*. Both subs radioed position reports to U-boat headquarters, which in turn ordered 11 boats from *Stürmer*, six from *Dränger*, nine from *Raubgraf*, plus 11 other U-boats in the area to attack the convoys. The subs were in position the following day.

James Oglethorpe was the first ship in HX-229 to be hit. *U-758* (Helmut Manseck) sent a torpedo into the freighter's starboard hull, which started fires and flooded the forward compartments. Thirty men were rescued by HMS *Pennywort*,

The French D-211 Pimpernelle (U.S. Navy ex-YMS-26) minesweeper drops a depth charge in the Atlantic on a training exercise. Depth setting and the speed of the craft were prime factors when rolling depth charges from a ship's stern. The YMS motor minesweepers were fitted with a 3-inch dual-purpose gun forward and a pair of 20-mm guns for antiaircraft protection at the stern. The craft still retains its U.S. Navy bow markings. *(National Archives/80GK-1689)*

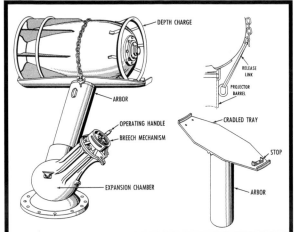

Depth charge projectors such as the "K-gun," illustrated, and the later "Y-guns," could launch either a 300-pound cylindrical depth charge or the 200-pound teardrop charge (Mark 9 or Mark 14) as shown. The range a K-gun could throw a depth charge was determined by the amount of powder used to launch it. Crews had premeasured charges capable of sending a Mark 9 depth charge 50, 75, and 120 yards. *(U.S. Navy)*

The standard method of delivering depth charges at the beginning of the war was the "rack." Rails enabled the charges to roll off the stern of a ship under their own weight, and could be manually released at the rack, or remotely from the ship's bridge. *(U.S. Navy)*

This view from the aft of the bridge on a patrol craft shows the force of a depth charge's explosion. The concussion from a depth charge coupled with the water pressure at deeper depths was used to implode a submarine's hull. During World War II, 781 U-boats were destroyed. *(National Archives/80GK-13753)*

and 14 men drowned when their lifeboat overturned, but the captain and another 30 sailors remained on board. *James Oglethorpe* remained afloat and could have been salvaged had it not been torpedoed by *U-91* the following afternoon. The captain and crew perished when *U-91*'s torpedo sank the crippled ship. In addition, *U-758*'s torpedoes also sank the Dutch ship *Zaanland*. *William Eustis*, a 7,196-ton Liberty Ship carrying 7,000 tons of sugar and 600 tons of foodstuffs, was heavily damaged by a torpedo from *U-435* (Siegfried Strelow). The crew abandoned ship and was rescued by HMS *Volunteer* (D-71).

Other U-boat successes against the ships of HX-229 on March 16-17 included *U-603* (Hans-Joachim Bertelsmann), which sank the Norwegian *Elin K* with four torpedoes; *U-600* (Bernhard Zurmühlen), which sank the tanker *Southern Princess* and damaged *Irénée Du Pont* with two torpedoes as well as the British merchantman *Nariva; U-384* (Hans-Achim von Rosenberg-Gruszynski) sank the British Liberty *Coracero; U-631* (Jürgen Krüger) sent the Dutch cargo ship *Terkoelei* to the bottom; and *U-91* crowned its successful day by sinking *Harry Luckenbach* with two torpedoes and subsequently finished off *William Eustis*, *Nariva*, and *Irénée Du Pont*. On March 18, just minutes before 1 P.M., the 7,191-ton freighter *Walter Q. Gresham* was hit by a torpedo from *U-221* (Hans Trojer) on the port side, aft. Within an hour the ship slid under, stern first. *U-221* sent *Canadian Star* to the bottom as well.

When HX-229 came under attack, the freighter *Matthew Luckenbach* left the convoy and steamed ahead on its

St. Louis (CL-49) moves past oiler Lakawanna (AO-40) in the right foreground, departing Tulagi, Solomon Islands, in late June or early July 1943. The cruiser took a torpedo during the Battle of Kolombangara in the early-morning hours of July 13. St. Louis returned to Tulagi, and then sailed to Espiritu Santo for temporary repairs. After overhaul at Mare Island, California, St. Louis returned in time to support the Marines on Bougainville. *(National Archives/80GK-3971)*

own. This romper, as opposed to a straggler, crossed the bow of *U-527* (Herbert Uhlig), which fired three torpedoes at 8:54 A.M., on the morning of March 19. Both torpedoes hit the port side, the first at the number two hatch and the second at the number four. The entire crew of 68 was rescued by USCG cutter *Ingham* (WPG-35). *Matthew Luckenbach* remained afloat, but was finally sent to the bottom by a single torpedo from *U-523* (Werner Pietzsch). Additional escort ships and long-range B-17s and B-24s were dispatched to cover the remainder of HX-229's voyage, preventing any further attacks on the convoy. This single wolf-pack engagement sank 13 freighters of 93,502 tons, and was one of the Allies' costliest encounters with U-boats.

By mid morning on March 17, the 12 U-boats of *Raubgraf* were forced to retire either due to insufficient fuel to continue the fight or battle damage. The remaining subs continued west until *U-338* (Manfred Kinzel) stumbled upon SC-122. This convoy fared much better than HX-229. Kinzel navigated his way past the convoy's screening destroyers and

Chandeleur (AV-10) at Apia, Samoa, on April 20, 1943, with a PBY-5 flying boat on deck. The PBY is ready for a complete overhaul as its control surfaces and outer wing panels have been removed. From July 1 through October 13, 1943, Chandeleur was the seaplane tender for Patrol Squadron 71 based at Espiritu Santo. *(National Archives/80GK-6985)*

fired five torpedoes, each scoring a hit. The freighters *Alderamin*, *Kingsbuy*, and *King Gruffydd* sank, and merchant ship *Fort Cedar Lake* was heavily damaged. *U-666* (Herbert Engel) sent a torpedo into the side of the Greek freighter *Carras*, but was in turn hit by depth charges from a 220 Squadron (Royal Air Force) B-17. *U-666* withdrew from the battle and sailed to St. Nazaire, France, for repairs. *U-333* (Werner Schwaff) finished off *Carras*. Subsequently, *U-663* (Heinrich Schmid) sank *Clarissa Radcliffe*, a straggler from SC-122. In all, SC-122 lost nine ships of 53,000 tons.

When combined, U-boats destroyed an impressive 22 ships of 146,502 tons during the described three-day period. Had they been able to sustain such a record of sinkings, the war's outcome would have been in doubt. U-boats would continue to menace Allied convoys in the North Atlantic, Gulf of Mexico, and the Caribbean, sinking ships throughout the remainder of the war. Increased use of airborne radar, increased convoy escorts, and hunter/killer carrier escort groups minimized the U-boat's effectiveness from mid-1943 through the end of the war.

Advancing Through the Pacific

Spring and summer 1943 saw the Allies island-hopping north from Guadalcanal to New Georgia, Kolombangara, and Bougainville. Airstrips on these islands would enable the Allies to neutralize the Japanese stronghold at Rabaul. To counter the Allied advance, the Japanese had been constructing airfields at Munda on New Georgia and at Vila-Stanmore on Kolombangara. Nightly U.S. cruiser and destroyer

▲ Motor torpedo boats and a PBY patrol bomber alongside destroyer tender Gillis (AVD-12) at Massacre Bay, Attu, Alaska, on June 21, 1943. After duty in the Aleutians, Gillis went into overhaul at the Puget Sound Naval Yard, Washington. In March 1945, the tender supported the invasion of Okinawa stationed at Kerama Retto. *(National Archives/80GK-9454)*

◄ Nicholas (DD-449) shells Kolombangara, New Georgia Island, Solomons, on the night of May 13 as part of Task Force 18. That night the destroyer's Number Three 5-inch gun jammed and subsequently exploded. Miraculously, no one was injured. Repaired at Noumea, New Caledonia, Nicholas escorted ships and served on antisubmarine patrol until July. On the fifth, the destroyer once again shelled Kolombangara. When Helena (CL-50) was sunk, the destroyer saved 291 men. *(National Archives/80GK-2751)*

Tractors towing track-equipped trailers unload supplies at Amchitka on July 23, 1943. By the end of July, the Japanese had evacuated their positions on Kiska. The only enemy the Americans had to deal with after the Japanese withdrawal was the weather. *(National Archives/80GK-8142)*

bombardments of both airfields went off without a hitch until the night of March 6–7, when cruisers *Montpelier* (CL-57), *Cleveland* (CL-55), and *Denver* (CL-58), with destroyers *Conway* (DD-507), *Cony* (DD-508), and *Waller* (DD-466), detected destroyers *Minegumo* and *Murasame* on radar at 12:57 A.M., off the eastern shore of Kolombangara Island in Kula Gulf. Both *Minegumo* and *Murasame* were sunk by gunfire, only 49 men survived from both ships. No damage was received by American forces.

To deny the Japanese a route to supply the airfield garrisons at Munda and Vila-Stanmore, the Americans landed at Segi Point, New Georgia, on March 21. During the next seven months, the Allies attempted to quarantine the Japanese garrisons while advancing through the Solomons. Near midnight on June 29-30, Rear Adm. Aaron S. Merrill's four

cruisers and four destroyers (Task Force 36.2.1) shelled the airfields at Vila-Stanmore and Buin-Shortland on Bougainville. The following morning, landings were made to capture the airfield at Munda, and at Rendova. The Japanese retaliated on the night of July 2 when cruiser *Yubari* and its destroyer squadron bombarded the American positions on Rendova.

On July 6, the three American light cruisers and four destroyers clashed with the "Tokyo Express" in Kula Gulf. Seven Japanese destroyer transports loaded with men and supplies bound for Kolombangara, battled it out with the superior U.S. force. *Suzukaze* and *Tanikaze* sank *Helena* (CL-50), and in exchange the Japanese lost destroyer *Niizuki*, while *Nagatsuki* beached on Kolombangara. Destroyers *Amagiri*, *Hatsuyuki*, and *Sukukaze* are also damaged but manage to escape American shellfire.

Yorktown (CV-10) was laid down at Newport News Ship Building and Dry Dock Co. on December 1, 1941, six days before the Japanese attack on Pearl Harbor. Originally named Bon Homme Richard, CV-10 was renamed Yorktown on September 26, 1942, after the first carrier Yorktown (CV-5) was sunk during the Battle of Midway. CV-10 transits the Panama Canal on July 11, 1943, while every officer and seaman not on duty monitors the delicate operation. TBF Avengers line the starboard flight deck while SBD dive-bombers sit on the port side. The port-side elevator has been lifted to near vertical to maneuver the ship through the canal. *(National Archives/80GK-15334)*

◀ Eugene "Gene" Kelly enlisted in the U.S. Navy on November 27, 1944, and is seen in a 1945 portrait of the actor in Washington, D.C. Lt. (jg) Kelly starred in and directed a number of films for the U.S. Navy, including a history of Franklin (CV-13). Kelly was discharged on May 13, 1946. *(National Archives/80GK-6029)*

▶ Lt. Cmdr. Douglas Fairbanks Jr. served aboard Ludlow (DD-438), Mississippi (BB-41), as executive officer of Goldcrest (AM-80), Washington (BB-56), Wasp (CV-7), and saw combat on board Wichita (CA-45) while escorting ships near Iceland. Fairbanks also trained with the British and commanded a PT-boat during the invasion of Southern France. *(National Archives/80GK-6663)*

Although the German and Italian surface navies were not a factor during the invasion of Sicily, the Luftwaffe hit the ships of the landing force hard. Sailors aboard Leonard Wood wait between sending waves of supplies ashore and watch as an unidentified ship burns in the distance. *(National Archives/80GK-2158)*

A landing craft (mechanized) from Leonard Wood (APA-12) leads a landing craft (small support)off Sicily on D-Day, July 10, 1943. The Western Naval Task Force sailed from ports in Algiers and Tunisia to land Gen. Patton's troops in the Gela Gulf region on the southern shore of Sicily. *(National Archives/80GK-2151)*

Landing ship (medium) LSM-152 steams away from the Gela Gulf area to await its next assignment, which was the invasion in the Anzio region south of Rome which was behind German lines. *(National Archives/80GK-14463)*

LST-394, LST-352, and LST-358 unload in the port town of Naples on the Italian mainland. British LCTs are in the background. The city endured heavy shelling. *(National Archives/80GK-14064)*

One week later, in nearly the same location as the Kula Gulf battle, Rear Adm. Walden L. Ainsworth's ships tangled with cruiser *Jintsu*, five destroyers, and four destroyer transports. At 1:00 A.M., the U.S. armada made radar contact, but the Japanese destroyers fired the first salvo of torpedoes at 1:08 A.M., one hitting the New Zealand cruiser HMNZS *Leander*. The American destroyers exchanged torpedoes, none of these hitting the enemy. Using radar controlled fire, 6-inch shells from the American cruisers *Honolulu* (CL-48) and *St. Louis* (CL-49) blanketed *Jintsu* which sank at 1:45 A.M., taking all hands with it. The Japanese destroyers turned tail and sailed north up The Slot with Ainsworth's ships in hot pursuit. Having reloaded their torpedo tubes, the Japanese destroyers turned, launched thirty-one underwater missiles, and then continued their retreat. *Honolulu* and *St. Louis* were struck in the bow resulting in light damage, but destroyer *Gwin* (DD-433) took a torpedo amidships, wrecking her engine room, killing two officers, and fifty-nine men. The ship was abandoned and the crew taken aboard *Ralph Talbot*, which subsequently scuttled the destroyer.

A PBY Catalina patrol bomber located Rear Adm. Nishimura Shoji's thirteen ship Tokyo Express moving down The Slot between Vella Lavella and Choiseul Island at 10:30 P.M., on July 19. Before sunrise, six TBF Avengers attacked Shoji's ships with 2,000-pound bombs, scoring a direct hit on destroyer *Yugure* and damaging heavy cruiser *Kumano*. Another dawn raid by five TBFs and eight B-25s failed to score any hits. While rescuing survivors from *Yugure*, more B-25s returned and sent *Kiyonami* to the bottom.

Rendova-based *PT-109* was patrolling Blackett Strait on the night of August 1-2 when it was rammed by *Amagiri*, sinking the boat. The crew would eventually be rescued, and its skipper, Lt. John F. Kennedy, would become America's thirty-fifth president.

Three days later, the Allies secured Munda, New Georgia. However, the Japanese airfield at Vila-Stanmore, across the gulf from Munda, was now in jeopardy, but they were not going to give up easily. Near midnight on August 6–7, destroyer transports of the Tokyo Express carrying 950 troops and 55 tons of supplies to Vila-Stanmore were caught in the gulf by *Craven* (DD-382), *Dunlap* (DD-384), and *Maury* (DD-401). *Arashi*, *Hagikaze*, and *Kawakaze* were sunk by the American destroyers' torpedoes while

Ships supporting Operation Husky, the joint U.S., British, and Canadian invasion of Sicily, staged through Algiers Harbor. The Germans raided the port on July 16, and two Liberty Ships burn in background beyond Savannah (CL-42) and the breakwater. (National Archives/80GK-3964)

Shigure, damaged, managed to escape. After losing three destroyers at what became known as the Battle of Vela Gulf, the Japanese evacuated the garrison at Vila-Stanmore, but left 10,000 others on Kolombangara that the Allies promptly bypassed.

Leap-frogging over Kolombangara, the Third Amphibious Force landed Allied troops at Vella Lavella further up the Solomons chain on August 15. Although nightly surface actions continued in the area after the landings, two enagements are worth note. Around midnight on August 17–18, the Battle of Vella Lavella ensued when four U.S. destroyers encountered four Japanese destroyers escorting four large landing craft, 17 landing barges, a pair of auxiliary subchasers, and three armed Daihatsu boats. Some barges were full of troops destined for Horaniu on Vella Lavella Island, while the empty barges were en route to evacuated Vila-Stanmore. At 1:00 A.M., *Sazanami* launched a torpedo salvo at the American ships, but failed to score any hits. The U.S. destroyers damaged *Isokaze* and sank both auxiliary sub chasers, two large landing craft, and one of the Daihatsus.

The Japanese continued to evacuate Kolombangara at night, and with New Zealand troops pushing across Vella Lavella they

decided to risk an evacuation of the remaining 600 troops on that island also. On the night of October 6–7, six Japanese destroyers escorting three destroyer transports, four sub-chaser transports, four patrol boats, and four landing craft headed for Vella Lavella to evacuate the remnants of the island's garrison.

Japanese floatplanes began dropping flares over the American destroyers. Sighting the ship illuminated by aircraft flares, Rear Adm. Matsuji Ijuin ordered the transports to retire until the Americans had been dealt a deathblow. Only *Selfridge* (DD-357), *Chevalier* (DD-451), and *O'Bannon* (DD-450) had been spotted, as *Raph Talbot*, *Taylor* (DD-468), and *Lavallette* (DD-448) were still more than 20 miles to the south, steaming at full speed to join in the fray. At 10:51 P.M., Ijuin's destroyers turned to port, exposing their flanks, and the American destroyers quickly launched 14 torpedoes. *Yugumo* returned torpedo and gunfire, followed by *Kazegumo*, which opened up with her deck guns. *Yugumo*, only 3,300 yards from the U.S. ships, took the brunt of the American fire. By 11:05 P.M., the Japanese destroyer was dead in the water, blazing from stem to stern, and subsequently sank.

Dace (SS-247) awaits commissioning at Electric Boat's Groton, Connecticut, facility on July 23, 1943. The sub played an important role at Leyte Gulf, Philippines, in October 1944, when Dace sank the 12,200-ton heavy cruiser Maya in the opening actions of the battle. *(National Archives/80GK-16049)*

Shot on board a submarine at the New London, Connecticut, Navy training base in August 1943, this sailor demonstrates the lack of room in the hull bunking above a practice torpedo. Every space in the submarine was used for vital equipment, the comfort of its officers and men a secondary consideration. Submariners had to "hot bunk," where as soon as one sailor woke up for his watch, another climbed into bed to sleep. *(National Archives/80GK-16016)*

Chevalier was hit in the forward magazine by a torpedo that severed the ship ahead of the bridge. To prevent the ship from plowing under, the engines were ordered to reverse at full speed, which caused the destroyer to back across *O'Bannon*'s path. The two ships collided. *O'Bannon* stayed by *Chevalier* to evacuate wounded, which kept her out of the hunt. *Selfridge* continued to pursue Japanese destroyers *Shigure* and *Samidare*.

Although out of range of *Selfridge*'s 5 inch guns, the two retreating destroyers sent torpedoes against their pursuer. The first two missed, and a third struck *Selfridge* on the port side.

The southern group of destroyers, *Ralph Talbot, Taylor,* and *Lavallette*, arrived in the area too late, only able to watch the Japanese ships retire on their radar screens. They did render assistance to *Chevalier*, which sank at 3:11 A.M., and assisted *Selfridge* and *O'Bannon* out of the area. Both destroyers returned to the West Coast for permanent repairs, returning to the fleet later the following spring.

During the battle, the Japanese sub chasers slipped past the melee and evacuated 589 men from Vella Lavella. The remaining garrison on neighboring Choiseul Island was bypassed, effectively completing the eviction of the Japanese from the New Georgia Island area and the central Solomons.

Husky and Avalanche: Allied Attacks in the Mediterranean

Having secured North Africa in Operation Torch, and routed Gen. Irwin Rommel's Afrika Korps from Tunisia, the Allied armies began preparations for the invasion of Sicily, and eventually the Italian mainland. Operation Husky, codename

▶ Franklin (CV-13), one of ten Essex-class carriers built, is ready for christening at Newport News Ship Building and Dry Dock Co., Newport News, Virginia, on October 14, 1943. The Essex-class carriers had an overall length of 872 feet and were 147 feet, 6 inches wide at the flight deck. Each ship in the class displaced 27,100 tons. Franklin was commissioned on January 14, 1944; Capt. James M. Shoemaker was the commanding officer. The carrier was in the thick of battle during the fast carrier sweeps of the Japanese home islands. *(National Archives/80GK-14016)*

for the joint U.S., British, and Canadian invasion of Sicily, was under the overall command of Gen. Dwight D. Eisenhower with Adm. of the Fleet Andrew B. Cunningham as Allied Naval Commander. The Western Naval Task Force, under Vice Adm. Henry K. Hewett, was to land Gen. George S. Patton's Seventh Army (six divisions) on the southern side of the island, while the Eastern Naval Task Force, under Vice Adm. Sir Bertram Ramsay, would take Lt. Gen. Sir Bernard Montgomery's Eighth Army (seven divisions) ashore on the eastern end.

When the Axis surrendered in North Africa on May 13, the Northwest African Air Force began softening up Sicily and striking airfields on the Italian mainland. For nearly 60 days, the aerial bombardment continued. Pantelleria, an island northwest of Malta halfway between Tunisia and Sicily, was captured on June 11. This island provided an advance base for fighters, as did Gozo, adjacent to Malta. On Gozo, Army engineers built a twin-strip fighter field in only 18 days—a feat expected to take months. It was operational on June 25.

The Western Naval Task Force sailed from ports in Algiers and Tunisia to land Patton's troops in the Gela Gulf region on the southern shore of Sicily. On the morning of

◀ French battleship Richelieu in New York Harbor destined for overhaul and refitting at the New York Naval Yard in November 1943. In addition to the battleship, cruisers Georges Leygues, Gloire, and Montcalm came to the United States for repair. The war ended before Richelieu could rejoin the battle. *(National Archives/80GK-3895)*

July 10, at 1:15 A.M., transports began lowering boats for the invasion. Patton's landings were lightly opposed, terrain being his Army's biggest obstacle, while Montgomery's landings were fought vigorously. Neither the Italian nor the German surface navies was a factor in the landings. Shore-based aircraft from the Italian mainland constantly harassed the invasion fleets, with the Eastern Naval Task Force suffering heavier attacks due to its proximity to the mainland.

Destroyer *Maddox* (DD-622) was 16 miles off shore on antisubmarine patrol when a lone Ju-87 "Stuka" dive-bomber scored a direct hit on the ship's after magazine at 4:58 A.M. *Maddox* went under in less than two minutes. Only 74 of her crew were rescued; seven officers and 203 men went down with the ship. Destroyer *Murphy* (DD-603) was straddled by near-misses and was lightly damaged. At 6:35 P.M., a Messerschmitt Bf-109 fighter skip-bombed *LST –313,* igniting the ships' cargo of trucks, half-tracks, ammunition, and mines. During the air attacks on the first day, collisions between *Roe* (DD-418) and *Swanson* (DD-443) as well as *LST-345* and submarine chaser *PC-621* caused minor damage.

The second day of operations saw cruisers and destroyers of the gunfire support squadrons turning back German Panzers advancing on Army units near the town of Gela. Shore bombardment played an integral part of the advance by Gen. Patton's Seventh Army. In addition, Patton used U.S. Navy amphibious craft to move tanks and artillery up the coast, avoiding Sicilian roads congested by the Allied armies. While the bombardment ships were killing tanks, Italian bombers rocked *Barnett* (APA-5) with near-misses—close enough to start fires and kill seven men. At 3:45 P.M., more than 30 German bombers attacked ships in the Gela anchorage. Almost simultaneously, three bombs hit the Liberty Ship *Robert Rowan.* Each one passed through a cargo hatch: the first bomb into the number one hold, and then out the ship's side without exploding; the second and third bombs hit the number two and three hatches and exploded in the holds, igniting the ship's cargo of 2,900 tons of ammunition, gas, and jeeps. The Liberty's crew plus 348 troops were rescued by landing craft and *Orizaba* (AP-24) about an hour after the bombing.

The ground war on Sicily ended on August 17, but German and Italian air attacks against Allied shipping in the Mediterranean continued through the end of the following year. The air war against Allied shipping heated up in September when the Italian mainland was invaded under Operation Avalanche. On September 3, the Italians ceased the fight against the Allied armies—although they did not

The 81,235-ton Cunard luxury liner Queen Mary, nearing the docks of New York Harbor, and its sister ship Queen Elizabeth transported troops across the Atlantic during 1943. Capable of carrying 15,000 soldiers each, the Queens steamed at 28.5 knots, eliminating the need for escorts, and were too fast for a U-boat to track. *(National Archives/80GK-5648)*

▲ Mechanic on Lexington (CV-16) changes a
spark plug on an F6F Hellcat prior to carrier
strikes on Mili and Kwajalein Islands.
(National Archives/80GK-15560)

▶ F6F Hellcats and TBF Avengers run up on
Yorktown's deck prior to air operations
over Tarawa, Jaluit, Mili, and Makin in the
Gilbert Islands beginning on November 19,
1943. After the Gilberts strikes, Yorktown
returned to Pearl Harbor on December 9,
making raids on Kwajalein and Wotje Atolls
en route. (National Archives/80GK-15092)

officially surrender until September 8, and the following
morning Operation Avalanche delivered Gen. Mark W.
Clark's Fifth Army to beaches in the Gulf of Salerno, 30 miles
south of Naples. At 3:30 A.M., on September 9, the Allies
went ashore and were met by fierce resistance. Here, as with
the landings in Sicily, naval shore bombardment kept German
tanks from reinforcing the beachhead area. Artillery on shore
scored hits on *LST-336, LST-375, LST-385,* and *LST-389.*
LST-386 struck a mine during its approach to shore. In
addition, tug *Nauset* (AT-89) was sunk by dive-bombers.

The morning of September 11 was clear, with visibility
unlimited. A dozen Focke-Wulf Fw-190 fighters
approached the roadstead at 9:30 A.M., screening Dornier
Do-217 twin-engine bombers. The Do-217s launched
radio-guided bombs from 18,000 feet, the first striking
Philadelphia (CL-41), causing light damage, and the second
hitting *Savannah* (CL-42) in the number three turret. The
missile traveled down through the turret and exploded,
blowing a hole in the ship's bottom and opening up hull
plates on her sides. Although nearly awash, the ship was
kept afloat and eventually sailed to Malta under its own
power for further repairs. On September 13, two more
radio-controlled bombing attacks were focused on
Philadelphia, which the ship managed to out maneuver.

Later that evening, *Rowan* (DD-405) was escorting
ships away from the Salerno beachhead back to Oran to
reload when German E-boats (similar to U.S. Navy PT-boats)
attacked the convoy. *Rowan* dodged the first volley of
torpedoes, but one from a second attack struck a magazine,
sending the destroyer to the bottom in less than one
minute. Of the ship's 273 officers and men, 202 perished
in the sinking.

By September 18, the Fifth Allied Army was moving
away from the beachhead area pushing up the Italian
peninsula toward the Bay of Naples and the Volturno River.
The next offensive landing, planned for the Anzio and
Nettuno areas south of Rome was to take place in early 1944.

Further Island Hopping in the Pacific

The Allied island-hopping campaign continued through
the end of the year. American and New Zealand troops went
ashore on Mono and Sterling Islands in the Treasury Islands
on October 27, followed by landings of the 1st Marine
Amphibious Corps at Cape Torokina on Bougainville Island.

The Japanese retaliated on the night of November 2–3 with a planned cruiser and destroyer attack on the transports off Cape Torokina as well as a counter landing at Mutupina Point by 250 soldiers from destroyer transports.

Allied patrol planes spotted the Japanese force, commanded by Vice Adm. Sentaro Omori, shortly after it sortied from Rabaul at 5 P.M., on November 1. At 9:20 P.M., an Allied patrol plane dropped a bomb close aboard light cruiser *Sendai*. Believing his force had been discovered, Omori ordered the transports to retire, while the destroyers and cruisers continued steaming southward in an effort to attack Allied transports off the cape the following morning. As the Japanese ships were sailing toward Bougainville, at 1:30 A.M., on November 2, a patrol plane dropped a bomb on cruiser *Haguro*, lightly damaging the ship. Minutes later, one of Omori's scout planes reported sighting the ships of Task

Force 39 (Rear Adm. Aaron Stanton Merrill) 50 miles west of Cape Torokina. Rather than reporting the full force of four light cruisers and eight destroyers, the Japanese pilot gave the count as one cruiser and three destroyers.

Merrill's cruisers picked up the Japanese armada on radar at 2:27 A.M. Task Force 39's cruisers were positioned across the mouth of the bay to prevent any Japanese ships from entering and attacking the transports. Eighteen minutes later, a Japanese scout dropped flares over Task Force 39, which enabled light cruiser *Sendai* to fix the American position. Eight American destroyers launched torpedoes one minute before the Japanese torpedo volley left its tubes. Neither side scored any hits due to the extreme range. *Sendai* took the brunt of the cruisers' radar-controlled fire, being hit at 2:52 A.M., and later sank.

During the rain of American shells, destroyers *Samidare* and *Shiratsuyu* collided, knocking both ships out of the

Hellcats come aboard Lexington (CV-16) after a strike on Kwajalein, December 4. Aircraft wait for the elevator to return from the hangar deck as another F6F comes aboard. Planes from the carrier sank a transport, damaged a pair of cruisers, and shot down 30 enemy planes that day. Later that evening, at 11:33 p.m., Lexington was struck by a torpedo and was forced to sail to Pearl Harbor for emergency repairs. *(National Archives/80GK-15290)*

engagement. Destroyer *Hatsukaze* cut in front of cruiser *Myoko*, and the smaller ship was heavily damaged and was later sunk by gunfire from *Spence* (DD-512). Three American destroyers were damaged in the engagement: *Foote* (DD-511) hit by a Japanese torpedo; *Spence* and light cruiser *Denver* by shellfire. At first light, almost 100 Japanese planes from Rabaul arrived overhead. Seventeen Allied aircraft engaged the flight, downing eight of the Japanese. Persistent, the dive-bombers and fighters began attacking the American ships, but only scored two hits on the stern of *Montpelier* (CL-57). The battle was over at 8:12 A.M. One Japanese cruiser and one destroyer were at the bottom, two cruisers and one destroyer were damaged, and nearly 30 aircraft had been shot down at a cost of four American ships damaged.

Fortunately for Merrill's ships, the Fifth Air Force B-25s, P-38s, and P-47s attacked Rabaul that morning, preventing a return strike against the American ships. In addition, Fifth Air Force fighters downed an additional 31 aircraft that day.

The Japanese quickly dispatched 19 cruisers and destroyers from Truk to Rabaul for another attack in the Empress Augusta Bay area. U.S. reconnaissance planes detected this arrival and Task Force 38 (Rear Adm. Frederick C. Sherman) with carriers *Saratoga* and *Princeton* (CVL-23) were sent to attack on November 5. Ninety-seven aircraft attacked the ships in Simpson Harbor, damaging four heavy cruisers, two light cruisers, and a pair of destroyers.

On November 11, the American carriers were back; this time Task Force 38 was joined by the carriers *Essex, Bunker Hill,* and *Independence* from Task Force 50.3 (Rear Adm. Alfred E. Montgomery). Destroyer *Suzunami* was sunk near Simpson Harbor's entrance, and three others were damaged. Heavy cruiser *Agano* was heavily damaged by an aerial torpedo and was towed to Truk for repairs. Light cruiser *Yubari* was also damaged by strafing aircraft. Both carrier raids ended any further Japanese plans to strike at the ships in Empress Augusta Bay.

The Bougainville campaign ended with the Battle of Cape St. George on the night of November 24–25, when five U.S. Navy destroyers commanded by Capt. Arleigh A. Burke surprised an equal number of Japanese destroyer transports evacuating troops from Buka to Rabaul. Destroyers *Charles Ausburne* (DD-570), *Claxton* (DD-571), *Converse* (DD-509), *Dyson* (DD-572), and *Spence* made radar contact with the Japanese at 1:41 A.M., November 25. Captain Burke sent three destroyers to launch torpedoes at the Japanese, while the remaining two ships prepared to provide cover fire had they

Kinugawa Maru was beached on Guadalcanal during the night of November 14–15, 1942. After dawn on November 15, Army and Marine fighters strafed Kinugawa Maru and three other beached transports. Throughout the day, planes from Enterprise attacked the ships and the supplies they had unloaded. Kinugawa Maru is seen one year later down by the stern, and a total wreck. *(National Archives/80GK-1467a)*

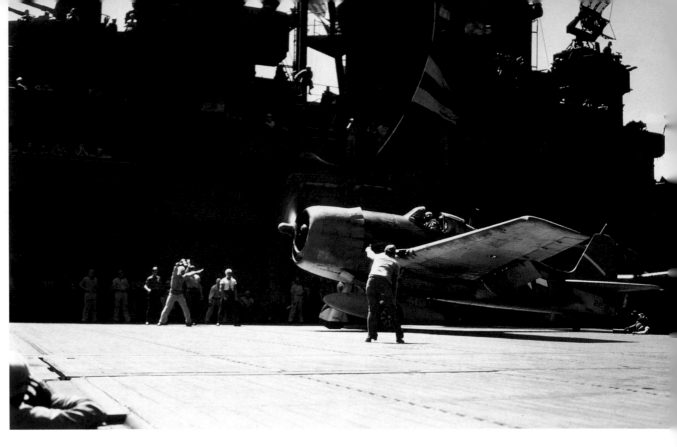

Lt. Cmdr. Jimmy Flatley, commander of VF-5, awaits the signal to launch from Yorktown's flight deck. Flatley's squadron was headed for the Marcus Islands on August 31, 1943. *(National Archives/80GK-16051)*

been discovered. Torpedoes found *Makinami* and *Onami*, which promptly sank, and the American destroyers began pursuing the three surviving ships. *Charles Ausburne*'s guns continually struck *Yugiri* as the remaining two destroyer transports, *Mizuki*—lightly damaged— and *Amagiri*, out distanced the American destroyers. *Yugiri* was sunk as dawn broke, forcing Burke's destroyers to retire out of the range of Rabaul-based Japanese air cover. So ended the battle: three Japanese destroyer transports sunk, one damaged, and the Americans retired without a scratch.

The Gilberts: Tarawa's Bloody Beach

The U.S. Marines Fifth Amphibious Corps were tasked with taking the Tarawa and Makin Atolls in Operation Galvanic. The Second Marine Division began landing on Betio Island at 9:13 A.M., on November 20, to capture its airfield. Betio was 11,400 feet long, approximately 1,800 feet at its widest point, and covered 300 square acres. The Japanese had 4,500 men defending this tiny speck of an island. Unfortunately for the Marines, the Japanese had sat on the island for more than a year with nothing to do but build defensive fortifications.

To ensure victory, Maj. Gen. Julian C. Smith landed more than 18,500 men of the Second Marine Division on the island. The only softening up the island received was done the morning of the invasion, followed by strikes from carrier aircraft as the Marines went ashore in LVTs—tracked landing craft capable of holding 25 men and equipped with two .50-

caliber machine guns, commonly referred to as "amphtracs." After the shore bombardment ceased, the Japanese reinforced the invasion beaches with riflemen and machine gunners setting up a vicious crossfire.

Supporting the landing troops was landing ship (dock) *Ashland* (LSD-1), which sent waves of landing craft loaded with Sherman tanks toward the beaches. A miscalculation in tidal currents prevented the landing craft from crossing the island's reef, forcing many tanks to wade ashore in water too deep for their intake systems. Many tanks flooded before reaching the beach. Similarly, landing craft had to disgorge the Marines out on the reef, and most were cut down by Japanese fire. By nightfall, a beachhead only 900 feet wide had been established. The following day, when the tide came in, the Marines took full advantage, flooding the beach with landing craft. More than 1,000 Marines and sailors died taking Tarawa, and only 17 Japanese were taken prisoner.

In a simultaneous landing, Makin Atoll received the attentions of the U.S. 27th Army Division, which put 6,500 men ashore to battle an estimated 800 defenders. Like Tarawa's garrison, Makin's defenders put up fierce resistance that took two days to suppress. The Army suffered 186 casualties, a vast difference from Tarawa, and took 104 prisoners.

The lessons learned on Tarawa's bloody beach saved further lives in amphibious operations during the next two years of the war.

A crippled Hellcat comes aboard Cowpens (CVL-25) during the November attacks on the Gilberts. A deck hand in yellow appears to be hesitating as to whether he should dive into the gun gallery, or hold his ground as the Hellcat loses its right wheel. *(National Archives/80GK-6693)*

A wounded aircrewman is taken below to Cowpens' sick bay after a strike mission over the Gilberts. *(National Archives/80GK-302)*

BUILDING BATTLESHIP IOWA

Having slid down the way, Iowa settles into the water on August 27, 1942. *(National Archives/80GK-13514)*

Iowa ready for launch at the New York Navy Yard late August 1942. Heavy chains hanging from Iowa's rail are used to slow the ship during launch. *(National Archives/80GK-13507)*

Tugs arrive to move Iowa to a fitting-out berth at New York Navy Yard. A portion of the battleship's superstructure had been completed when this photo of Iowa was taken in late 1942. The ship's triple 16-inch gun turret was installed at the fitting-out berth. *(National Archives/80GK-875)*

A beehive of workers covers the upper decks of the battleship in October 1942, as workers install the Mark 7, 16-inch/.50-caliber guns in the forward turret, while others lay deck planks. *(National Archives/80GK-522)*

A welder joins steel plates on the deck of Iowa near one of the ship's three main battery turrets. Iowa was completed six months later. *(National Archives/80GK-512)*

Iowa's commissioning ceremony was held on the aft deck on February 22, 1943, at the New York Navy Yard. The destroyer at right rear is Wainwright (DD-419). *(National Archives/80GK-823)*

Iowa (BB-61) is named for a Sioux Indian tribe that once lived on the plains of the Missouri Territory, and the 29th state admitted to the Union. BB-61 is the third U.S. Naval ship to bear the name. Iowa was the first of its class that also included New Jersey (launched December 7, 1942), Missouri (January 29, 1944), Wisconsin (December 7, 1943), and the unfinished Kentucky. Iowa-class battleships displaced 45,000 tons and had a length of 887 feet, 3 inches with a beam of 108 feet, 2 inches.

On June 27, 1940, the ship's keel was laid down at the New York Navy Yard, and two years later was launched on August 27, 1942. Iowa was sponsored by the vice president of the United States' wife, Mrs. Henry A. Wallace. Twelve Babcock & Wilcox boilers drove geared turbines that turned four propellers with a combined 200,000 shaft horsepower, which gave the

Iowa-class ships a top speed of 35 knots. Iowa was armed with nine 16-inch/.50-caliber cannons in three triple-gun turrets, 20 5-inch/.38-caliber dual-purpose guns, 80 40 mm antiaircraft guns, as well as 50 20 mm cannons for close-in antiaircraft protection.

Iowa's first assignment was to transport President Franklin D. Roosevelt from the U.S. East Coast to Casablanca on his journey to the Teheran Conference in the fall of 1943. The ship's combat debut took place during the January 29 to February 3 invasion of the Marshall Islands. The ship's World War II combat tour was entirely in the Pacific Theater, and Iowa was Adm. William F. Halsey's flagship during the September 2, 1945, surrender ceremonies in Tokyo Bay.

Since landing in the Gulf of Salerno on September 9, 1943, the Allies had moved up the Italian peninsula—the British on the eastern side and the Americans on the western side. After landing at Taranto, the British took Bari, advancing north to capture the airfield complex at Foggia. From Foggia, American long-range heavy bombers began striking the heart of Germany. By December, the U.S. Fifth Army and British Eighth Army had reached a stalemate with Field Marshall Albert Kesselring's troops at the Winter Line—a defensive barrier stretching from the Tyrrhenian to the Adriatic Sea, passing though the town of Cassino, 70 miles south of Rome.

In an effort to break the Winter and later the Gustav Lines, the British conceived a plan to land troops near Anzio and Nettuno, approximately 40 miles behind German lines. Dubbed Operation Shingle, the American Third Division (Gen. Lucian Truscott), the First British Infantry Division (Maj. Gen. W. R. C. Penny), three battalions of U.S. Army Rangers, and two British Commandos were to land simultaneously with a push against the Gustav Line by the Fifth and Eighth Armies.

Embarking at points in the Gulf of Naples, the ships arrived off Anzio around midnight on January 21–22, 1944, and at 2:00 A.M., landing craft were hitting the beaches. Due to a lack of mine removal on the British landing beaches, LCIs, LSTs, and other amphibious craft did not hit the shore until nearly 7:00 A.M. On the American landing beaches, 5-inch rockets were shot at the sand to explode the land mines. The first Americans walked ashore unopposed at H-hour, 2:00 A.M. Subsequent waves, landing 45 minutes later, faced stiff machine-gun fire from the area's German defenders. At daylight, ships in the shore bombardment group began shelling targets for the advancing troops, and the Luftwaffe appeared overhead. LCI-20 was sunk by dive-bombers, and later in the day *Portent* (AM-106) stuck a mine and sank.

The following evening, British destroyers *Janus* and *Jervis* caught the full fury of a Luftwaffe attack. A torpedo bomber scored a hit on *Janus*, and *Jervis* was struck by a German guided bomb. On January 24, Luftwaffe bombers heavily damaged *Plunkett* (DD-431) and minesweeper *Prevail* (AM-107), and *Mayo* (DD-422) hit a mine that ripped open the starboard hull, killing five.

Although a beachhead was firmly established, the German Luftwaffe relentlessly harassed the Allied fleet, sinking two cruisers, three destroyers, three LSTs, an LCI, and a British hospital ship. On land, the fighting was fierce. Nearly four months after coming ashore at Anzio, the Fifth Army finally broke through the Gustav Line on May 11, joined up with the American Third Division, and began the advance on Rome.

Continuing Advances in the Pacific

In the Pacific, Operation Flintlock to secure the Marshall Islands got under way with the January 31-February 1 landings on the islands of the Kwajalein Atoll. Comprising 97 islands—only six and one-third square miles habitable,—the atoll stretches for 66 miles. The four major islands of the atoll are Roi and Namur in the north (connected by a sandbar), Ebadon to the west, and Kwajalein 40 miles to the south. Pre invasion air attacks had destroyed all aircraft and the hangar facilities on Roi, eliminating Japanese air power from threatening the invasion fleet. Ships of the fire support group softened up the beaches in preparation for the landings, killing many of the estimated 3,700 Japanese defenders. After some delay, the Fourth Marine Division went ashore on Roi and Namur beginning at 11:57 A.M. Roi was virtually deserted. The few Japanese that were there put up some resistance, but were quickly eliminated. By nightfall, construction equipment was coming ashore to repair the island's airfield for use by the Americans.

The amphtracs landing on Namur were greeted by an anti tank ditch just behind the beach. To surmount this obstacle, Marines disembarked and moved ahead on foot. Facing a pocket of determined resistance, the Marines were gaining the upper hand until a Japanese blockhouse exploded with tremendous force. No one was sure why the bunker exploded, whether the Japanese detonated it in a suicide action, or if the Marines had placed demolition charges and blown the building. However, 20 Marines lost their lives, most killed by flying shrapnel. During the night of February 1–2, a number of banzai charges were made against the Marines, but by noon the following day Namur was secured.

The awesome power of an Iowa-class battleship is demonstrated in this one gun broadside. Notice that the forward deck is clear, except for three sailors in the bow gun tub. The 16-inch guns could throw a one-ton shell more than 20 miles. *(National Archives/80GK-1620)*

A British hospital ship loads wounded soldiers from the Italian campaign at Naples Harbor, early in 1944. Although hospital ships were painted white with red crosses and sailed fully illuminated, the Luftwaffe attacked and sank a number of them during the advance up the Italian peninsula. *(National Archives/80GK-13841)*

The Army's Seventh Infantry Division assault on Kwajalein Island was preceded by the occupation of neighboring Enubuj and Ennylabegan Islands on January 31. Both islands are to the northwest of Kwajalein, each received softening-up bombardments from *Washington* (BB-56) and *New Orleans* (CA-32). Both islands were secured by 1:00 P.M. The Army troops encountered light resistance. Enubuj became an artillery fire support base for the invasion of Kwajalein, while Ennylabegan served as an overhaul stop for amphtracs and DUKW amphibious trucks.

Prior to the invasion of Kwajalein, the island was pounded by more than 2,000 14 - and 16-inch shells from battleships *Idaho, Indiana, Massachusetts, Mississippi, New Mexico, Pennsylvania,* and *Washington*. On invasion morning, shellfire from *Mississippi* and *Pennsylvania* greeted the Japanese defenders as the sun rose. *New Mexico* and three cruisers joined the shelling, which continued until 8:40 A.M., to allow carrier-based SBDs, TBFs, and F6Fs to bomb and strafe the island. When the planes had cleared the area, the shelling began anew. Artillery from Enubuj joined in the fray, bombarding the defending Japanese from all sides. At 9:30 A.M., the first waves hit the beaches on the island's

French destroyer escort Senegalais, formerly the Cobesier (DE-106), participated in the sinking of U-371 off the Algerian coast. A sailor paints a U-boat kill marking on the funnel following the sinking on May 4. U-371 was located on radar as it attempted to attack a convoy guarded by Menges (DE-320). The American destroyer was torpedoed as it attacked the sub. Menges was subsequently towed to Bougie, Algeria, and later returned to the fleet. U-371 was sunk through the combined efforts of Senegalais, and U.S. destroyers Joseph E. Campbell (DE-70) and Pride (DE-323). *(National Archives/80GK-1606)*

southwestern side. Heavy fighting broke out when the Americans approached the island's warehouse area built to store supplies for Japanese in the Marshalls. Pillboxes, concrete blockhouses, and a tank trap blocked the Army's advance. Air strikes combined with shellfire from *Idaho* and three destroyers broke the impasse, and the troops moved forward. Fighting continued through February 5, when the last pockets of Japanese either surrendered—about 40 men did so—or were killed by American troops.

The Allies captured the remaining islands in the Marshalls by the end of April, by passing Wotje (3,500 estimated defenders as of January 1944), Maloelap (3,300), Jaluit (3,500), and Mili (5,500). The Japanese garrisons on these four islands remained there, facing regular naval bombardment or air attacks until the war was over.

Eniwetok Atoll was the next objective of the American amphibious forces. Like Kwajalein, the atoll was heavily bombarded in the days before the invasion. To prevent Japanese aircraft from interfering with the operation, carrier air strikes simultaneous with the Eniwetok landings worked over Truk (Operation Hailstone) on February 16 and 17, Jaluit on February 20, and airfields in the Marianas on February 22. Aside from being an important port and airfield bastion, the Navy estimated there were more than 20,000 troops at Truk.

Operation Hailstone employed the carriers of Task Force 58, which included *Enterprise, Yorktown*, and *Belleau Wood*

(CV-24) of Task Group 58.1, Rear Adm. John W. Reeves; *Essex* (CV-9), *Intrepid* (CV-11), *Cabot* (CVL-28) of TG-58.2, Rear Adm. A. E. Montgomery; as well as *Bunker Hill* (CV-17), *Monterey*, and *Cowpens* (CV-25) of TG-58.3, Rear Adm. F. C. Sherman. Supporting the carriers were more than six battleships, 10 cruisers, 25 destroyers, and 10 submarines of Task Force 50 under the command of Vice Adm. Raymond A. Spruance. In two days of attacks, carrier air strikes sank 26 transports, six destroyers/destroyer transports, and shot down 270 aircraft, and strafed the port facilities, fuel farm, and warehouse areas. To keep pressure on the Japanese, Truk was again struck on April 29 and 30, destroying another 104 aircraft in aerial combat and on the ground.

The 22nd Marine Regiment landed on Engebi Island, Eniwetok Atoll, on February 17. Suffering only light casualties, the island was declared secured the following afternoon. Parry and Eniwetok, the other major islands in the atoll, were heavily defended and were not secured until February 21.

In the ensuing months, American carriers raided by-passed Choiseul Island in the Solomons; destroyed the airfields, port installations, and attacked shipping at Palau, Yap, Ulithi, and Woleai in the Western Caroline Islands (March 30-April 1); and the Allies invaded Hollandia, New Guinea (April 21–24). The Japanese were being pushed back from strategic bases, which the Allies then rebuilt to support the fleet as it advanced toward the home islands.

Stevens (DD-479) was assigned to Task Group 52.8, providing fire support for Operation Flintlock, the January 31–February 1 landings on the islands of the Kwajalein Atoll. After Flintlock, Stevens operated in the Solomon Islands, and provided fire support for the invasion of Guam and later the Philippines. This destroyer has been fitted with an aircraft catapult and derrick where the Number Three 5-inch gun was usually mounted. *(National Archives/80GK-13835)*

(I5PL.87IBS3523AC5M3O)(I-O-2I)(2-17-I640)(6.375'26400)(07°28'N151°51'E)(DUBLON IS. TRUK)RESTRICTED

Strike photo from the February 17 raid on Truk during Operation Hailstone showing the port facilities of Dublon Island. Carrier aircraft from Task Force 58 sank 26 transports, six destroyers and destroyer transports, and shot down 270 aircraft. *(Nicholas A. Veronico Collection)*

Capturing Enemy Secrets

U-505's career began on a solid note. Axel-Olaf Loewe, the sub's first commander, was a plank-owner, and supervised its construction from the time it was laid down at Deutsche Werft yard in Hamburg. Loewe commanded the boat on three patrols that sank seven ships for 37,789 tons. Not the best record of ships sunk, but not the worst either. On the third patrol, Loewe was stricken by appendicitis, and the boat returned from the Caribbean to Lorient after being out for 79 days.

Peter Zschech sailed the boat on five patrols, the first to Trinidad where he sank the British 7,773-ton *Ocean Justice*. Three days later while running on the surface, an aircraft attacked the sub, killing a watch officer and a lookout, and wounding two others. An episode of bad luck, but things on board *U-505* were going to get worse. Zschech was only out 12 days on his second patrol when he was forced back to Lorient due to depth-charge damage suffered on July 13, 1943. On its third patrol with Zschech, *U-505* was only two days out of Lorient before it was recalled. The fourth patrol under this captain lasted 12 days before the boat returned for

Green flag raised, a catapult crew launches a Vought OS2U Kingfisher for an afternoon patrol. Battleship and cruiser scout planes played an invaluable role sighting targets ashore, spotting the fall of a ship's bombardment, sighting enemy ships, and rescuing sailors and airmen. *(National Archives/80GK-4594)*

New Mexico (BB-40) recovers an OS2U during the Tinian Island campaign on June 14. A pick-up mat is streamed behind the ship, which turns to put the mat in the calm waters of the ship's lee side. *(National Archives/80GK-6692)*

repairs. On the fifth sortie, during a very heavy and accurate depth-charge attack, Zschech put a pistol to his head and took his life in the control room—in front of his crew. First officer Paul Meyer returned the boat and its shaken crew to Lorient on November 11, 1943. The fact that the boat's first two commanders experienced varying degrees of misfortune while on patrol was enough to give the U-boat a reputation, and a bad one at that.

U-505 departed the submarine base at Lorient, France, on March 16, 1944, to patrol the tropical waters off equatorial Africa. Oberleutnant zur See (comparable to a U.S. Navy lieutenant, junior grade) Harald Lange was in command of the boat, assisted by first officer Paul Meyer. Lange was 40, quite old when compared to his 22-to 24-year-old counterparts. Before the sub sailed, the boat was provisioned and given updated naval codes. When the boat left Lorient, 59 men were on board.

Two months after Lange and *U-505* left for Africa, Capt. Daniel Gallery and Task Group 22.3 sailed from Hampton Roads, Virginia, on May 15, to patrol off the western coast of Africa. Gallery commanded the group from *Guadalcanal* (CVE-60), with Cmdr. Frederick S. Hall commanding the subordinate destroyers *Chatelain* (DE-149), *Flaherty* (DE-135), *Jenks* (DE-665), *Pillsbury* (DE-133), and *Pope* (DE-134). The Wildcat fighters and Avenger bombers of Composite Squadron Eight (VC-8) on board

OS2U about to be recovered by Quincy (CA-71). The floatplane has taxied up onto a sled where a hook in the bottom of the float snags the mat. The aircraft is then towed at the ship's speed and its engine can be shut down while a crane's cable is attached to the plane. Once connected, the floatplane is then hoisted on board. *(National Archives/80GK-1954)*

Aratama Maru, a converted sub tender of 6,784 tons, was sunk at the entrance to Talafoll Bay, Guam. April 8 was a productive day for Cmdr. Slade Cutter and the crew of Seahorse (SS-304). After sending Aratama Maru to the bottom, Cutter sank Kizugawa Maru, a 1,915-ton cargo ship, and the following day put the 4,467-ton freighter Bisaku Maru on the bottom as well. *(National Archives/80GK-4092)*

During wartime, traditions were maintained on the home front. Each day the honor guard of the Tomb of the Unknown Soldier at Arlington National Cemetery respectfully maintains a vigil over the gravesite. Washington, D.C., can be seen in the distance. *(National Archives/80GK-14039)*

Guadalcanal formed hunter-killer teams that would work in concert with the surface ships to destroy submarines. Prior to Gallery's May patrol, his hunter-killer group blew *U-515* to the surface and destroyed the sub. Recognizing that his task group might have had the opportunity to board *U-515* had they been prepared, Gallery began training for the next opportunity. During World War II, the Allies had captured one U-boat and boarded two others: *U-570* surrendered to a 269 Squadron (Royal Air Force) Hudson bomber piloted by Squadron Leader J. H. Thompson on August 27, 1941, the sub becoming HMS *Graph*; *U-110* was boarded by the British, who took off code books and attempted to tow the sub before it foundered on May 11, 1941; and on October 30, 1942, *U-559* was blown to the surface, and an *Enigma* coding machine was recovered before the sub sank, taking a Royal Navy officer and sailor with it.

Gallery's opportunity to board an enemy submarine came on June 4. Using high-frequency direction finding to home in on the sub's daily reports to headquarters, combined with information from Allied cryptanalysts, Task Force 22.3 was given a point to begin the search for *U-505* in the waters between Dakar and the Cape Verde Islands.

Architects of the American victory gather for a lunch meeting, from left: Chiefs of Staff Gen. Henry H. "Hap" Arnold, Army Air Forces; Adm. William D. Leahy, U.S. Navy; Adm. Ernest J. King, U.S. Navy; and Gen. George C. Marshall who, after the war, was responsible for the plan to rebuild the nations that were once America's enemies. *(National Archives/80GK-14010)*

Lange had sailed as far south as Monrovia, Liberia, before turning north on May 27, for the return voyage to France. Shipping targets had eluded *U-505* on this patrol, too. Short on fuel, Lange decided to sail between the coast of Africa and the Cape Verde Islands rather than take the longer route to the west through the open ocean.

Task Force 22.3 searched for *U-505* for nearly two weeks before it, too, ran short on fuel. On June 4, Gallery turned his ships north for Casablanca where they could refuel. At 11:10 A.M., *Chatelain's* sonar detected something cruising under the surface. The contact was evaluated as a submarine, and the destroyer launched depth charges using the forward-firing "Hedgehog" mount. These charges only explode if a direct hit is made, and none did.

Two Wildcat fighters, piloted by John W. Cadle Jr. and Wolffe W. Roberts, were vectored toward *Chatelain,* and *Jenks* and *Pillsbury* were sent to assist as well. Having the advantage of height, the fighters were able to spot the sub's outline and marked its location with machine-gun fire. Eleven minutes after the first contact, *Chatelain* fired more depth charges. *U-505* broached the surface one minute later. *U-505* fired a torpedo at the destroyer, and upon seeing it, *Chatelain* sent a torpedo toward the sub. Both shots missed and the destroyers began shelling the sub. One German sailor was killed during the shelling.

Overhead, Cadle and Roberts reported that the Germans were abandoning ship. Hearing this, Gallery ordered the destroyers to secure their fire. Cmdr. Hall ordered *Pillsbury* to draw near the sub and launch a boarding party. Simultaneously, *Chatelain* and *Jenks* sent boats to rescue the sub's crew.

Nine men from *Pillsbury* boarded *U-505* and, disregarding the possibility of being shot by a German crewmember or being wounded by booby traps, Lt. (jg) Albert L. David went below, followed by Stanley E. Wdowiak, radioman second class, and Arthur Knispel, torpedoman's mate third class. With water rushing in from a sea strainer, one of the men found the vent's cap and secured it. The flooding was stopped, but the rudder was hard to starboard and *U-505's* electric motors were propelling it in a right-hand turn. In addition, the sub hung on the surface in a precarious position, its decks awash. Believing that *U-505* would go under at any moment, David and the men secured the code books, maps, and cipher machines, and passed them topside.

Fifty-nine men were rescued from the sea, including Lange, albeit injured. *Pillsbury* came alongside

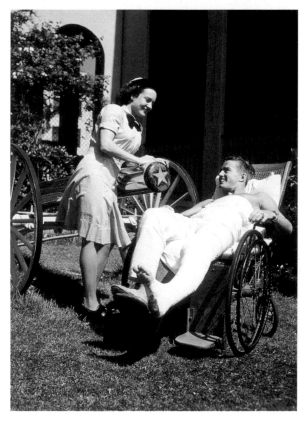

San Diego Naval Hospital WAVE apprentice 1st Class Reiba McNeill spends time with patient Seaman First Class Richard Insico, wounded in the Pacific. Men who were sent home from the battle front to recover often suffered grievous wounds. The need to keep men alive and repair the damage done in battle advanced medical science during the war years. *(National Archives/80GK-5458)*

The American flag flies over the captured U-505 with escort carrier Guadalcanal (CVE-60) in the background. Capt. Daniel Gallery commanded Task Group 22.3, consisting of Guadalcanal plus destroyers Chatelain (DE-149), Flaherty (DE-135), Jenks (DE-665), Pillsbury (DE-133), and Pope (DE-134). On June 4, Chatelain made sonar contact with U-505. The sub was subsequently depth charged to the surface, boarded by U.S. sailors, and towed to Bermuda—the first time the U.S. Navy captured an enemy man-of-war since the War of 1812. U-505's code books and cipher machines were invaluable to the Allied war effort. *(U.S. Navy via Museum of Science and Industry)*

While the war raged in both the Atlantic and Pacific Theaters, Missouri (BB-63) was undergoing its shakedown cruise in June. A 16-inch salvo wings its way to a target from the forward turret. *(National Archives/80GK-4546)*

the sub to begin salvage operations, but *U-505*'s diving planes split the destroyer's fuselage open, flooding an engine room. *Guadalcanal* undertook towing operations and, due to the lack of fuel, slowly began steaming for Dakar. Fearing German spies would spot the captured sub and report it to Nazi headquarters, who would in turn change the naval codes only two days before the invasion of France, Gallery was ordered to sail for Bermuda. The oiler *Kennebec* (AO-36) and fleet tug *Abnaki* (ATF-96) were dispatched to refuel the task group and take the sub in tow.

The captured sub reached Port Royal Bay, Bermuda, on June 19 after sailing more than 1,700 miles. *U-505* was the first foreign man-of-war captured by the United States since the War of 1812. In addition, the Task Group was awarded the Presidential Unit Citation; Wdowiak and Knispel each received the Navy Cross, Cmdr. Earl Trosino—who managed the salvage operation in the first hours—received the Legion of Merit; and Lt. David was awarded the Medal of Honor for his actions.

In all, *U-505* was an intelligence bonanza, netting more than 1,100 pounds of codes and coding machines, plus an *Elektra-Sonne* navigation system used by U-boats to fix their position with great accuracy.

Operation Overlord: D-Day in France

After months of preparation, planning, and stockpiling of men, ships, and weapons, the Allies were prepared to assault the European Continent. From January to May 1944, more than 589,000 men arrived in the United Kingdom in preparation for the invasion. The Germans expected the Allies to come ashore at Calais on the French coast. Calais is situated at the narrowest point along the Strait of Dover between England and France. The Germans had heavily reinforced the Atlantic seawall with a vast network of shore batteries, beach obstacles, and minefields.

The site chosen for the landings was along the Normandy region coastline in the Bay of the Seine, roughly between Le Harve on the north and Cherbourg on the Cotentin Peninsula in the south. After months of training soldiers in how to assault the beaches and sailors in how to handle landing craft and larger amphibious ships, a target date was set for Operation Neptune, the amphibious assault phase of Operation Overlord (the invasion of France).

Gen. Dwight D. Eisenhower was selected Supreme Commander of the Allied Expeditionary Force. Managing the naval aspect of the invasion was Sir Bertram Ramsay (Royal

Cruiser Alaska (CB-1) as viewed from a battleship's 5-inch/.38-caliber gun mount during a fall 1944 training cruise. Alaska was commissioned on June 17 and entered the war on January 15, 1945, participating in the Iwo Jima campaign. *(National Archives/80GK-5583)*

FM-2s, General Motors' license-built version of the Grumman F4F Wildcat, land aboard Charger (AVG-30) during carrier qualifications in Chesapeake Bay. Charger trained both sailors and airmen in the intricacies of carrier operations. *(National Archives/80GK-1601)*

On April 28, 1944, nine German E-boats attacked eight tank landing ships during an invasion rehearsal at Scadtan Sands Beach, England, sinking LST-507 and LST-531. LST-289 arrives at Portsmouth, England, after taking an E-boat torpedo in the stern. *(National Archives/80GK-2054)*

Navy) who served as Supreme Naval Commander for the operation. Two men were responsible for getting the troops to the beaches: Rear Adm. Alan G. Kirk commanded the Western Naval Task Force, landing troops on the American beaches code-named "Utah" and "Omaha"; Rear Adm. Sir Philip Vian (Royal Navy) commanded the Eastern Naval Task Force that landed Commonwealth troops at "Gold," "Juno," and "Sword" beaches.

The invasion troops were boarded on ships at every dock, beach, and pier in Southern England on May 28. U.S. forces were supported by and transported in 931 ships, while the British and Commonwealth Armies sailed in 1,796 ships of all types. The invasion ships were ready on June 3, but the weather was not cooperating. June 4 was not any better, and the fifth was predicted to be miserable, too. Forecasters predicted a break in the weather on June 6, and close to midnight on June 4, Gen. Eisenhower gave the invasion order. The invasion armada sortied the following morning. On the night of June 5–6, more than 13,000 American paratroopers landed in the early-morning hours behind the beaches. At 5:00 A.M., as the ships approached the landing areas, coastal batteries opened up.

Facing the soldiers coming ashore were beach obstacles designed to snare landing craft, antiship mines, antipersonnel mines along the beaches and down to the tide line, one armored division, two mobile infantry divisions, and three additional divisions of standard infantry. Six armored divisions plus the German 15th Army were within a day's march of reinforcing the army at the beachhead.

Minesweepers moved in, clearing channels for the fire support and amphibious ships beginning at 2:00 A.M., June 6. Troops began reaching the beach at 6:30 A.M. to face withering fire from the German defenders. *LCI-93* and *LCI-553* plus *LCT-612* were shelled by shore batteries and subsequently sank.

The quiet weapons—undersea mines—took a heavy toll: Destroyer *Corry* (DD-463), anti-submarine patrol craft *PC-1261*, 11 tank landing craft, and five infantry landing craft were sent to the bottom. Casualties from these ships were enormous, and those that survived had a long swim to the beach in full combat gear. In spite of German resistance, both active and passive, more than 21,000 men and more than 1,700 tanks, half-tracks, trucks, and jeeps were ashore at Utah beach by 6:00 P.M.

German casemated gun emplacements were the target of the day for the fire support ships. Gunfire support was called for by Army units on the ground, and the fall of the shot was monitored by Navy pilots flying from land bases in Britain.

American troops faced stiffer resistance, and increased German fortifications at Omaha beach. Troops here faced a long trip over the open sand, liberally sown with antipersonnel mines, to a concrete seawall topped with barbed wire. To give the soldiers tactical surprise, the Normandy

◀◀ Given the go-ahead to assault the Normandy beaches in France, medics and litter bearers embark onto an LCT for the trip across the English Channel. *(National Archives/RG-111C-1133)*

◀ Although this photograph was taken during a D-Day rehearsal, this is what it looked like when hundreds of tank landing ships hit the Normandy beaches. The shallow-draft LSTs could beach themselves at the surf line and disgorge men, tanks, trucks, and artillery. Here an M-4 Sherman charges up the beach. *(National Archives/RG-111C-564)*

▼ In the days following the assault on the Normandy beaches, those Germans not killed were taken prisoner and held in pens on the beaches. They were then transported by DUKWs, amphibious trucks seen behind the pen's fence, to ships off shore, and then on to England. Many German prisoners of war were transferred to camps in the United States and Canada. *(National Archives/RG-HIS-6)*

beaches did not receive any preinvasion bombardment, either by air or ship, in the weeks prior to the assault. All the German defenses were intact. Shore bombardment by the destroyers, cruisers, and battleships of the invasion fleet turned the tide of battle at Omaha beach. Firing on targets, often within yards of American troops, many of the destroyers closed to within 800 yards of the beach—often touching bottom. As the troops moved away from the beaches, gunfire support ships were hitting targets as far as 10 miles inland.

The Allied armies ashore consolidated their position and soon began moving across the French countryside. To counter the invasion, the Luftwaffe moved aircraft from Italy and Germany to deal with the invasion fleet. Radio-guided bombs, employed with success off the coast of Italy, were used to attack the invasion fleet. Allied air superiority over the French coast limited their effectiveness. German undersea mines continued to extract a high price for sailing in French coastal waters, sinking or heavily damaging a number of ships before the area was cleared.

To supply the advancing armies, the British devised two types of emergency harbors to be constructed off the invasion beaches. "Mulberry A" was constructed at Omaha beach. It was built using concrete caissons that had been floated across the channel from England and flooded, sinking in position to form a breakwater. "Mulberry B" was built off the beach near Arromanche. "Gooseberry" harbors were built at both Omaha and Utah beaches by sinking obsolete or war-weary ships in

Gleaves (DD-423) and British light cruiser HMS Didd lay smoke off the beachhead during the invasion of south France. Gleaves supported U.S. Army Rangers in their landings on the beaches of southern France and also provided shore bombardment support. *(National Archives/80GK-1933)*

40 feet of water to form a breakwater. Small craft were able to operate or take shelter from the sea behind the Gooseberries. The artificial harbors proved their worth on the night of June 18–19. Strong winds and heavy seas wreaked havoc on the hundreds of ships and small craft supporting the invasion. The storm lasted for three days and completely wrecked Mulberry A.

Operation Neptune was concluded on June 25 when U.S. Navy battleships knocked out the Hamburg Battery. Four 280 mm cannons with a range of 40,000 yards harassed Allied shipping until *Texas* and *Arkansas* began to slug it out. One cannon was put out of action before the Navy declared the duel a draw. Cherbourg fell on June 26 and, after mopping up small pockets of resistance, the Cotentin Peninsula came completely under Allied control. The land battle began working its way across France, and the U.S. Navy turned its attentions to its next assignment: Operation Dragoon.

Beginning on April 29, the Allied air forces in the Mediterranean began bombarding bridges, rail yards, and shore installations in preparation for Operation Dragoon—the invasion of Southern France. The assault armada sailed from Oran, Algeria; Calvi, Corsica; Brindisi, Taranto, Naples, and Palermo, Italy, and arrived off the French coast between Toulon and Cannes at 10:00 P.M., August 14. At 5:14 A.M. the following morning, paratroopers were dropped behind the beachhead, followed by glider-borne troops at 9:26 A.M. Minesweepers applied their craft to within 150 yards of the landing beaches, but unlike the shore at Normandy, the sea bottom drops off rapidly between Toulon and Cannes, dramatically reducing the effectiveness of undersea mines. At 8:00 A.M., August 15, Allied troops stormed ashore to open a second front in France. The weather was favorable and

Operation Dragoon: On D-Day-plus 5, August 20, trucks and supplies come ashore from DUKWs and LCTs at Saint Raphaël, halfway between Cannes and St. Tropez. Landings were made at Saint Raphaël, as the French had built an airfield behind the beach. Bordering the town is the Argens River, where the French had also constructed a seaplane base. Both aerodromes were prime targets for the U.S. Army. *(National Archives/80GK-2112)*

resistance was relatively light. One month later, the beaches were closed and the ports of Toulon, Marseilles, and Port de Bouc handled all incoming supplies. Eliminating pockets of German resistance across France was the order of the day, while other Allied armies moved toward Germany.

Operation Forager and the Marianas Turkey Shoot

Operation Forager's goal was to capture Guam, Saipan, and Tinian in the Marianas group, islands the Japanese believed were part of their homeland. Allied submarines had prevented reinforcements from reaching the Marianas since mid-April, sinking almost every ship destined for the islands. Task Force 58 under Vice Adm. Marc A. Mitscher began bombing and strafing the airfields, port facilities, and coastal batteries on Guam, Rota, Saipan, Tinian, and the Pagan Islands on June 12. The invasion was set for June 15.

The first amphtracs went ashore on Saipan at 8:44 A.M. The second wave hit the beach at 9:00 A.M. Brutal Japanese

mortar and artillery fire pinned down the invaders on the beach, and shore batteries heavily damaged infantry landing craft (gunboats) LCI(G)-451 and LCI(G)-726. Early in the morning on June 16, at 3 A.M., a banzai charge of more than 700 men attacked the Marines on the beaches. Tanks and shellfire from ships off shore brought the Japanese suicide attacks to a halt at sunrise.

When word of the Saipan landings reached Adm. Soemu Toyoda late on June 15, he enacted Operation *A-Go*. Vice Adm. Jisaburo Ozawa, at Tawi Tawi in the Sulu Archipelago, prepared to engage the American fleet in Japan's much sought-after "decisive battle" with the American fleet. Unfortunately for Adm. Ozawa, his ships had been located by submarines *Bonefish* (SS-223), *Harder* (SS-257), and *Puffer* (SS-268), which cut three destroyers and two tankers from the fleet. Japanese submarines sent to scout for the American Task Force received a most unwelcome reception. Seventeen boats were sunk during May, six by *England* (DE-635). Having

Biloxi (CL-80) 40-mm quad in action during the spring of 1944. Notice how the spent shells are ejected forward from the gun mount. During Operation Forager, Biloxi bombarded Saipan and covered the amphibious landings on the island. The ship was active in every major engagement in the Pacific through the end of April 1945, when it was sent for overhaul on the West Coast. Biloxi was back in battle by July 18, 1945, when the ship bombarded Wake Island. (National Archives/80GK-14525)

A battleship's 5-inch gun crews prepare to fire on the beaches at Saipan during fire support for the June 15 invasion. Men on deck pass and handle ammunition, while the gun crew awaits the order to commence firing. Bombardment from ships off-shore usually obliterated beach obstacles and any enemy waiting for the Army and Marines en route to the beaches. *(National Archives/80GK-14162)*

been warned of Ozawa's approach, Vice Adm. Mitscher postponed the invasion of Guam until the Japanese fleet could be dealt with.

On the morning of June 19, the American carriers launched a strike against the airfields on Guam. Hellcats downed nearly 40 Japanese planes during the early-morning strike. The real action began at 10:00 A.M., in what became known as the Battle of the Philippine Sea. Sixty-nine planes,

the first of four waves from Ozawa's carriers, were picked up on radar more than 150 miles from the carrier. Hellcats were immediately launched and 41 Japanese aircraft were destroyed before the enemy could approach the ships. Of the few that got through the American fighter curtain, one struck *South Dakota* (BB-57) while the remainder were shot down by antiaircraft fire. Moments after the first Japanese wave was launched, *Albacore* (SS-218, Cmdr. J. W. Blanchard) shot a

single torpedo into the side of the enemy's newest carrier, *Taiho.* The torpedo struck the 31,000-ton ship's aviation fuel tanks and exploded in a huge fireball.

The Japanese carriers then sent a second attack wave that consisted of 130 aircraft, 98 of which were shot down by combat air patrol Hellcats or antiaircraft fire. The third wave of 47 aircraft flew to the wrong target area, although a dozen were shot down by marauding U.S. Navy fighters.

Miles from the American carriers, *Cavalla* (SS-244, Cmdr. H. J. Kossler) was shadowing Ozawa's ships, and came into position to launch torpedoes at one of the Japanese carriers. At 11:18 A.M., six underwater missiles from *Cavalla* streaked toward *Shokaku,* three hitting and sinking the 30,000-ton carrier.

The fourth and final Japanese wave of the day launched 82 aircraft from *Junyo, Ryuho,* and *Zuikaku*

Hornet (CV-12) steaming with other carriers during June 1945. SB2C Helldivers and F6F Hellcats line the deck. Behind are Bon Home Richard (CV-31) and two other carriers in the distance. *(National Archives/80GK-5702)* toward the American fleet. A young lieutenant with Fighter Squadron 16, named Alex Vraciu, was launched in a Hellcat (Bureau number 40194) from *Lexington* to meet the fourth wave. Vraciu said, "We ran into a batch of 'em. Forty or 50—a rambling mass. Sure enough, there they were, about 2,000 or 3,000 feet below. Our purpose was to keep them together. We knew if they started to separate, the torpedo planes would go down below and the dive-bombers would pick their targets.

"I started to go down and another Hellcat had designs on the same Judy I was going after, so I aborted my run to keep from colliding with him. I then started after another Judy on the formation's edge. I got him, and he started down in flames. I pulled up, coming from the rear and saw two in a loose wing formation. I got the rear one, moved up, dipped the wing and then got the next one. Number four seemed to be breaking formation. I worked in real close and got a short burst to the wing root. He caught fire and went down.

"Then I saw a group of three Judys beginning to make their dive-bombing run. I got the tail-ender in the wing root. The next Judy was about one-fifth of the way down in his dive. I must have hit his bomb, as he blew up in a big explosion. I started for the last one, but he ran into a solid wall of steel thrown up from the battleship below. I looked around and saw nothing but Hellcats in the sky. Glancing backwards, all I could see was a 35-mile-long pattern of flaming oil slicks in the water."

Vraciu shot down six Judys in eight minutes, bringing his total of confirmed victories to 18. During the retaliatory strike on June 20 against the Japanese fleet, Vraciu downed his 19th Japanese plane, a Zeke. From June 12 to 19, Vraciu single-handedly sank a 6,500-ton cargo ship (June 12) in Tanapag Harbor, Saipan, with a direct hit on the ship's stern, and shot down eight aircraft—six on a one-hop. For his

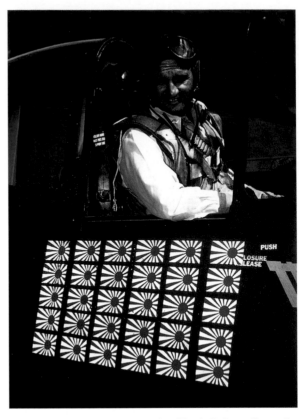

Lt. Cmdr. David McCampbell, commander of Essex's Air Group 15, scored the first of his 34 confirmed kills over Saipan on June 11. Seen sitting in his F6F Hellcat later in October 1944, McCampbell received the Medal of Honor, a Navy Cross, the Legion of Merit, a Silver Star, three Distinguished Flying Crosses, and an Air Medal for his service during World War II. *(National Archives/80GK-2178)*

A jubilant Lt. Alex Vraciu holds up six fingers representing the gaggle of "Judy" dive-bombers he destroyed in one sortie on June 19, during the Marianas Turkey Shoot. Vraciu downed the six dive-bombers in eight minutes. *(U.S. Navy via Alex Vraciu)*

A load of bombs comes across to a carrier somewhere in the Pacific. The well-traveled ammunition transport has a full load of bombs on its deck, ready to be transferred, four at a time. *(National Archives/80GK-5282)*

New Mexico (BB-40) loads 14-inch shells prior to the invasion of Guam in July 1944. The battleship expended hundreds of shells preparing the beaches for invasion and to support troops once they had established a beachhead by shelling pockets of enemy resistance. *(National Archives/80GK-14228)*

actions, Vraciu received the Navy Cross and a Distinguished Flying Cross.

At the Battle of the Philippine Sea, the U.S. Navy lost 30 aircraft, and one battleship took a bomb hit, causing minor damage. The Japanese were essentially put out of the carrier aviation business with this engagement. Two IJN carriers were on the bottom and 346 planes had been destroyed. A sailor who heard the final tally of Japanese aircraft destroyed that day, dubbed the action "The Great Marianas Turkey Shoot."

The following day, June 20, American scout planes searched for the Japanese carriers. At 3:40 P.M., a TBF spotted the Japanese fleet approximately 275 miles from the American armada. At 4:20 P.M., the U.S. carriers sent 216 planes to sink the Japanese carriers, which were steaming at the extreme limit of the American planes' range. When the dive-bombers, torpedo bombers, and fighters arrived over Ozawa's fleet, they quickly crippled tankers *Gen'yo Maru* and *Seiyo Maru*, and sank carrier *Hiyo* in a torpedo attack. Carrier *Zuikaku*, battleship *Haruna*, and six other ships were damaged by American planes.

In what became known as "The Mission Beyond Darkness," the U.S. Navy planes returned to their carriers after sundown; many short on fuel were forced to ditch, or landed on the wrong carriers. Destroyers recovered most of the downed flyers; 49 airmen were lost.

Saipan was in American hands by June 27, having cost the Americans 3,426 men. More than 24,000 Japanese were buried on the island, and only 1,780 were captured. And now that the threat of Japanese carrier attacks had been eliminated, the Third Marine Division, First Provisional Marine Brigade, and the Army's 77th Infantry landed on Guam on July 21. The Japanese put up a fierce resistance, taking 1,435 American lives, and wounding 5,646 others. On July 24, the U.S. Marines landed on Tinian, securing it in only seven days while suffering 386 killed and 1,816 wounded.

Retaking the Philippines

Gen. MacArthur's triumphant return to the Philippines began on October 17, at 6:30 A.M., when minesweepers cleared the approaches to Leyte Gulf. The following day, U.S. Army Sixth Ranger Battalion captured Calicoan, Dinagat, Homonhon, and Suluan Islands, the gatekeepers of Leyte Gulf. Suluan's defenders radioed a warning of the island's assault to Adm. Toyoda, who ordered Operation *SHO-1* to defend Leyte from the American attack.

With the gulf's approaches clear, the gunfire support ships under Rear Adm. Jesse Oldendorf approached the beaches off Tacloban and Dulag on the eastern shore of Leyte.

Tennessee (BB-43) bombarding Japanese forces on Guam, July 19, 1944. Notice how close the battleships come to the shore to give fire support to the troops on the beach. *(National Archives/80GK-14224)*

Oldendorf's ships began bombarding the landing areas and other targets of opportunity at dawn on October 20. Four divisions of MacArthur's Sixth Army began arriving on the beaches at 10:00 A.M. Accurate mortar fire harassed the landing craft and troops on the beach, but resistance was considered light. In a tactic that would prove costly both at Leyte, and later Okinawa, the Japanese fought a rear-guard action while luring the invaders off the beach toward defensive positions in the hills. That afternoon, MacArthur rode a landing craft to the beach with Philippine President Sergio Osmeña and proclaimed to the Philippine people, "I have returned."

Unloading continued at the beachhead for the next several days, while the Japanese ships of Operation *SHO-1* steamed south toward Leyte Gulf. Submarine *Darter* (SS-227, Cmdr. D. H. McClintock) spotted the armada on October 22, and the ships passed near Manila Bay where *Bream* (SS-243, Cmdr. W. G. Chapple) torpedoed heavy cruiser *Aoba*, which suffered heavy damage. The next day, *Darter* and *Dace*

Biloxi (CL-80) fires its 6-inch guns in preparation for the invasion of Guam on July 12. The light cruiser's armament consisted of 12 6-inch/.47-caliber guns in four triple mounts, 12 5-inch/.38-caliber dual-purpose antiaircraft and antishipping guns in six paired mounts, twenty four 40-mm antiaircraft guns, and nineteen 20-mm cannons. *(National Archives/80GK-2850)*

Solace (AH-5) anchored off shore of Guam on July 23. For the next three days, the hospital ship took on wounded from the assault beaches and the ships off shore. More than 500 wounded were transported and cared for en route to Kwajalein. On August 5, Solace returned to Guam for another load of 500 wounded sailors and Marines. *(National Archives/80GK-5631)*

On September 25, Pennsylvania (BB-38) sailed for Manus, Admiralty Islands, where she was left in an advance base section dry dock for repairs to her hull. Eleven days later, the battleship joined the Central Philippine Attack Force's Fire Support Group commanded by Rear Adm. Jesse B. Oldendorf. *(National Archives/80GK-2106)*

(SS-247, Cmdr. B. D. Claggett) each sent a heavy cruiser to the bottom—the former sank 12,000-ton *Atago* as well as damaging cruiser *Takao*, and the latter, 12,200-ton *Maya*.

The Japanese planned to use their remaining carriers (the Northern Force) as bait to lure Adm. Halsey's carrier's north, away from the Leyte invasion beaches. Then, in a two-pronged attack (Central and Southern Forces), Toyoda's battleships and cruisers would surprise the American fleet and destroy it while riding at anchor. Due to a lack of fuel and poor timing on the part of the Japanese, the plan was not executed well. The result was a three-day engagement known as the Battle for Leyte Gulf that involved four separate battles: On October 24, the Battle of the Sibuyan Sea; the night of October 24–25, the Battle for Surigao Strait; and in the early morning hours of October 25, the Battles of Sumar and Cape Engaño.

Japan's lack of air superiority in the Leyte area was effectively demonstrated during the Battle of the Sibuyan Sea. This aircraft-versus-surface ship duel saw more than 100 planes attack Adm. Kurita's force while steaming through the Mindoro Strait into the Sibuyan Sea. Eighteen planes were shot down by Japanese antiaircraft gunners, but battleship *Musashi* was sunk by a combination of aerial torpedoes and bombs delivered with precision by the American flyers.

The Battle of Surigao Strait began when U.S. carrier planes spotted Vice Adm. Nishimura's Central Force consisting of battleships *Fuso* and *Yamashiro* steaming in company with three heavy cruisers, a light cruiser, and four

destroyers in the Sibuyan Sea, east of Mindoro at 11:30 A.M. Adm. Oldendorf's ships (six battleships, four heavy cruisers including the Royal Australian Navy's *Shropshire*, four light cruisers, four destroyer divisions, and 39 PT-boats) sortied from Leyte Gulf to meet the on rushing enemy ships. At 10:36 P.M., on the evening of the 24th, *PT-131*'s radar picked up the Japanese armada. The PTs attacked in three boat sections, but none scored any torpedo hits.

The destroyers of Destroyer Squadron 54 (Desron 54) under the command of Capt. Jesse G. Coward split into two columns for a torpedo attack against the advancing Japanese column. *McDermut* and *Monssen* were to the port of the Japanese, and *Remey, McGowan,* and *Melvin* were to the starboard. At 3:00 A.M., on October 25th, the destroyers to starboard launched first—torpedoes slapped into the water, racing toward Nishimura's column. Moments later, the port destroyers launched. Battleship *Fuso* was hit and began to burn, destroyer *Yamagumo* exploded and rapidly went under, while destroyers *Michishio* (taking on water fast, later to sink), *Asagumo* (bow blown off), and *Yamashiro* were heavily damaged. Desron 24 followed up with a torpedo attack of its own. *Michishio* was dealt the *coup de grace* and another hit was scored on *Yamishiro*. At 3:51 A.M., Nishimura's remaining ships, *Yamashiro, Mogami,* and *Shigure,* steamed into the concentrated firepower of Adm. Oldendorf's cruisers and battleships, which mauled the Japanese ships using radar-controlled fire. *Mogami* turned tail first at 3:55, but was caught in a barrage from *Portland*. *Yamashiro* took two

torpedo hits from destroyer *Newcomb* at 4:04, and was on its way to the bottom. Cruisers *Denver* and *Columbia* pursued the retreating Japanese and sank *Asagumo*, and air attacks after daybreak saw *Mogami* and *Abukuma* sunk. Only *Shigure* sailed away to fight again.

Later that morning, at 6:46 A.M., the Battle off Samar began when Adm. Kurita's Center Force appeared on the radar screens of Adm. Clifton Sprague's escort carrier group, codenamed "Taffy Three." Two minutes after they were discovered, the Japanese Center Force's four battleships, six cruisers, and 11 destroyers opened fire. Sprague's six lightly armed and armored escort carriers and seven destroyers and destroyer escorts were no match for the big guns of the Japanese. A squall line came in just as the Japanese began firing for range. Sprague ordered his ships to steer into the wind and launch every aircraft not already on patrol. Taffy One and Taffy Two, hearing Sprague's predicament, launched planes, but they were 20 minutes' flying time away. Taffy Three's escorts began a delaying action, shelling and firing torpedoes at the enemy while the escort carriers steamed away from danger. Destroyer *Johnston* (DD-557) was hit by battleship and cruiser fire, and subsequently abandoned at 9:50. Twenty minutes later, DD-557 slid under the surface. Destroyers *Heermann* (DD-532), *Hoel* (DD-533), and *Samuel B. Roberts* (DE-413) were sunk shortly thereafter.

The Japanese cruisers were able to overtake the fleeing escort carriers and damage *Gambier Bay*, which could not keep up and fell behind. Losing its way, *Gambier*

Coates (DE-685) cruises in the Caribbean in 1944. The destroyer escort was named for Charles Coates of Oakland, California, who perished on board Juneau (CL-52) when the ship was torpedoed on November 13, 1942, near Guadalcanal. Commissioned on January 24, 1944, DE-685 served as a training ship based at Miami for the duration of the war. *(National Archives/80GK-14140)*

Interior view of an LSD (landing ship, dock) en route to Morotai on September 14. When the ship's docking bay is flooded and the rear ramp is lowered, the landing craft in the center of the ship can sail out for the invasion beaches. *(National Archives/RG-111C-153)*

Halford (DD-450) ship's insignia on the cupola of the torpedo mount. Halford was at sea for 75 days during Operation Forager, the invasion of the Marianas. After bombarding Tinian, Halford participated in the "Marianas Turkey Shoot" portion of the Battle of Leyte Gulf, and then shelled the landing beaches at Guam. *(National Archives/80GK-3977)*

High-velocity aerial rockets (HVARs) come up to the flight deck on Lexington's ammunition elevator. Hellcats used HVARs to devastate the invasion beaches. At Leyte Gulf, Lexington's aircraft joined in sinking battleship Musashi, and carriers Chitose, Zuikako, and Zuiho. *(National Archives/80GK-4821)*

Iowa (BB-61) refuels from Cahaba (AO-82) prior to the Battle of Leyte Gulf. Cahaba is also servicing a carrier, as seen from its deck. Refueling two ships in calm seas was a test of seamanship. Executing the same maneuver in rough weather was the ultimate test. U.S. Navy sailors did it often, and did it well. *(National Archives/80GK-6112)*

Under a cloudy sky, 4.5-inch rockets arc toward a beach in the Philippines, fired from a landing craft infantry. (*National Archives/80GK-4343*)

Bay (CVE-73) received the full attention of the Japanese cruisers and was sunk at 9:07 A.M. Four minutes later, the Japanese cruisers broke off their pursuit of the escort carriers and retired.

During the afternoon of October 25, Adm. Halsey's scout planes located Adm. Ozawa's Northern Force (battleships *Hyuga* and *Ise*, carriers *Zuikaku, Zuiho, Chitose,* and *Chiyoda*, three light cruisers, and nine destroyers). Halsey had gone north to pursue the Japanese carriers, and in doing so left the escort carriers off Sumar unprotected. When the scout notified him of Ozawa's location, Halsey had to gather his carrier forces. A rendezvous was set for 11:45 P.M. At 2:05 A.M., October 26, night fighters located Ozawa's ships 205 miles northeast of Cape Engâo. At first light, scout planes again searched for the Japanese, locating them at 7:10 A.M., only 150 miles away. Prior to contact, Adm. Mitscher launched his strike aircraft at 6:00 A.M., with instructions to orbit at a halfway point between the American carriers and the 2:05 A.M. position report. By 8:00 A.M., Helldivers were attacking the Japanese column, followed by torpedo-carrying Avengers. *Zuiho* was hit by one bomb, but it did not do much damage. *Chitose* was the recipient of half a dozen bombs, and the light carrier went down at 9:37 A.M. *Zuikaku* was struck by a torpedo and began listing, and destroyer *Akitsuki* was blown out of the water during the attack.

A second strike was launched at 8:35 A.M., and bombs from those aircraft started fires on *Chiyoda*. The light carrier began to list, and was sunk later in the day by shellfire from American cruisers. The third strike of the day focused on *Zuikaku*, which sank at 2:14 P.M., and *Zuiho*. The latter carrier put up a brave fight but was finally sent to the bottom at 3:30 P.M. Two more strikes during the day caused further damage to the already battered Japanese ships, but no additional ships were sunk by aircraft. The day's final victim was light cruiser *Tama*, sunk by a torpedo spread from *Jallao* (SS-368, Cmdr. J. B. Icenhower). Fierce fighting on, above, and under the seas around Leyte continued through January 1945 as the war slowly moved north, island-hopping through the Philippines en route to the Japanese home islands.

After Thanksgiving, the U.S. Navy began softening up Luzon Island in the Philippines in preparation for landings early in 1945. On November 25, Rear Adm. Gerald F. Bogan's Task Group 38.2 and Rear Adm. Frederick C. Sherman's Task Group 38.3 worked over

everything afloat off the Luzon's shores. Heavy cruiser *Kumano* was sunk by planes from *Ticonderoga* (CV-14), and a coastal convoy was mauled by TBMs, Hellcats, and Curtiss SB2C Helldivers from *Ticonderoga, Essex,* and *Langley* (CVL-27). Japanese suicide planes known as *kamikaze,* or "Divine Wind," struck *Essex, Hancock* (CV-19), and *Intrepid.*

Sailors always keep a watchful eye on the weather, but sometimes they guess wrong. Unfortunately, Adm. Halsey's Third Fleet was caught at sea by a typhoon on December 18. The storm sank destroyers *Hull* (DD-350), *Monaghan* (DD-354), and *Spence* (DD-512). Four light carriers, four escort carriers, light cruiser *Miami* (CL-89), 11 destroyers and destroyer escorts, an oiler, and a tug were also damaged in the storm.

The year ended with the invasion of Mindoro Island, Philippines, on December 15. The invasion was lightly opposed by ground forces, and American troops quickly moved ashore. An airfield was constructed outside the town of San José, for use by the Army Air Forces in supporting landings farther north in the Philippines. The field was operational on December 24, and on December 26 every available aircraft (92 fighters including P-38s, 13 B-25 medium bombers, and five P-61 night fighters) attacked Rear Adm. Masatomi Kimura's force, sent to destroy the transports off San José. Cruisers *Ashigara* and *Oyodo,* supported by six destroyers, were headed for the roadstead, but their attack was broken up by Army Air Force aircraft. Every ship in the Japanese force was damaged and destroyer *Kiyoshimo* was sunk by *PT-223.*

By the end of 1944, the sun was setting on the Japanese Empire as California (BB-44) and Tennessee (BB-43) steam toward their next engagement in the Pacific. The Allied navies were landing troops closer and closer to the home islands, which the Japanese were to defend fanatically. *(National Archives/80GK-3709)*

SHIPBOARD LIFE

Cards, especially poker, were a great way to pass time between battles. Sailors on board New Mexico work to win each other's paychecks. Is it possible that the sailor in the upper left has already lost his shirt? *(National Archives/80GK-1723)*

On board ships of the fleet, physical fitness was combined with sports. One of the results was boxing matches among sailors as well as sailors from other ships. This match on the quarterdeck of Iowa (BB-61) drew a standing-room-only crowd on June 5 while waiting for the Marianas campaign to begin. The catapult plane is a Vought OS2U Kingfisher. *(National Archives/80GK-1617)*

A jive band on New Mexico's stern serenades off-duty sailors in the South Pacific. Whenever two musicians come together a jam session usually breaks out, and the ships of the U.S. Navy had many excellent bands. *(National Archives/80GK-1722)*

Imagine being stuck on a ship in the middle of the Pacific Ocean, or anchored off an uninhabited island. How much fun can a seaman have there? Fun is what you make of it, and sailors on O'Bannon (DD-450) made themselves a kayak-catamaran constructed from jettisoned drop tanks. Not only fun, but mobile, too. *(National Archives/80GK-3983)*

Life on board ship was not all combat followed by periods of relaxation. There is always time for spit and polish. Sailors on Biloxi (CL-80) stand for a personnel inspection. A pair of Curtiss SO3C Seagulls are secured on the catapults. *(National Archives/80GK-2832)*

Even a navy at war can take time out to honor its traditions. When crossing the Equator it is traditional to hold a "Neptune Party." Neptunus Rex, God of the Sea, arrives to preside over the ceremony converting polliwogs into the Order of the Shellbacks. Carrier Wasp's decks have plenty of room for the initiation ceremonies. *(National Archives/80GK-811)*

Polliwogs become Shellbacks after experiencing "the solemn mysteries of the ancient order of the deep." Many of the Navy's ceremonies present participating sailors with appropriately adorned certificates. *(National Archives/80GK-821)*

The year 1945 opened with the Allies marching across Europe to end Hitler's reign of terror. In spite of the Nazi counter offensive in the Ardennes, known as the Battle of the Bulge. Allied armies were closing in on Germany from both the east and west. From a surface navy standpoint, the Kreigsmarine was essentially out of the war. However, Nazi U-boats continued to prowl the seas, and as late as April were torpedoing ships off the U.S. East Coast. German submarines were still a formidable foe, but Allied shore-based antisubmarine patrols, hunter-killer escort carrier groups, and signals intelligence were taking its toll. From January 1 through May 7, when Germany unconditionally surrendered to the Allies at Reims, France (effective May 9), the Kreigsmarine lost 172 U-boats, killing an estimated 7,740 men.

On the other side of the globe, the Japanese were suffering defeat after defeat as vast Allied armadas moved toward Japan. By January 1945, the battle to conquer the Japanese entrenched on Leyte was reaching its climax, and operations moved north to invade the Philippine island of Luzon. On January 9, at 9:30 A.M., Task Force 77, under the command of Vice Adm. Thomas C. Kinkaid, landed the U.S. Sixth Army at Lingayen Gulf on the eastern shore of Luzon, about 100 miles north of Manila. From Lingayen Gulf, the Sixth Army seized the Central Luzon Plain and then drove south toward Manila, but the island would not be secured until the end of June.

Ships in Lingayen Gulf supporting the landings were subject to constant kamikaze attacks, and at 7:00 A.M., on January 9, Japanese suicide planes struck the task force. Light cruiser *Columbia* (CL-56) was the morning's first casualty when three kamikaze planes from Nichols Field, Luzon, attacked the anchorage. *Columbia* was the target of two prior suicide plane attacks on previous days, and this morning's kamikaze strike hit the forward main battery director, where the plane's bomb exploded, killing 24 and wounding 68. One plane slightly damaged the destroyer escort *Hodges* (DE-231), knocking off the ship's radio antenna and foremast before crashing into the gulf, and the third was driven off by antiaircraft fire. Shortly after 1:00 P.M., a Val dive-bomber made a suicide attack on the

battleship *Mississippi* (BB-41), striking the ship's port side. Twenty-three men died instantly and another 63 were wounded. The kamikazes' toll on Allied sailors and ships was heavy in relation to Japanese losses of one plane and pilot per successful attack. Vice Adm. John S. McCain's Task Force 38.1, built around carriers *Wasp* (CV-18), *Hornet* (CV-12), *Monterey* (CV-26), and *Cowpens* (CV-25), struck at airfields in the Ryukyus and Pescadores Islands, along the Indo-China coast, as well as the island of Formosa in an effort to suppress kamikaze attacks.

During the evening of February 7, *PT-356* and *PT-373* reconnoitered Manila Bay. This was the first time since Corregidor surrendered in 1942 that U.S. ships had been in the bay. After a fierce, month-long, house-to-house battle, Manila was finally secured on March 4. It took until the end of June to bring Luzon completely under Allied control.

The U.S. Navy also played a major role in the march across Europe. Although the U.S. Army maintained its own fleet of assault craft, the boats were too light to handle the Rhine River's swift current. To facilitate the Army's crossing of the river at Oppenheim, Germany, Navy landing craft capable of transporting armor and personnel were dispatched overland to the river's banks. Task Group 122.5, consisting of 96 mechanized (LCM) and vehicle/personnel landing craft (LCVP), 52 officers, and 820 men began operations on the Rhine on March 11 at Bad Neuenahr, Germany. When not ferrying troops and vehicles, the boats of Task Group 122.5 aided Army Engineers in bridge-construction work. When the Rhine operation was completed, the Navy had transported more than 30,000 troops as well as 3,100 vehicles including tanks, artillery pieces, trucks, and other vehicles. On the return trips across the river, the boats evacuated the wounded and transported prisoners.

While the battle raged in the Pacific and across Germany, Churchill, Stalin, and Roosevelt met at Yalta, Crimea, U.S.S.R., from February 4 to 11, to discuss the war's prosecution. The "Big Three" reaffirmed their commitment to the policy of demanding an unconditional surrender from Germany, to study reparations from the Nazis, and to divide Germany into

Jerry S. Foley, a Liberty Ship built by the St. Johns River Shipbuilding Co. yard in Jacksonville, Florida, rides at anchor in Manila Harbor with a destroyed Japanese ship in the foreground. Jerry S. Foley was launched in October 1944, and was scrapped at Brownsville, Texas, in 1971. *(National Archives/80GK-15738)*

Alaska (CB-1) was at both the invasion of Iwo Jima and, later, Okinawa. Marine Cpl. Osborne Cheek (left), and mount captain Sgt. George Lewell atop a 5-inch/.38-caliber gun mount during firing practice in preparation for the invasion of Iwo Jima in February 1945. *(National Archives/80GK-3037)*

four occupied zones at the conclusion of hostilities. In addition, the Soviet Union agreed to open another front against the Japanese within three months of the conclusion of hostilities in Europe. The Yalta Conference attendees also came to an agreement to ask France and China to sponsor the founding of the United Nations; the first meeting was held April 25, 1945, in San Francisco.

Fighting for Every Inch of Soil: Iwo Jima

The Volcano Islands in the Nanpo Shoto group lie halfway between Saipan and Tokyo. Iwo Jima, the 11 and one-quarter-square-mile (four and one-half miles long by two and one-half miles wide) island in the center of the chain, was the perfect location for an air base. When the island was secured, fighters could escort Saipan- and Tinian-based B-29s to Tokyo and return, plus crippled B-29s would have an emergency airfield. The southern tip of the island is dominated by 556-foot-tall Mount Suribachi, which has a commanding view of the island to the north and the surrounding seas.

The Japanese had completed two airfields—one in the southern section plus one in the middle section of the island, and were in the process of building a third in the northern area when the island came under attack from U.S. forces. Land-based B-24s from the Marianas began daily bombing raids of the islands and, on February 16 at 6 A.M., the bombardment ships of Task Force 54 arrived to soften up the beaches. Battleships *Arkansas, Idaho* (BB-42), *New York, Nevada, Tennessee,* and *Texas,* along with heavy cruisers *Chester, Pensacola, Salt Lake City,* and *Tuscaloosa* plus their attending destroyers began pounding the island at 7:07 A.M. Cannon shells rained down on the island until 4:00 P.M., when the ships retired off the coast to wait for daylight. The following morning the routine resumed.

When LCI(G)s (Landing Craft Infantry gunboats) attempted to deliver underwater demolition teams to reconnoiter the beach area, they came under heavy fire from Japanese coastal batteries. Battleships of the gunfire support group closed the beaches and fired point-blank at the gun emplacements. In spite of the severe bombardment the island took, the Japanese defenders were well dug in, supported by a system of caves and tunnels. From this defensive system, the Japanese, under the command of Gen. Tadamichi Kuribayashi, would defend the island "to the death."

The Japanese Navy attempted to send three submarines equipped with *Kaiten,* a torpedo guided to the target by a

◀ Nevada (BB-36) shells Iwo Jima on D-Day, February 19, 1945. A concrete blockhouse on the island was frustrating the Marines' advance. The battleship had scored a direct hit on it with its secondary battery, but Japanese troops must have reoccupied it. At 11:00 a.m., Nevada's skipper Capt. H. L. Grosskopf ordered the ship's main batteries to take the bunker out. Using armor-piercing shells, the blockhouse was leveled. *(National Archives/80GK-3510)*

Mount Suribachi under bombardment on the morning of D-Day, February 19. Landing craft can be seen approaching the beach and smoke is visible from the battle raging at the foot of the volcano. *(National Archives/80GK-3509)*

Aerial view of the Iwo Jima invasion looking down island from the southwest during the initial landings on February 19, 1945. Mount Suribachi can be seen in the distance as well as a portion of the invasion and fire support armadas. *(National Archives/80GK-2973)*

New Mexico (BB-40) and two other battleships, Idaho (center) and either California or Tennessee in the distance, close to support the landings at Iwo Jima. The battleships' big guns softened up the beaches, but had a hard time finding the Japanese network of tunnels and caves dug into the island. *(National Archives/80GK-3706)*

Hansford (APA-106) honor guard firing a salute during burial at sea of a Marine who died of his wounds during the battle of Iwo Jima while the ship was en route to Saipan. From Iwo Jima's February 19, D-Day through March 27, the U.S. Marines lost 5,931 men killed and 17,272 wounded, and the Navy lost 881 men with an additional 1,917 men wounded. *(National Archives/80GK-3167)*

man riding the underwater missile, to attack U. S. ships off Iwo Jima. Two were sunk, and a third returned to base after being hunted for more than two days.

Iwo Jima's D-Day was the morning of February 19. Heavy fire from Task Force 54's ships pummeled the beaches, as 68 LTV (A) Amphtrac landing tanks headed for shore. At 9:00 A.M., the first Amphtracs hit the beach. The beach of the eastern landing zone rises in steps, the first 15 feet high. Volcanic ash and sand bogged down the Amphtracs, which quickly came under Japanese mortar fire. Ships of the gunfire force and carrier aircraft supported the 4th and 5th Marine Divisions as they slowly moved up and off the beaches. On D-Day, more than 30,000 troops were landed.

The Japanese defenders were so well dug in that every yard of ground gained by the Marines was an individual battle. Many of the defenders' gun positions were underground with only the mortar's barrel protruding. Each of these emplacements had to be located and dispatched by Marines on the ground using flame throwers, hand grenades, and support fire from tanks. On the morning of February 23, 40 men from the 28th Marines, led by 1st Lt. H. G. Schreier, climbed Mount Suribachi. Fighting off the last Japanese observation troops on the summit, a Marine tied a small American flag to a length of iron pipe and raised it at 10:20 A.M. Subsequently, an 8-foot-long flag from *LST-779* was carried up the hill and raised. The second raising was captured on film by Associated Press photographer Joe Rosenthal to become the most memorable photo of World War II.

While the Marines were taking Mount Suribachi, the Japanese were being pushed to the north and Seabees (construction battalions) were improving the southern airfield. By March 16, the island was declared "secure," but scattered resistance, oftentimes heavy, continued until the last days of May. Early on the morning of March 26, more than 350 Japanese soldiers charged the Seventh Army Air Force and Seabee encampments near Hirawa Bay. During the three-hour rampage, approximately 250 Japanese were killed in exchange for 53 American lives and another 119 wounded.

The first B-29, low on fuel, landed on Iwo Jima on March 4. Iwo Jima's usefulness as an airbase for homeward bound B-29s is illustrated by the fact that more than 2,400 of the bombers made emergency landings there by the time the war ended. Many of these crews might have perished had they been forced to ditch in the sea.

Although always a threat, Iwo Jima's remoteness prevented kamikaze attacks from becoming a reality. Six

Norton Sound (CAV-1) at anchor in Tanapag Harbor, Saipan, in April 1945. Saipan provided an excellent harbor to support the invasion of Okinawa. Ships damaged by kamikaze attacks were brought to Saipan for seaworthiness repairs before continuing to Pearl Harbor or the West Coast for overhaul. *(National Archives/80GK-16199)*

Indiana (BB-58) fires a salvo at Kamashi, Honshu Island, 250 miles north of Tokyo, site of Imperial Japanese Iron Works. This is the first bombardment of the Japanese home islands, and is seen from the battleship South Dakota. (National Archives/80GK-6035)

aircraft attacked, one of which crashed into *Saratoga* on February 21, destroying 42 aircraft, killing 123 men, and wounding an additional 192. Escort carrier *Bismarck Sea* (CVE-95) was hit that evening. Fires touched off explosions on-board the carrier, which eventually sank, taking 218 men with her. Additionally, *LST-477*, net-cargo ship *Keokuk* (CMC-6), and escort carrier *Lunga Point* (CVE-94) sustained light damage from kamikaze attacks.

Operation Iceberg: Invading Okinawa

Planning for Operation Iceberg, the invasion of the Ryukyu Islands, began in the summer of 1944. The Ryukyus encompass 55 islands between Formosa and the southern most Japanese home island of Kyushu. Okinawa, the largest of the Ryukyus, is located at the center of the island chain and is approximately 900 miles southwest of Tokyo. The Japanese had constructed five airfields on Okinawa in the central and southern sections of the island: Yotan, Kadena, and Naha were the largest. Previous amphibious operations always landed troops away from airfields as the Japanese were known

Boston (CA-69) steams with Iro Saki, Japan, in background. The cruiser was launched on August 26, 1942, and commissioned June 30, 1943. Arriving at Pearl Harbor on December 6, 1943, Boston bombarded islands from Kwajalein to Honshu until the end of the war. (National Archives/80GK-6522)

Franklin (CV-13) had closed to within 50 miles of the Japanese coast on March 19 where she was attacked by a single Judy bomber. Two bombs found their target, one exploding on the flight deck among planes ready to take off, and the second penetrating into the hangar deck. Rockets, bombs, fuel, and entire aircraft began to explode, heavily damaging the carrier. The amount of damage is evident in this view of the carrier sailing up New York's East River in April 1945. (National Archives/80GK-4763)

to defend them to the last man. The assault on Okinawa was going to be different. The nearest land plane base was more than 1,000 miles away, and Okinawa's airfields would enable Army aircraft to supplement and later relieve Navy carrier planes from the task of suppressing enemy air attacks.

Kamikaze attackers scored more than 170 hits on Allied ships during the Philippine campaign, and U.S. military planners attempted to deal with the threat of suicide planes before the invasion fleet arrived off the island. Army Air Force B-29s were diverted from the strategic fire-bombing of Japan to reconnoiter Okinawa. Reconnaissance was followed by B-29 bombing raids of the Tachiarai Army and Oita Naval Airfields, as well as the Omura aircraft plant on Kyushu.

Task Force 58's carriers also attacked airfields on Formosa, as well as Kyushu, Shikoku, and Honshu in the Japanese home islands on March 18 and 19. Japanese planes counterattacked with fury on March 18. The carriers of Task Force 58.4, steaming 75 miles south of Shikoku, took the brunt of the day's attacks: *Enterprise* was struck by a bomb that fortunately failed to detonate, *Intrepid* suffered a

Upon her return to New York, church services were held on Franklin's hangar deck to remember the 724 killed and 265 wounded. Heroism was commonplace on board the carrier that March morning, and two men were recognized with the Medal of Honor for their actions that day. (National Archives/80GK-5056)

near-miss from a Betty bomber—fragments from the plane ricocheted from the sea onto the carrier, killing two and wounding 43, and *Yorktown* fought off three Yokosuka D4Y Judy bombers, one of which scored with a bomb hit on the signal bridge that killed five and wounded 26.

The following morning, *Franklin* had closed to within 50 miles of the Japanese coast to launch strikes against shipping at the Kure and Kobe naval bases as well as the Inland Sea. The carrier had launched one strike and was preparing another when, at 7:08 A.M., a lone Judy dropped two bombs on the carrier. One bomb passed through the flight deck and exploded in the hangar bay, wrecking the forward elevator and starting tremendous fires. The second bomb exploded on the flight deck amid planes ready to launch. Fires ignited fuel, bombs, and aircraft. As the flames reached the F4U Corsairs on deck armed with the new 11.75-inch "Tiny Tim" rockets, they "cooked-off"—shooting over the deck like flying telephone poles. Except for those men with firefighting and damage-control duties, *Franklin*'s crew was ordered off the ship. The officers and sailors remaining behind risked their lives to fight fires as the ship began to list 13 degrees to starboard.

At 3:00 A.M. the following morning, the 106 officers and 604 sailors who remained on board were able to restore power

▲ Franklin, port side view of damage to flight deck. *(National Archives/80GK-4778)*

◄ Franklin, damaged in Japan's Inland Sea, returned to the Brooklyn Navy Yard under her own power on April 28, 1945. *(National Archives/80GK-4761)*

◀ Sangamon (CVE-26) was originally built as an oiler. On February 25, 1942, the ship nosed into the Norfolk Navy Yard for conversion into an escort carrier. On May 4, 1945, after reloading at Kerama Retto, the carrier was steaming away from the islands when kamikaze planes were reported 29 miles from the ship. One kamikaze crashed within 25 yards of the ship, and a second scored a direct hit on the center of the flight deck with a bomb, and subsequently crashed into the ship. Sangamon returned to the Norfolk Navy Yard for permanent repairs but the war ended before they could be completed. The ship was striken from the Navy inventory on November 1, 1945, and subsequently scrapped. (National Archives/80GK-6317)

to the carrier. *Franklin* withdrew from the area under tow from *Pittsburgh* (CA-72) until the carrier's speed was restored to 15 knots. The ship sailed to Pearl Harbor for seaworthiness repairs, and then to the naval yard at Brooklyn, New York, where *Franklin* arrived on April 28, 1945, for overhaul.

Acts of bravery were commonplace on *Franklin*, and two were singled out for the nation's highest honor: Ship's Chaplain Lt. Cmdr. Joseph T. O'Callahan organized firefighting and rescue efforts belowdecks when not tending to the wounded and dying. He also ordered firefighters to wet down ammunition magazines to prevent them from exploding. In addition, Lt. (jg) Donald Gary found 300 men trapped in a smoke-filled mess compartment. Gary led the men to safety, making three trips through flame and smoke to evacuate them. Both O'Callahan and Gary were awarded the Medal of Honor for their actions on March 19.

Three minutes later, *Wasp* was hit by an armor-piercing bomb that traveled through the flight deck, destroyed an aircraft on the hangar deck, split water and aviation fuel lines

▶ Bunker Hill (CV-17) ablaze after two kamikaze planes struck the carrier on May 11, 1945. A Cleveland-class cruiser has come to Bunker Hill's aid. More than 390 men were killed and 264 were wounded. The ship sailed for Bremerton, Washington, for permanent repairs, and returned to the Pacific Fleet in September. *(National Archives/80GK-5274)*

Gunners on Makin Island (CVE-93) practice on March 21, 1945, four days before the escort carrier arrived in Okinawan waters. The carrier supported the invasion, and remained in the vicinity for 67 days. Aircraft from Makin Island's Composite Squadrons 84 and 91 flew 2,558 ground support and reconnaissance missions before being relieved on June 1. (National Archives/80GK-5171)

before penetrating a third deck and exploding in the galley. The damage to the flight deck was repaired within the hour, but the bomb took a heavy toll on the crew, 269 wounded and 101 dead.

The carriers returned to work over Okinawa in concert with Rear Adm. Morton L. Deyo's fire support group, Task Force 54. The big guns of battleships *Tennessee* (flagship), *Arkansas, Colorado, Idaho, Maryland, Nevada, New Mexico* (BB-40), *New York, Texas,* and *West Virginia*, seven heavy and three light cruisers, 24 destroyers, plus eight destroyer escorts blasted the shores of Okinawa for five days in preparation for the April 1 assault.

Kerama Retto, a group of rocky islands seven miles off Okinawa's southwestern tip, was invaded on March 26 beginning at 8:00 A.M. The landings were unopposed. The Japanese fled into the hills, and the following evening on the island of Zamami Jima, two counter attacks saw 106 Imperial Army troops give their lives for the Emperor. Further resistance was spotty, and the Kerama Retto was deemed secure two days later. While exploring the islands, more than 250 Japanese suicide boats were discovered camouflaged along the shores and in caves. Each boat was 18 feet long and carried a pair of 250-pound depth charges. The intent was to have a suicide boat drop the charges against the hulls of Allied ships where the depth bombs would explode under the keel, sinking the ship.

On March 29, 30 Martin PBM Mariner patrol bombers arrived at Kerama Retto to set up shop. The Mariners provided antisubmarine patrols for ships of the forthcoming

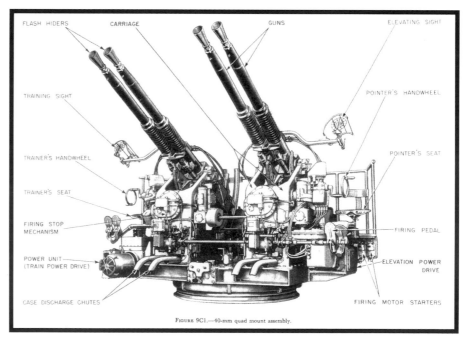

FIGURE 9C1.—40-mm quad mount assembly.

The U.S. Navy ship-based 40-mm quad gun mount is the type of rapid-firing cannon used to repel thousands of air attacks on ships patrolling the waters off Okinawa. (U.S. Navy)

West Virginia (BB-48) 40-mm quad gun mount and crew stand by as the ship covers the landings on Ie Shima off the west coast of Okinawa on April 16, 1945. West Virginia's quad 40-mm guns destroyed two kamikaze planes off Ie Shima on April 12. *(National Archives/80GK-4710)*

LST-647 moves toward Kerama Retto on April 1, 1945, with LST-885 in the background. This photo was taken from West Virginia. A roadstead was established at Kerama Kaikyo to serve as a rest and refueling area for ships involved in the Okinawa campaign. *(National Archives/80GK-3821)*

invasion of Okinawa. In addition, the Kerama Kaikyo roadstead was established between the islands with torpedo nets protecting the ships at anchor. Here refueling and other logistics tasks could be accomplished in the protection of the roadstead.

On April 1, Task Force 54 began to shell Okinawa at 6:40 A.M. Fifty-five minutes later the firing stopped to allow carrier planes to strafe the landing beaches. At 8:00 A.M., wave after wave of landing craft headed for the beaches at Hagushi, on the western side of the island near Yontan and Kadena airfields. The first assault wave hit the beach at 8:32 A.M., and, two hours later, both Kadena and Yontan were in American hands. Japanese resistance varied from light to non existent. By late afternoon, more than 50,000 men had gone ashore at Hagushi beach. At 7:10 P.M., while unloading cargo, the attack transport *Alpine* (APA-92) was hit by a kamikaze plane that crashed through the deck, starting fires in the number

Idaho (BB-42), main batteries to starboard, fires 14-inch/.50-caliber shells point-blank at Okinawa prior to the beach assault on April 1, 1945. Photo shot from the stem of West Virginia. Idaho supported both the Iwo Jima and Okinawa landings. On April 12, off Okinawa, the ship shot down five Japanese planes before being damaged at the waterline by a kamikaze that narrowly missed the battleship. *(National Archives/80GK-3829)*

two, three, and four holds, killing 21 and wounded 26. *Alpine* finished unloading and withdrew from the battle for repairs.

Achernar (AKA-53), named for the brightest star in the constellation Eridanus, was struck by a suicide plane at 12.43 A.M., on the morning of April 2. Six were killed and 41 wounded. Fires were extinguished, the flooding was stopped, and *Achernar* continued to unload. The ship withdrew to San Francisco for repairs on April 19 and was back at Okinawa two months later.

The U.S. Marines overran the northern part of Okinawa, which was lightly defended. Japanese Lt. Gen. Mitsuru Ushijima, commander of the island's defenders, had concentrated his troops in the southern part of Okinawa, intending to let the numerically superior Allied forces land, and then counterattack when the Marines were out of range of Task Force 54's big guns. Using this tactic, Ushijima believed he could wipe out the Allied force and retake the island. In the

Isherwood (DD-520) steams off Ie Shima in the days before April 16, when the destroyer was transferred to take Laffey's position at radar picket station number one. Isherwood was hit by a kamikaze on April 22 near dusk. The plane struck the number three gun mount and started numerous fires. One cooked off a depth charge on a stem rack, which heavily damaged the after engine room. More than 80 men were killed or wounded. The valiant destroyer served the U.S. Navy until September 11, 1961, when she was transferred to the navy of Peru as Guise (DD-72). *(National Archives/80GK-4732)*

Midway (CVB-41, Aircraft Carrier Large) was the first ship of its class, and was laid down on October 27, 1943, by Newport News Ship Building and Dry Dock Co., Newport News, Virginia. At 986 feet long, Midway was more than 100 feet longer than the Essex-class carriers that were the backbone of the Pacific Fleet during the war. Three ships of this class were built (CVB-42 Franklin D. Roosevelt and CVB-43 Coral Sea). Midway was launched on March 20, 1945, and commissioned September 10, eight days after the Japanese officially surrendered in Tokyo Bay. *(National Archives/80GK-3518)*

meantime, the vast armada of American and British ships effectively quarantined the island, preventing any Japanese reinforcement. Having captured three-quarters of the island with minimal effort, the U.S. Marines entered a two-month battle to secure the southern part of the island on April 7.

Submarines *Threadfin* (SS-410) and *Hackleback* (SS-295) were patrolling the Bungo Suido, the channel between the home islands of Kyushu and Shikoku around 8:00 P.M., on April 6. Both submarine skippers were surprised to see battleship *Yamato*, light cruiser *Yahagi,* and destroyers *Asashimo, Fuyutsuki, Hamakaze, Hatsushimo, Isokaze, Kasumi, Suzutsuki,* and *Yukikaze,* which had sortied from Tokuyama, Honshu, at 3:20 P.M. The *Yamato* group was to arrive off Okinawa during Operation *Ten-Go,* a massed kamikaze attack on the American Fleet. Whatever ships remained afloat after the suicide planes had done their job, were the *Yamato* group's objective. The Japanese ships carried only enough fuel for a one-way trip. After successfully engaging the Allied fleet, *Yamato* and its cruiser and destroyer were ordered to beach themselves after the attack to provide bombardment support to the island's defenders.

Threadfin and *Hackleback's* sighting gave Adm. Mitscher enough time to sail Task Force 58 north, within range of *Yamato's* anticipated position the following day. At dawn on April 7, search planes were launched to find the Japanese

Midway sponsor's party (left to right) maid of honor Miss Fredricka Patterson; Rear Adm. D. L. Cox, Newport News Ship Building and Dry Dock Co., superintendent of ship building; Mrs. Bradford Williams Ripley II, ship's sponsor from Dayton, Ohio; and Lt. George Gay—sole survivor of VT-8 at the Battle of Midway; and Mrs. William Aycrigg, prior to christening the carrier on March 20, 1945, at Newport News Ship Building and Dry Dock Co. *(National Archives/80GK-3517)*

Franklin D. Roosevelt passed away on April 12 at 3:30 p.m., while the president was vacationing in Warm Springs, Georgia. His funeral procession and casket passes Constitution Avenue toward the White House on April 14, 1945. (National Archives/80GK-3997)

battlegroup. A scout from *Essex* (CV-9) spotted the ships at 8:23 A.M., and a pair of Kerama Retto based PBMs followed the Japanese armada throughout most of the morning, sending continuous position reports. The American task force launched another scouting force at 9:15 A.M. to monitor *Yamato's* progress, and at 10:00 A.M. began launching the main striking force of 131 torpedo bombers, 180 fighters, and 75 dive-bombers.

Yamato sighted 150 aircraft 50 miles to the south at 12:32 P.M. Two minutes later the ships opened fire with everything they had, including *Yamato's* 18-inch main batteries. First a group of dive-bombers targeted *Yamato*, one of which was shot down. Two bombs hit near the aft mast and the Number Two auxiliary gun. One torpedo struck the battleship at 12:45 P.M. At 1:33, 20 torpedo planes attacked, three of their "fish" striking *Yamato* amidships. One torpedo bomber was shot down and two more torpedoes found their mark. One half hour later, the dive-bombers were back, this time scoring three hits, followed by four additional torpedoes. At 2:20 P.M., *Yamato* was listing 20 degrees to port. Three minutes later, the ship's magazines exploded, sending the world's largest battleship to the bottom of the sea. The light cruiser *Yahagi* withstood the onslaught of 12 bombs and seven torpedoes before finally sinking. Destroyers *Asashimo, Hamakaze, Isokaze,* and *Kasumi* were also sunk or scuttled while the remaining four destroyers returned to Sasebo for repairs. The Japanese lost 3,655 officers and men (2,488 from *Yamato* alone), versus the American losses of 10 planes and 12 airmen.

Coinciding with *Yamato's* demise, the Japanese opened Operation *Ten-Go*, a nearly two-month-long kamikaze assault on ships stationed around Okinawa. The massed attacks were known as *kikusui,* or floating chrysanthemum, and 10 were

America's 33rd president, Harry S. Truman, of Missouri, was unaware of America's program to build the atomic bomb when he took the highest political office in the United States. Many credit Truman's decision to use the bomb for shortening the war and saving millions of Allied and Japanese lives. (National Archives/80GK-15861)

downed nine planes, and combat air patrol aircraft dispatched a few more, but four bombs and six kamikaze planes had hit the ship by the time the attack was over, around 10:00 A.M. In addition, the ship was strafed, one bomb exploded in the water, narrowly missing the destroyer, and a seventh kamikaze crashed short of striking the ship. *Laffey* was dead in the water with 32 of its crew killed and 71 wounded. Although the destroyer had been badly mauled, it sailed under its own power to the West Coast for repairs and eventually rejoined the fleet.

In all, 1,465 aircraft made suicide attacks under Operation *Ten-Go*, another 435 suicide attacks were launched by aircraft from other units and those based at Formosa, 1,351 harassed the fleet either through bombing or strafing, and surviving records indicate that an additional 3,700 dive-bombing and torpedo sorties were recorded by Japanese naval aircraft. Twenty-one ships were sunk, 43 were scrapped as a result of kamikaze attacks, and another 23 ships needed repairs that took more than one month.

Okinawa was secured on June 21. That day the Marines finally pushed to the south coast of the island. With Allied victory at hand, Gen. Ushijima committed suicide the following morning, and the Marines began mopping up small pockets of resistance.

Changing World Leadership

America's 32 president, Franklin D. Roosevelt, the man who led the nation from the depths of economic depression in 1932 to the brink of total victory in 1945, died of a cerebral hemorrhage at Warm Springs, Georgia, on April 12 at 3:30 P.M. Roosevelt was succeeded by Harry S. Truman, a senator from Missouri, who had only taken the office of vice president in January 1945. Truman continued Roosevelt's fighting spirit and he put the Axis powers on notice in his April 16 State of the Union address: "So that there can be no possible misunderstanding, both Germany and Japan can be certain, beyond any shadow of a doubt, that America will continue the fight for freedom until no vestige of resistance remains!"

The transition of power had been smooth in the United States, but chaos reigned in Berlin a little more than two weeks later. On April 30, under the constant bombardment of Soviet artillery, Adolph Hitler and his new bride Eva Braun committed suicide in the Reich Chancellery bunker just minutes before 4:00 P.M.. Control of the German government passed to Adm. Karl Dönitz, who called upon his U-boats to cease fire at 8:00 A.M., on May 5. On May 7, surrender terms were reached at Gen. Dwight D. Eisenhower's headquarters in Reims, France. The surrender was effective at midnight on May 8. The Allies accepted the surrender of 168 U-boats, and the Japanese took control of six U-boats (*U-181, U-195, U-219, U-862,* and the ex-Italian submarines *U-IT24* and *U-IT25*).

U-boats had sunk 2,575 Allied ships, taking more than 45,000 lives. In exchange, 781 U-boats were lost in

Less than a month after President Roosevelt died, Adolph Hitler committed suicide in his Berlin headquarters. Adm. Karl Dönitz surrendered all Nazi forces effective at midnight on May 8. German U-boats surrendered to the nearest ship or port. U-858 is brought to anchor at Cape Henlopen, Delaware, after being surrendered at sea. With megaphone on her conning tower is Lt. Cmdr. Willard D. Michael, officer in charge of the enemy vessel. After the war, the U.S. Navy used the U-boat as a target and sunk the craft in 600 feet of water northeast of Cape Cod, Massachusetts. The Sikorski HNS-1 flying overhead represents a new technology for the U.S. Navy, while the blimp would soon be phased out of service. *(National Archives/80GK-3319)*

launched between April 6 and June 22. To provide an early-warning net around Okinawa, the U.S. Navy positioned 16 destroyers on radar picket stations within a 100-mile radius of Zampa Misaki, a point near Yontan airfield. Each destroyer sailed within a 5,000-yard patch of ocean, providing the ships anchored off Okinawa with an early-warning radar network. The picket ships took a beating from the kamikazes, none worse than *Laffey* (DD-724).

The destroyer arrived at Radar Picket Station Number One on April 14, after Operation *Ten-Go* had begun. Upon steaming into position, the destroyer immediately went to battle stations to repel an attack of more than 50 kamikaze planes, of which 13 were shot down. The following day, the Japanese launched the third-largest attack of the *Ten-Go* operation when 315 aircraft attacked the fleet off Okinawa, 165 making suicide attacks. Kamikazes hit *Laffey* the hardest of any ship during the war. Beginning at 8:27 A.M., 23 Japanese planes converged on *Laffey*. The destroyer's gunners combat or to accidents, and more than 32,000 German sailors gave their lives.

London, New York, and cities all over the Allied nations celebrated the end of the war in Europe, but the joy was short-lived as there was still an enemy to fight.

In mid-April, Truman welcomed delegates to the first United Nations assembly in San Francisco via a radio address. At the same time, the new president was briefed about America's effort to build an atomic bomb under the codename "Manhattan Project." Truman took this knowledge to the July 17 through August 2 Potsdam Conference, named for the city west of Berlin where the conference was held. Truman, Stalin, Churchill, and later Clement Attlee, who succeeded Churchill as prime minister, established four-nation rule over Germany and its Russian, British, American, and French zones of occupation. In addition, the Potsdam Declaration was presented to Japan, calling for its unconditional surrender or total annihilation.

One City, One Bomb: Hiroshima and Nagasaki

Having secured Okinawa, the fast carrier task forces maintained pressure on the Japanese by striking targets in and around the home islands. From July 10 to August 15, carrier

continued on page 148

GIs stationed in Germany were understandably anxious to return home after the surrender of Germany. West Point (AP-23) steaming past Ellis Island and the Statue of Liberty on July 11, 1945, was one of the first ships to return from Europe. Returning servicemen were welcomed home with open arms. *(National Archives/80GK-5780)*

Cruiser Salem (CA-139) at anchor in Toulon, France. Salem was one of the last ships laid down during the war. The ship's keel was laid on July 4, after victory in Europe, and before the final outcome in the Pacific was assured. *(National Archives/80GK-11921)*

JAPAN SURRENDERS

Instrument of Surrender

We, acting by command of and in behalf of the Emperor of Japan, the Japanese Government and the Japanese Imperial General Headquarters, hereby accept the provisions set forth in the declaration issued by the heads of the Governments of the United States, China, and Great Britain on 26 July 1945 at Potsdam, and subsequently adhered to by the Union of Soviet Socialist Republics, which four powers are hereafter referred to as the Allied Powers.

We hereby proclaim the unconditional surrender to the Allied Powers of the Japanese Imperial General Headquarters and of all Japanese armed forces and all armed forces under the Japanese control wherever situated.

We hereby command all Japanese forces wherever situated and the Japanese people to cease hostilities forthwith, to preserve and save from damage all ships, aircraft, and military and civil property, and to comply with all requirements which may be imposed by the Supreme Commander for the Allied Powers or by agencies of the Japanese Government at his direction.

We hereby command the Japanese Imperial General Headquarters to issue at once orders to the Commanders of all Japanese forces and all forces under Japanese control wherever situated to surrender unconditionally themselves and all forces under their control.

We hereby command all civil, military, and naval officials to obey and enforce all proclamations, and orders and directives deemed by the Supreme Commander for the Allied Powers, to be proper to effectuate this surrender and issued by him or under his authority and we direct all such officials to remain at their posts and to continue to perform their non-combatant duties unless specifically relieved by him or under his authority.

We hereby undertake for the Emperor, the Japanese Government, and their successors to carry out the provisions of the Potsdam Declaration in good faith, and to issue whatever orders and take whatever actions may be required by the Supreme Commander for the Allied Powers or by any other designated representative of the Allied Powers for the purpose of giving effect to that Declaration.

We hereby command the Japanese Imperial Government and the Japanese Imperial General Headquarters at once to liberate all Allied prisoners of war and civilian internees now under Japanese control and to provide for their protection, care, maintenance, and immediate transportation to places as directed.

The authority of the Emperor and the Japanese Government to rule the state shall be subject to the Supreme Commander for the Allied Powers who will take such steps as he deems proper to effectuate these terms of surrender.

Signed at Tokyo Bay, Japan, at 0904 on the second day of September, 1945.

Mamoru Shigmitsu (Foreign Minister),
By Command and in behalf of the Emperor of Japan and the Japanese Government

Yoshijiro Umezu (General),
By Command and in behalf of the Japanese Imperial General Headquarters

Accepted at Tokyo Bay, Japan, at 0908 on the second day of September, 1945, for the United States, Republic of China, United Kingdom, and the Union of Soviet Socialist Republics, and in the interests of the other United Nations at war with Japan.

Douglas MacArthur,
Supreme Commander for the Allied Powers

C. W. Nimitz,
United States Representative

Hsu Yung-Chang,
Republic of China Representative

Bruce Fraser,
United Kingdom Representative

Kuzma Derevyanko,
Union of Soviet Socialist Republics Representative

Thomas Blamey
Commonwealth of Australia Representative

L. Moore Cosgrave,
Dominion of Canada Representative

Jacques Le Clerc,
Provisional Government of the French Republic Representative

C. E. L. Helfrich,
Kingdom of the Netherlands Representative

Leonard M. Isitt,
Dominion of New Zealand Representative

General of the Army Douglas MacArthur affixes his signature to the surrender documents on board battleship Missouri, while Gen. Jonathan Wainwright and British Gen. Sir Arthur Percival look on. MacArthur signed on behalf of all Allied nations. Foreign Minister Mamoru Shigemitsu signed the documents at 9:04 a.m. (Tokyo Time). *(National Archives/RC-111C-1587)*

Japanese shipyard workers were diligently working to supply their navy with the tools of the trade. These midget subs, in an assembly shed at the Mitsubishi Shipyards, were to be used in defense of the home islands. Photographed September 17, 1945, as Allied troops occupied Japan. *(National Archives/80GK-6490)*

After defeating both Germany and Japan in 1945, the U.S. Navy began storing a large number of ships for future use. Ships of every class from battleship and aircraft carrier to submarine and net tender were stored in reserve fleets on the West and East Coasts as well as the Gulf of Mexico. Eight Victory Ships and an LST await an uncertain fate in storage at Suisun Bay, California. *(Nicholas A. Veronico)*

Continued from page 145

planes raided Tokyo five times (July 10, 18, 30, and August 13 and 15); Hokkaido/Northern Honshu twice (July 14–15 and August 9–10); and targets of opportunity in the Inland Sea and Kure Naval Base area on July 24–25.

Surface elements of the fast carrier forces bombarded military targets on the island of Honshu between July 14 and August 9 (Kamaishi, July 14; Hitachi on the night of July 17–18; Omura, night, July 22–23; Shiono Misaki, night, July 24–25; Hamamatsu, night, July 29–30; Shimizu, night, July 30–31; and Kamaishi again on August 9). The port city of Muroran on the island of Hokkaido was shelled during daylight hours on July 15.

From Tinian Island in the Marianas, six B-29 bombers from the 509th Bomb Group headed for the home islands in the early morning hours of August 6. Three planes departed to reconnoiter the weather over the prime target, Hiroshima, the secondary, Kokura, and the alternate, Nagasaki. At 2:45 A.M., the B-29 christened *Enola Gay,* after Col. Paul Tibbets' mother, lifted off the Tinian runway. A pair of camera, and scientific-instrument-laden B-29s followed at two-minute intervals, Maj. Charles W. Sweeney in *The Great Artiste* and Capt. George W. Marquardt's *No. 91,* met *Enola Gay* over Iwo Jima for the trip north. *Enola Gay* was carrying an atomic bomb to drop on Hiroshima, a city that had been spared from the nightly B-29 fire-bombing raids. President Truman had authorized use of the atomic bomb, equal to 20,000 tons of TNT, only days before during his return trip from the Potsdam Conference.

Enola Gay arrived over Hiroshima at 31,600 feet, traveling at 328 miles per hour. At 8:15 A.M., Hiroshima time, the bomb was dropped from *Enola Gay.* Fifty seconds later, it exploded 2,000 feet above the ground, vaporizing 4.7 square miles and engulfing the city in a firestorm. More than 71,000 were instantly killed, and thousands more died from radiation-related diseases in the ensuing months and years. The mushroom cloud from the blast climbed more than 50,000 feet into the air and was visible for more than 400 miles. *Enola Gay* safely returned to Tinian, and the world entered the age of atomic warfare.

After the bombing, President Truman called for the surrender of Japan in a radio broadcast beamed to Japan, but no action was taken by the Japanese government.

On August 9 at 3:49 A.M., Maj. Sweeney left Tinian in the B-29 *Bock's Car* headed for Kokura. Here the weather obscured the target and Sweeney flew to the alternate, Nagasaki. At 10:58 A.M., Nagasaki time, the second atomic bomb was dropped. The U.S. Strategic Bombing Survey, conducted after the war, concluded that more than 35,000 were killed instantly at Nagasaki.

Sadly, one of America's worst naval tragedies occurred during the bombings. The cruiser *Indianapolis* (CA-35) had delivered the parts to assemble the atomic bombs on Tinian on July 26—racing from San Francisco to the island, more than 5,000 miles in 10 days. Departing Tinian on July 28, the cruiser staged through Guam en route to Leyte. On July 30, at 12:15 A.M., two torpedoes from *I-58* struck the ship forward on the starboard side: one under the Number One turret and the second farther aft. *Indianapolis* rolled over and sank in less than 12 minutes. Those who did not perish in the initial explosions boarded rafts or swam, buoyed only by their life jackets.

When the ship did not reach Leyte on July 31, it was not reported as overdue because of a clerical error. On August 2, at 10:25 A.M., Lt. (jg) Wilbur C. Gwinn, in a Lockheed PV-1 Ventura patrol bomber, spotted men in the water. At first he counted 30, then 90, then 150. Gwinn dropped his aircraft's life rafts and radioed for help. The survivors had been spotted after three and one-half days in the water. Of the ship's 1,199 men, it was estimated that 800 were able to abandon ship. Less than 40 percent survived their wounds, sharks, or exposure—only 316 men were rescued.

Victory Over Japan

Many in the Japanese government had been contemplating a total Allied victory since the invasion of Okinawa and, coincidentally, the government was meeting to review the surrender terms when the bomb was dropped on Nagasaki. Russia had entered the war against Japan the previous day, and in combination with the atomic bombings, the Japanese government subsequently announced that they would accept the terms of the Potsdam declaration. Working through the Swiss, word of the Japanese acceptance was sent to the United States. The British and Soviet governments were contacted by the Swedes on Japan's behalf.

Subjects of the Japanese Empire learned of the war's end through a radio broadcast of a message from the Emperor on August 15. During a press conference at 7:00 P.M., on August 14 (Washington, D.C., time and date) President Truman announced that war with Japan had ended, and that a two-day national holiday would celebrate the Allied victory. In addition, Gen. Douglas MacArthur was named Supreme Allied Commander for the occupation of Japan, and he would preside over the surrender ceremonies in Tokyo Bay.

Elements of the U.S. Third Fleet and the British Pacific Fleet began to arrive in Tokyo Bay on August 27, including the battleship *Missouri*, flagship of Adm. Halsey. Adm. Nimitz and Gen. MacArthur arrived at Yokohama by air on August 29. Adm. Nimitz selected *Missouri* as the site for the surrender ceremonies, which were slated to take place on September 2.

The destroyer *Lansdowne* (DD-486) delivered the Japanese delegation to the *Missouri* at 8:56 A.M. Foreign

Minister Mamoru Shigemitsu and Army Gen. Yoshijiro Umezu were piped aboard the battleship escorted by representatives of the Army, Navy, and Imperial Foreign Office. On *Missouri's* starboard quarterdeck near Turret Number Two, Gen. MacArthur opened the ceremony with brief remarks. At 9:04 A.M., Shigemitsu signed the surrender documents officially ending the war, followed by Gen. Umezu. MacArthur then signed on behalf of all Allied nations, followed by representatives of every nation involved in the conflict. The ceremony was over at 9:25 A.M., and was followed by a demonstration of air power. More than 450 carrier planes paraded over *Missouri,* followed by 462 B-29 heavy bombers.

General MacArthur's closing comment after the surrender documents had been signed were words of hope for a world ravaged by 1,364 days of total war: "Let us pray that peace be now restored to the world and that God will preserve it always."

The war was over both in Europe and the Pacific, and it was time for America's fighting men and women to come home. Large numbers of America's vast armada of ships were put into storage, and the war workers returned to their lives. The time had come for the nation, and for the world, to begin rebuilding. The world had become smaller, and life was now challenged by the war's aftermath in the Atomic Age.

Chandeleur (AV-10) approaches Golden Gate after war's end in November 1945. Like the Statue of Liberty on the East Coast, San Francisco's Golden Gate Bridge was the first or last sign of home many a soldier, sailor, or airman saw. Chandeleur was based at Kerama Retto, beginning March 28, to support seaplanes participating in the Okinawan campaign. Seaplanes associated with the tender were responsible in part for the sinking of I-8 on March 31, and spotting battleship Yamato on April 7. Yamato was subsequently sunk by carrier planes that afternoon. *(National Archives/80GK-6781)*

SHIPS PRESENT AT PEARL HARBOR, DECEMBER 7, 1941, 8:00 A.M.

Note: Ships listed by hull number. (*) Denotes ships sunk during the air raid. *Arizona, Oklahoma,* and *Utah* were not returned to service. Source: Naval Historical Center.

Battleships
Pennsylvania (BB-38) (in dry dock)
Arizona (BB-39)*
Nevada (BB-36)
Oklahoma (BB-37)*
Tennessee (BB-43)
California (BB-44)*
Maryland (BB-46)
West Virginia (BB-48)*

Heavy Cruisers
New Orleans (CA-32)
San Francisco (CA-38)

Light Cruisers
Raleigh (CL-7)
Detroit (CL-8)
Phoenix (CL-46)
Honolulu (CL-48)
St. Louis (CL-49)
Helena (CL-50)

Submarines
Narwhal (SS-167)
Dolphin (SS-169)
Cachalot (SS-170)
Tautog (SS-199)

Destroyers
Allen (DD-66)
Schley (DD-103)
Chew (DD-106)
Ward (DD-139, patrolling Channel entrance to Pearl Harbor)
Dewey (DD-349)
Farragut (DD-348)
Hull (DD-350)
MacDonough (DD-351)
Worden (DD-352)
Dale (DD-353)
Monaghan (DD-354)
Aylwin (DD-355)
Selfridge (DD-357)
Phelps (DD-360)
Cummings (DD-365)
Reid (DD-369)
Case (DD-370)
Conyngham (DD-371)
Cassin (DD-372 – in dry dock)
Shaw (DD-373 – in floating dry dock)
Tucker (DD-374)
Downes (DD-375 – in dry dock)
Bagley (DD-386)
Blue (DD-387)
Helm (DD-388)
Mugford (DD-389)
Ralph Talbot (DD-390)
Henley (DD-391)
Patterson (DD-392)
Jarvis (DD-393)

Minelayer
Oglala (CM-4)*

Minesweepers
Turkey (AM-13)
Bobolink AM-20)
Rail (AM-26)
Tern (AM-31)
Grebe (AM-43)
Vireo (AM-52)

Coastal Minesweepers
Cockatoo (AMC-8)
Crossbill (AMC-9)
Condor (AMC-14)
Reedbird (AMC-30)

Destroyer Minelayers
Gamble (DM-15)
Ramsay (DM-16)
Montgomery (DM-17)
Breese (DM-18)
Tracy (DM-19)
Preble (DM-20)
Sicard (DM-21)
Pruitt (DM-22)

Destroyer Minesweepers
Zane (DMS-14)
Wasmuth (DMS-15)
Trever (DMS-16)
Perry (DMS-17)

Patrol Gunboat
Sacramento (PG-19)

Destroyer Tenders
Dobbin (AD-3)
Whitney (AD-4)

Seaplane Tenders
Curtiss (AV-4)
Tangier (AV-8)

Small Seaplane Tenders
Avocet (AVP-4)
Swan (AVP-7 – on marine railway dock)

Seaplane Tenders, Destroyers
Hulbert (AVD-6)
Thornton (AVD-11)

Ammunition Ship
Pyro (AE-1)

Oilers
Ramapo (AO-12)
Neosho (AO-23)

Repair Ships
Medusa (AR-1)
Vestal (AR-4)
Rigel (AR-11)

Submarine Tender
Pelias (AS-14)

Submarine Rescue Ship
Widgeon (ASR-1)

Hospital Ship
Solace (AH-5)

Stores Issue Ships
Castor (AKS-1)
Antares (AKS-3, at Pearl Harbor entrance)

Ocean Tugs
Ontario (AT-13)
Sunnadin (AT-28)
Keosanqua (AT-38, at Pearl Harbor entrance)
Navajo (AT-64, 12 miles outside Pearl Harbor entrance)

Miscellaneous Auxiliaries
Utah (AG-16)*
Argonne (AG-31)
Sumner (AG-32)

SHIPS PRESENT AT TOKYO BAY, SEPTEMBER 2, 1945

Note: Ships are listed alphabetically by type. U.S. Navy ships have hull numbers and Allied ships have pendant numbers. HMAS—Australian; HMS—British; HMNZS—New Zealand.

Battleships
Colorado (BB-45)
HMS *Duke of York* (17)
Idaho (BB-42)
Iowa (BB-61)
HMS *King George V* (41)
Mississippi (BB-41)
Missouri (BB-63)
New Mexico (BB-40)
South Dakota (BB-57)
West Virginia (BB-48)

Light Aircraft Carriers
Bataan (CVL-29)
Cowpens (CVL-25)

Escort Carriers
HMS *Ruler* (D.72)
HMS *Speaker* (D.90)
Salamaua

Heavy Cruisers
Boston (CA-69)
Chicago (CA-136)
Quincy (CA-71)
St. Paul (CA-73)
HMAS *Shropshire* (96)

Light Cruisers
Detroit (CL-8)
HMNZS *Gambia* (48)
HMAS *Hobart* (I.63)
HMS *Newfoundland* (59)
Oakland (CL-95)
Pasadena (CL-65)
San Diego (CL-53)
San Juan (CL-54)
Springfield (CL-66)
Wilkes-Barre (CL-103)

Destroyers
Ault (DD-698)
Benham (DD-796)
Blue (DD-744)
Buchanon (DD-484)
Caperton (DD-650)
Clarence K. Bronson (DD-668)
Cogswell (DD-651)
Colahan (DD-658)
Cotten (DD-669)
Cushing (DD-797)
De Haven (DD-727)
Dortch (DD-670)
Frank Knox (DD-742)
Gatling (DD-671)
Halsey Powell (DD-686)
Healy (DD-672)
Hilary P. Jones (DD-427)
Hughes (DD-410)
Ingersoll (DD-652)
Kalk (DD-611)
Knapp (DD-653)
Lansdowne (DD-468)
Lardner (DD-487)
Madison (DD-425)
Mayo (DD-422)
HMAS *Napier* (G.97)
HMAS *Nizam* (G.38)
Nicholas (DD-449)
Perkins (DD-877)
HMS *Quality* (G.62)
Robert K. Huntington (DD-781)
Southerland (DD-743)
Stockham (DD-683)
Taylor (DD-468)
HMS *Teazer* (R.23)
HMS *Tenacious* (R.45)
HMS *Terpsichore* (R.33)

Twining (DD-540)
Uhlmann (DD-687)
Wadleigh (DD-689)
HMS *Wager* (R.98)
Wallace L. Lind (DD-703)
HMAS *Warramunga* (I.44)
Wedderburn (DD-684)
HMS *Whelp* (R.37)
HMS *Wizard* (R.72)
Wren (DD-568)
Yarnell (DD-541)

Destroyer Escorts
Goss (DE-444)
Kendall C. Campbell (DE-443)
Lyman (DE-302)
Major (DE-796)
Roberts (DE-749)
Waterman (DE-740)
Weaver (DE-741)
William Seiverling (DE-441)
Ulvert M. Moore (DE-442)

Frigates
HMS *Derg* (K.257)
HMAS *Gascoyne* (K.354)

Sloops
HMS *Crane* (U.23)
HMS *Whimbrel* (U.29)

Destroyer Minelayers
Gwin (DM-33)
Thomas E. Fraser (DM-24)

Destroyer Minesweepers
Ellyson (DMS-19)
Fitch (DMS-25)
Gherardi (DMS-30)
Hambleton (DMS-20)

Hopkins (DMS-13)
Jeffers (DMS-27)
Macomb (DMS-23)

Submarines
Archerfish (SS-311)
Cavalla (SS-244)
Gato (SS-212)
Haddo (SS-255)
Hake (SS-256)
Muskallunge (SS-262)
Pilotfish (SS-386)
Razorback (SS-394)
Runner (SS-275)
Sea Cat (SS-399)
Segundo (SS-398)
Tigrone (SS-419)

Submarine Chasers
PC-466
PCE(R)-848
PCE(R)-849
PCE(R)-850
PCE-877

Motor Gunboats
PGM-16
PGM-26
PGM-32

Minesweepers
HMAS *Ballarat* (K.34)
HMAS *Cessnock* (J.175)
HMAS *Ipswich* (J.186)
Pheasant (AM-61)
HMAS *Pirie* (J.189)
Pochard (AM-375)
Revenge (AM-110)
Token (AM-126)
Tumult (AM-127)

Source: Naval Historical Center – Commander in Chief, U.S. Pacific Fleet and Pacific Ocean Areas (CINCPAC/CINCPOA) A16-3/FF12 Serial 0395, 11 February 1946: Report of Surrender and Occupation of Japan.

Auxiliary Motor Minesweepers
YMS-177
YMS-268
YMS-276
YMS-343
YMS-362
YMS-371
YMS-390
YMS-415
YMS-426
YMS-441
YMS-461
YMS-467

Auxiliary Minelayers
Picket (ACM-8)

General Communications Vessels
Ancon (AGC-4)
Mount Olympus (AGC-8)
Teton (AGC-14)

High-Speed Transports
Barr (APD-39)
Horace A. Bass (APD-124)
Burke (APD-65)
Gosselin (APD-126)
Hollis (APD-86)
Pavlic (APD-70)
Reeves (APD-52)
John Q. Roberts (APD-94)
Runels (APD-85)
Sims (APD-50)
Wantuck (APD-125)
William M. Pattison (APD-104)

Tank Landing Ships
LST-567
LST-648
LST-717
LST-718
LST-789
LST-846
LST-1083
LST-1139

Landing Ships, Dock
Catamount (LSD-17)
Shadwell (LSD-15)

Landing Crafts, Infantry
LCI(L)-438
LCI(L)-441
LCI(L)-450
LCI(L)-457
LCI(L)-458
LCI(L)-469
LCI(L)-726
LCI(L)-752
LCI(L)-798

Medium Landing Ships
LSM-13
LSM-15
LSM-71
LSM-101
LSM-208
LSM-252
LSM-284
LSM-290
LSM-362
LSM-368
LSM-371
LSM-419
LSM-488

Landing Ships, Vehicle
Monitor (LSV-5)
Ozark (LSV-2)

Attack Transports
Bosque (APA-135)
Botetourt (APA-136)
Briscoe (APA-65)
Cecil (APA-96)
Clearfield (APA-142)
Cullman (APA-78)
Darke (APA-157)
Dauphin (APA-97)
Deuel (APA-160)
Dickens (APA-161)
Hansford (APA-106)
Highlands (APA-119)
Lavaca (APA 180)
Lenawee (APA-195)

Mellette (APA-156)
Missoula (APA-211)
Rutland (APA-192)
St. Mary's (APA-126)
Sherburne (APA-205)
Sheridan (APA-51)
Talladega (APA-208)

Transport
General Sturgis (AP-137)

Attack Cargo Ships
Libra (AKA-12)
Medea (AKA-31)
Pamina (AKA-34)
Sirona (AKA-43)
Skagit (AKA-105)
Todd (AKA-71)
Tolland (AKA-64)
Whiteside (AKA-90)
Yancy (AKA-93)

Cargo Ship
Lesuth (AK-125)

Civilian Cargo Ships
St. Lawrence Victory (U. S.)
Winthrop Victory (U. S.)

Stores Issue Ship
Cybele (AKS-10)

Repair Ship
Delta (AR-9)

Landing Craft Repair Ship
Patroclus (ARL-19)

Oilers
Chiwawa (AO-68)
Mascoma (AO-83)
Neches (AO-47)
Niobrara (AO-72)
Tamalpais (AO-96)

Civilian Oilers
Carelia (British)
City of Dieppe (British)
Dingledale (British)
Fort Wrangell (British)
Wave King (British)

Gasoline Tanker
Genesee (AOG-8)

Destroyer Tender
Piedmont (AD-17)

Hospital Ships
Benevolence (AH-13)
Marigold (U.S. Army)
HMHS *Tjitjalengka* (Dutch)

Seaplane Tenders
Cumberland Sound (AV-17)
Hamlin (AV-15)

Small Seaplane Tenders
Gardiners Bay (AVP-39)
Mackinac (AVP-13)
Suisun (AVP-53)

Submarine Tender
Proteus (AS-19)

Submarine Rescue Ship
Greenlet (ASR-10)

Fleet Ocean Tug
Moctobi (ARF-105)
Wenatchee (ATF-118)

Auxiliary Ocean Tug
ATA-205

Ocean Tug, Old
Woodcock (ATO-145)

APPENDIX

U.S. NAVY SHIP LOSSES BY TYPE

Note: Ships are listed alphabetically by type.

When Arizona exploded and sank, the battleship took 1,177 men with her. The ship's hull serves as the final resting place for those officers and men. The 184-foot-long memorial was dedicated in 1962 and features an entry room, central observation gallery, and the shire room located on the Ford Island side of the memorial, where the names of all 1,177 men who perished on board the Arizona are engraved. *(Nicholas A. Veronico)*

Battleships

Arizona (BB-39) destroyed by Japanese aircraft bombs at Pearl Harbor, Hawaii, December 7, 1941, and stricken from the Navy List, December 1, 1942.

Oklahoma (BB-37) capsized and sank after being torpedoed by Japanese aircraft at Pearl Harbor, Hawaii, December 7, 1941.

Aircraft Carriers

Hornet (CV 8) sunk after being torpedoed by Japanese aircraft during the Battle of Santa Cruz, Solomon Islands, October 26, 1942.

Lexington (CV-2) sunk after being torpedoed by Japanese aircraft during the Battle of the Coral Sea, May 8, 1942.

Princeton (CVL-23) sunk after being bombed by Japanese aircraft during the Battle of Leyte Gulf, Philippine Islands, October 24, 1944.

Wasp (CV-7) sunk after being torpedoed by Japanese submarine *I-19* south of Guadalcanal, Solomon Islands, September 15, 1942.

Yorktown (CV-5) damaged by aircraft bombs on June 4, 1942, during the Battle of Midway and sunk after being torpedoed by Japanese submarine *I-168*, June 7, 1942.

Aircraft Carriers, Escort

Bismarck Sea (CVE-95) sunk by kamikaze aircraft off Iwo Jima, Volcano Islands, February 21, 1945.

Block Island (CVE-21) sunk after being torpedoed by German submarine *U-549* northwest of the Canary Islands, May 29, 1944.

Gambier Bay (CVE-73) sunk by gunfire of Japanese warships during the Battle of Leyte Gulf off Samar, Philippine Islands, October 25, 1944.

Liscome Bay (CVE-56) sunk after being torpedoed by Japanese submarine *I-175* off Gilbert Islands, November 24, 1943.

Ommaney Bay (CVE-79) sunk by kamikaze attack south of Mindoro, Philippine Islands, January 4, 1945.

St. Lo (CVE-63) sunk by Japanese aircraft during the Battle of Leyte Gulf off Samar, Philippine Islands, October 25, 1944.

Heavy Cruisers

Astoria (CA-34) sunk by gunfire of Japanese warships off Savo, Solomon Islands, August 9, 1942.

Chicago (CA-29) sunk after being torpedoed by Japanese aircraft off Rennel, Solomon Islands, January 29–30, 1943.

Houston (CA-30) sunk by gunfire and torpedoes of Japanese warships in Sunda Strait, Netherlands East Indies, March 1, 1942.

Indianapolis (CA-35) sunk after being torpedoed by Japanese submarine *I-58* in the Philippine Sea, July 29, 1945.

Northampton (CA-26) torpedoed by the Japanese destroyer *Oyashio* on November 30, 1942, during the Battle of Tassafaronga and sank on December 1, 1942.

Quincy (CA-39) sunk by gunfire and torpedoes of Japanese warships off Savo, Solomon Islands, August 9, 1942.

Vincennes (CA-44) sunk after being torpedoed by Japanese warships off Savo, Solomon Islands, August 9, 1942.

Light Cruisers

Atlanta (CL-51) scuttled off Lunga Point, Guadalcanal, Solomon Islands, after being damaged by gunfire from Japanese warships during the Battle of Guadalcanal, November 13, 1942.

Helena (CL-50) sunk after being torpedoed by Japanese warships during the Battle of Kula Gulf, Solomon Islands, July 6, 1943.

Juneau (CL-52) sunk by the Japanese submarine *I-26* after being torpedoed during the Battle of Guadalcanal, November 13, 1942.

Destroyers

Aaron Ward (DD-483) sunk after being bombed by Japanese aircraft off Tagoma Point, Guadalcanal, Solomon Islands, April 7, 1943.

Abner Read (DD-526) sunk by kamikaze attack in Leyte Gulf, Philippine Islands, November 1, 1944.

Barton (DD-599) sunk after being torpedoed by Japanese warships off Savo, Solomon Islands, November 13, 1942.

Beatty (DD-640) sunk after being torpedoed by German aircraft off Cape Bougaroun, Algeria, November 6, 1943.

Benham (DD-397) sunk after being damaged by a torpedo from a Japanese warship off Guadalcanal, Solomon Islands, November 15, 1942.

Blue (DD-387) scuttled after being torpedoed by the Japanese destroyer *Kawakaze* in Savo Sound, Solomon Islands, August 22, 1942.

Borie (DD-215) sunk as a result of damage received on the November 1, 1943, ramming of the German submarine *U-405* in the North Atlantic, north of the Azores, November 2, 1943.

Bristol (DD-453) sunk after being torpedoed by the German submarine *U-371* off Cape Bougaroun, Algeria, October 12, 1943.

Brownson (DD-518) sunk by Japanese aircraft off Cape Gloucester, New Britain Island, December 26, 1943.

Buck (DD-420) sunk after being torpedoed by the German submarine *U-616* off Salerno, Italy, October 9, 1943.

Bush (DD-529) sunk after being hit by three kamikaze aircraft off Okinawa, Ryukyu Islands, April 6, 1945.

Callaghan (DD-792) sunk after being hit by one kamikaze aircraft off Okinawa, Ryukyu Islands, July 28, 1945.

Chevalier (DD-451) sunk after being torpedoed by a Japanese destroyer and damaged in a collision with USS *O'Bannon* (DD-450) off Vella Lavella, Solomon Islands, October 7, 1943.

Colhoun (DD-801) sunk after being hit by four kamikaze aircraft off Okinawa, Ryukyu Islands, April 6, 1945.

Cooper (DD-695) sunk after being torpedoed in Ormoc Bay, Leyte, Philippine Islands, December 3, 1944.

Destroyers (continued)

Corry (DD-463) sunk by a mine off Utah Beach, Normandy, France, June 6, 1944.

Cushing (DD-376) sunk by gunfire from Japanese warships off Savo, Solomon Islands, November 13, 1942.

De Haven (DD-469) sunk after being bombed by Japanese aircraft off Savo, Solomon Islands, February 1, 1943.

Drexler (DD-741) sunk after being hit by two kamikaze aircraft off Okinawa, Ryukyu Islands, May 28, 1945.

Duncan (DD-485) sunk after being damaged by gunfire from Japanese off Savo, Solomon Islands, October 12, 1942.

Edsall (DD-219) sunk by Japanese warships south of Java, Netherlands East Indies, March 1, 1942.

Evans (DD-552) seriously damaged by four kamikaze aircraft, May 11, 1945, off Okinawa, Ryukyu Islands, and not repaired after the end of the war.

Glennon (DD-620) sunk by a mine and gunfire from German shore batteries off Quineville, Normandy, France, June 10, 1944.

Gwin (DD-433) sunk after being torpedoed by Japanese destroyers in Kula Gulf, Solomon Islands, July 13, 1943.

Haggard (DD-555) seriously damaged by kamikaze aircraft, April 29, 1945, off Okinawa, Ryukyu Islands, and not repaired after the end of the war.

Halligan (DD-584) sunk after striking a mine off Okinawa, Ryukyu Islands, March 26, 1945.

Hammann (DD-412) sunk after being torpedoed by the Japanese submarine *I-168* northeast of Midway Island, June 6, 1942.

Henley (DD-391) sunk after being torpedoed by the Japanese submarine *RO-108* off Cape Cretin, New Guinea, October 3, 1943.

Hoel (DD-533) sunk by Japanese warships off Samar, Philippine Islands, October 25, 1944.

Hugh W. Hadley (DD-774) seriously damaged by an aircraft bomb and two kamikaze aircraft, May 11, 1945, off Okinawa, Ryukyu Islands, and not repaired after the end of the war.

Hull (DD-350) foundered during a typhoon in the Philippine Sea, December 18, 1944.

Hutchins (DD-476) seriously damaged by a Japanese suicide boat, April 27, 1945, in Buckner Bay, Okinawa, Ryukyu Islands, and not repaired after the end of the war.

Ingraham (DD-444) sunk after a collision in fog with the USS *Chemung* (AO-30) in the North Atlantic, August 22, 1942.

Destroyers (continued)

Jacob Jones (DD-393) sunk after being torpedoed by the German submarine *U-578* off Cape May, New Jersey, February 28, 1942.

Jarvis (DD-393) sunk by Japanese aircraft south of Guadalcanal, Solomon Islands, August 9, 1942.

Johnston (DD-557) sunk by Japanese warships off Samar, Philippine Islands, October 25, 1944.

Laffey (DD-459) sunk by the Japanese battleship *Hiei* off Savo, Solomon Islands, November 13, 1942.

Lansdale (DD-426) sunk after being torpedoed by German aircraft off Cape Bengut, Algeria, April 20, 1944.

Leary (DD-158) sunk after being torpedoed by the German submarine *U-275* in the North Atlantic, December 24, 1943.

Leutze (DD-481) seriously damaged by one kamikaze aircraft, April 6, 1945, off Okinawa, Ryukyu Islands, and not repaired after the end of the war.

Little (DD-803) sunk after being hit by four kamikaze aircraft off Okinawa, Ryukyu Islands, May 3, 1945.

Longshaw (DD-559) destroyed by Japanese shore batteries after running aground off Naha airfield, Okinawa, Ryukyu Islands, May 18, 1945.

Luce (DD-522) sunk after being hit by two kamikaze aircraft off Okinawa, Ryukyu Islands, May 3, 1945.

Maddox (DD-622) sunk after being bombed by German aircraft off Gela, Sicily, July 10, 1943.

Mahan (DD-364) sunk after being hit by three kamikaze aircraft in Leyte Gulf, Philippine Islands, December 7, 1944.

Mannert L. Abele (DD-733) sunk by kamikaze aircraft and glider bomb attack off Okinawa, Ryukyu Islands, April 12, 1945.

Meredith (DD-434) sunk by Japanese aircraft near San Cristobal, Solomon Islands, October 15, 1942.

Meredith (DD-726) sunk by German aircraft after being damaged by a mine in the Bay of the Seine, Normandy, France, June 9, 1944.

Monaghan (DD-354) foundered during a typhoon in the Philippine Sea, December 18, 1944.

Monssen (DD-436) sunk by gunfire from Japanese warships off Savo, Solomon Islands, November 13, 1942.

Morris (DD-417) seriously damaged by kamikaze aircraft, April 6, 1945, off Okinawa, Ryukyu Islands, and not repaired after the end of the war.

Morrison (DD-560) sunk after being hit by four kamikaze aircraft off Okinawa, Ryukyu Islands, May 4, 1945.

Destroyers (continued)

Newcombe (DD-586) seriously damaged by three kamikaze aircraft, April 6, 1945, off Okinawa, Ryukyu Islands, and not repaired after the end of the war.

O'Brien (DD-415) torpedoed September 15, 1942, by Japanese submarine *I-15* north of Espiritu Santo, New Hebrides Islands, and foundered off Samoa en route to base, October 19, 1942.

Parrott (DD-218) scrapped after being damaged beyond repair in a collision with the SS *John Norton* at Hampton Roads, Virginia, May 2, 1944.

Peary (DD-226) sunk by Japanese aircraft at Darwin Harbor, Australia, February 19, 1942.

Perkins (DD-377) sunk in collision with HMAS *Duntroon* off Cape Vogel, New Guinea, November 29, 1943.

Pillsbury (DD-227) sunk by Japanese warships east of Christmas Island, Indian Ocean, March 1-4, 1942.

Pope (DD-225) sunk by Japanese aircraft in the Java Sea, Netherlands East Indies, March 1, 1942.

Porter (DD-356) sunk after being torpedoed by Japanese submarine *I-21* near Santa Cruz Island, east of the Solomon Islands, October 26, 1943.

Preston (DD-379) sunk by Japanese cruiser *Nagara* off Savo, Solomon Islands, November 14, 1942.

Pringle (DD-477) sunk by kamikaze attack off Okinawa, Ryukyu Islands, April 16, 1945.

Reid (DD-369) sunk after being hit by two kamikaze aircraft off Limasawa Island, Philippine Islands, December 11, 1944.

Reuben James (DD-245) sunk after being torpedoed by German submarine *U-562* south of Iceland, October 31, 1941.

Rowan (DD-405) sunk after being torpedoed by German motor torpedo boat off Salerno, Italy, September 11, 1943.

Shubrick (DD-639) seriously damaged by one kamikaze aircraft, May 29, 1945, off Okinawa, Ryukyu Islands, and not repaired after the end of the war.

Sims (DD-409) sunk by Japanese aircraft during the Battle of the Coral Sea, May 7, 1942.

Spence (DD-512) capsized during a typhoon in the Philippine Sea, December 18, 1944.

Stewart (DD-224) captured by the Japanese after being scuttled in a dry dock at Surabaya, Java, Netherlands East Indies, March 2, 1942.

Strong (DD-467) sunk after being torpedoed by Japanese destroyer off New Georgia, Solomon Islands, July 5, 1943.

Sturtevant (DD-240) sunk by a mine off Marquesas Key, Florida, April 26, 1942.

Thatcher (DD-514) seriously damaged by one kamikaze aircraft off Okinawa, Ryukyu Islands, May 20, 1945, and not repaired after the end of the war.

Truxtun (DD-229) wrecked in a gale at Chamber's Cove, Newfoundland, February 18, 1942.

Tucker (DD-374) sunk by a mine in Segond Channel, New Hebrides, August 4, 1942.

Turner (DD-648) sunk by explosion off Sandy Hook, New Jersey, January 3, 1944.

Twiggs (DD-591) sunk by a kamikaze aircraft after being torpedoed off Okinawa, Ryukyu Islands, June 16, 1945.

Walke (DD-416) sunk by gunfire and torpedoes from Japanese warships off Savo, Solomon Islands, November 14, 1942.

Warrington (DD-383) foundered in a hurricane north of the Bahamas Islands, September 13, 1944.

William D. Porter (DD-579) sunk after being hit by one kamikaze aircraft off Okinawa, Ryukyu Islands, June 10, 1945.

Worden (DD-352) wrecked off Amchitka, Aleutian Islands, January 12, 1943.

Destroyers, Escort

England (DE-635) seriously damaged by one kamikaze aircraft, May 9, 1945, off Okinawa, Ryukyu Islands, and not repaired after the end of the war.

Eversole (DE-404) sunk after being torpedoed by Japanese submarine *I-45* east of Leyte, Philippine Islands, October 28, 1944.

Fechteler (DE-157) sunk after being torpedoed by German submarine *U-967* northeast of Oran, Algeria, May 5, 1944.

Fiske (DE-143) sunk after being torpedoed by German submarine *U-804* north of Azores, August 2, 1944.

Frederick C. Davis (DE-136) sunk after being torpedoed by German submarine *U-546* in the North Atlantic, April 24, 1945.

Holder (DE-401) scrapped after being torpedoed by German aircraft off Algiers, Algeria, April 11, 1944.

Leopold (DE-319) sunk after being torpedoed by German submarine *U-255* south of Iceland, March 10, 1944.

Oberrender (DE-344) damaged beyond repair by a kamikaze attack off Okinawa, Ryukyu Islands, May 9, 1945.

Rich (DE-695) sunk by a mine off Normandy, France, June 8, 1944.

Samuel B. Roberts (DE-413) sunk by Japanese warships during the Battle of Leyte Gulf off Samar, Philippine Islands, October 25, 1944.

Shelton (DE-407) sunk after being torpedoed by Japanese submarine *RO-41* off Morotai Island, October 3, 1944.

Underhill (DE-682) sunk by Japanese human torpedo northeast of Luzon, Philippine Islands, July 24, 1945.

Submarines

Albacore (SS-218) sunk after striking a mine north of Hokkaido, Japan, November 7, 1944.

Amberjack (SS-219) probably sunk by Japanese torpedo boat *Hiyodori* and Japanese sub chaser *No. 18* off Rabaul, New Britain Island, February 16, 1943.

Argonaut (APS-1) sunk by Japanese destroyers *Maikaze* and *Isokaze* off New Britain Island, January 10, 1943.

Barbel (SS-316) sunk by Japanese aircraft southwest of Palawan, Philippine Islands, February 4, 1945.

Bonefish (SS-223) sunk by Japanese warships in Toyama Wan, Honshu, Japan, June 19, 1945.

Bullhead (SS-332) sunk by Japanese aircraft north of Bali, Lesser Sunda Islands, August 6, 1945.

Capelin (SS-289) missing off Halmahera Island, December 1943.

Cisco (SS-290) sunk by Japanese warships and aircraft in the Sulu Sea, September 28, 1943.

Corvina (SS-226) sunk after being torpedoed by Japanese submarine *I-176* southwest of Truk, Caroline Islands, November 16, 1943.

Darter (SS-227) stranded on Bombay Shoal, off Palawan, Philippine Islands, and destroyed to prevent capture, October 24, 1944.

Dorado (SS-248) probably sunk in error by U.S. aircraft in the Caribbean Sea, October 12, 1943.

Escolar (SS-294) probably sunk after striking a mine in the Yellow Sea, October 17, 1944.

Flier (SS-250) sunk while on the surface by a mine in Balabac Strait, Philippine Islands, August 13, 1944.

Golet (SS-361) sunk by Japanese warships off north Honshu, Japan, June 14, 1944.

Grampus (SS-207) probably sunk by Japanese destroyers *Minegumo* and *Murasame* off New Georgia, Solomon Islands, March 5, 1943.

Grayback (SS-208) sunk by Japanese aircraft in the East China Sea, February 6, 1944.

Grayling (SS-209) probably sunk by Japanese freighter *Hokuan Maru* west of Luzon, Philippine Islands, September 9, 1943.

Grenadier (SS-210) sunk by Japanese aircraft off Penang, April 22, 1943.

Growler (SS-215) probably sunk by Japanese warships in the South China Sea, November 8, 1944.

Grunion (SS-216) missing off Kiska, Aleutian Islands, at the end of July 1942. Probably sunk by the Japanese submarine *I-25*, July 30, 1942.

Gudgeon (SS-211) missing off the Marianas Islands, April 18, 1944.

Submarines (continued)

Harder (SS-257) sunk by Siamese destroyer *Pra Ruang* off Caiman Point, August 24, 1944.

Herring (SS-233) sunk by Japanese shore batteries off Matsuwa Island, Kurile Islands, June 1, 1944.

Kete (SS-369) missing in the Central Pacific, March 20, 1945.

Lagarto (SS-371) sunk by Japanese minelayer *Hatsutaka* in the Gulf of Siam, May 3, 1945.

Perch (SS-176) scuttled after being damaged by Japanese destroyers *Sazanami* and *Ushio* north of Java, Netherlands East Indies, March 3, 1942.

Pickerel (SS-177) missing off northern Honshu, Japan, April 3, 1943.

Pompano (SS-181) missing east of Honshu, Japan, September 3, 1943.

R-12 (SS-89) foundered during exercises off Key West, Florida, June 12, 1943.

Robalo (SS-273) sunk by an internal explosion or a mine off Palawan, Philippine Islands, July 26, 1944.

Runner (SS-275) missing off the Kuril Islands, June 26, 1943.

S-26 (SS-131) sunk after collision with submarine chaser *PC-460* in the Gulf of Panama, January 24, 1942.

S-27 (SS-132) lost by grounding on a reef off St. Makarius Point, Amchitka, Aleutian Islands, June 19, 1942.

S-28 (SS-133) failed to surface during training exercises with the USCGC *Reliance* (WPC-150) off Pearl Harbor, Hawaii, July 4, 1944.

S-36 (SS-141) lost by grounding on Taka Bakang Reef, Makassar Strait, January 20, 1942.

S-39 (SS-144) lost by grounding south of Rossel Island, Louisiade Archipelago, August 14, 1942.

S-44 (SS-155) sunk by Japanese escort ship *Ishigaki* off Paramushiro, Kuril Islands, October 7, 1943.

Scamp (SS-277) probably sunk by Japanese patrol vessel off Tokyo Bay, Japan, November 11, 1944.

Scorpion (SS-278) missing in the western Pacific, March 6, 1944.

Sculpin (SS-191) sunk by Japanese destroyer *Yamagumo* off Truk, Caroline Islands, November 19, 1943.

Sealion (SS-195) sunk by Japanese aircraft at Cavite, Luzon, Philippine Islands, December 10, 1941, and destroyed to prevent capture, December 25, 1941.

Seawolf (SS-197) sunk in error by destroyer escort USS *Richard M. Rowell* (DE-403) off Morotai, October 3, 1944.

Shark (SS-174) probably sunk by Japanese destroyer *Yamakaze* east of Menado, Celebes, February 11, 1942.

158

Submarines (continued)

Shark (SS-314) sunk by Japanese destroyer *Harukaze* in Luzon Strait, Philippine Islands, October 24, 1944.

Snook (SS-279) missing in Okinawa, Ryukyu Islands, area (possibly sunk by a Japanese submarine), April 1945.

Swordfish (SS-193) missing south of Kyushu, Japan, January 12, 1945.

Tang (SS-306) sunk by own torpedo off Formosa, October 24, 1944.

Trigger (SS-237) sunk by Japanese aircraft and warships in Nansei Shoto, Ryukyu Islands, March 28, 1945.

Triton (SS-201) sunk by Japanese destroyers north of Admiralty Islands, March 15, 1943.

Trout (SS-202) sunk by Japanese destroyer *Asahimo* southeast of Okinawa, Ryukyu Islands, February 29, 1944.

Tullibee (SS-284) sunk by own torpedo north of Palau, Caroline Islands, March 26, 1944.

Wahoo (SS-238) sunk by Japanese aircraft and Japanese submarine chasers 15 and 43 in Soya Strait, Japan, October 11, 1943.

Source: Naval Historical Center

U.S. Navy

Antrim, Richard N., Commander, U.S. Navy, Makassar, Celebes, Netherlands East Indies, April 1942.

Bennion, Mervyn S. (posthumous), Captain, U.S. Navy, USS *West Virginia*, Pearl Harbor, December 7, 1941.

Bigelow, Elmer C. (posthumous), Watertender First Class, U.S. Naval Reserve, USS *Fletcher*, February 14, 1945.

Bulkeley, John D., Lieutenant Commander, Commander of Motor Torpedo Boat Squadron 3, U.S. Navy, Philippine waters, December 7, 1941 to April 10, 1942.

Bush, Robert E., Hospital Apprentice First Class, U.S. Naval Reserve, serving as Medical Corpsman with a rifle company, 2d Battalion, 5th Marines, 1st Marine Division, Okinawa Jima, Ryukyu Islands, May 2, 1945.

Callaghan, Daniel J. (posthumous), Rear Admiral, U.S. Navy, off Savo Island, November 12–13, 1942 .

Cromwell, John P. (posthumous), Captain, U.S. Navy, Submarine Coordinated Attack Group, USS *Sculpin*, off Truk Island, November 19, 1943.

David, Albert L. (posthumous), Lieutenant, Junior Grade, U.S. Navy, USS *Pillsbury*, off French West Africa, June 4, 1944.

Davis, George F. (posthumous), Commander, U.S. Navy, USS *Walke*, Lingayen Gulf, Luzon, Philippine Islands, January 6, 1945.

Dealey, Samuel D. (posthumous), Commander, U.S. Navy, USS *Harder.*

Evans, Ernest E. (posthumous), Commander, U.S. Navy, USS *Johnston*, off Samar, October 25, 1944.

Finn, John W., Lieutenant, U.S. Navy [then a Chief Petty Officer], Naval Air Station, Kaneohe Bay, December 7, 1941.

Flaherty, Francis C. (posthumous), Ensign, U.S. Naval Reserve, USS *Oklahoma*, Pearl Harbor, December 7, 1941.

Fluckey, Eugene B., Commander, U.S. Navy, Commanding USS *Barb*, along coast of China, December 19, 1944 to February 15, 1945.

Fuqua, Samuel G., Captain, U.S. Navy, USS *Arizona* [then Lt. Cmdr.], Pearl Harbor, December 7, 1941.

Gary, Donald A., Lieutenant, Junior Grade, U.S. Navy, USS *Franklin*, Japanese Home Islands near Kobe, Japan, March 19, 1945.

Gilmore, Howard W. (posthumous), Commander, U.S. Navy, USS *Growler*, Southwest Pacific from January 10 to February 7, 1943.

Gordon, Nathan G., Lieutenant, U.S. Navy, commander of Catalina patrol plane, Kavieng Harbor, Bismarck Sea, February 15, 1944.

Hall, William E., Lieutenant, Junior Grade, U.S. Naval Reserve, Coral Sea, May 7-8, 1942.

Halyburton, William D. JR. (posthumous), Pharmacist's Mate Second Class, U.S. Naval Reserve, serving with 2d Battalion, 5th Marines, 1st Marine Division, Okinawa Shima in the Ryukyu Chain, May 10, 1945.

Hammerberg, Owen F. P. (posthumous), Boatswain's Mate Second Class, U.S. Navy, West Loch, Pearl Harbor, February 17, 1945.

Herring, Rufus, G., Lieutenant, U.S. Naval Reserve, LCI (G) 449, Iwo Jima, February 17, 1945.

Hill, Edwin J. (posthumous), Chief Boatswain, U.S. Navy, USS *Nevada*, Pearl Harbor, T.H., December 7, 1941.

Hutchins, Johnnie D. (posthumous), Seaman First Class, U.S. Naval Reserve, USS LST 473, Lae, New Guinea, September 4, 1943.

Jones, Herbert C. (posthumous), Ensign, U.S. Naval Reserve, USS *California*, Pearl Harbor, December 7, 1941.

Keppler, Reinhardt J. (posthumous), Boatswain's Mate First Class, U.S. Navy, USS *San Francisco*, Solomon Islands, November 12–13, 1942.

Kidd, Isaac C. (posthumous), Rear Admiral, U.S. Navy, USS *Arizona*, Pearl Harbor, December 7, 1941.

Lester, Fred F. (posthumous), Hospital Apprentice First Class, U.S. Navy, attached to the 1st Battalion, 22nd Marines, 6th Marine Division, Okinawa Shima in the Ryukyu Chain, June 8, 1945.

McCampbell, David, Commander, U.S. Navy, Air Group 15, first and second battles of the Philippine Sea, June 19, 1944.

McCandless, Bruce, Commander, U.S. Navy, USS *San Francisco*, Battle off Savo Island, November 12–13, 1942.

McCool, Richard M., Lieutenant, U.S. Navy, USS LSC(L)(3) 122, off Okinawa, June 10–11, 1945.

O'Callahan, Joseph T., Commander (Chaplain Corps), U.S. Naval Reserve, USS *Franklin*, near Kobe, Japan, March 19, 1945.

O'Hare, Edward H., Lieutenant, U.S. Navy, Fighting Squadron 3, South Pacific, February 20, 1942.

O'Kane, Richard H., Commander, U.S. Navy, commanding USS *Tang*, vicinity Philippine Islands, October 20–23, 1944.

Parle, John J. (posthumous), Ensign, U.S. Naval Reserve, USS LST 375, Sicily, July 9-10, 1943.

Peterson, Oscar V. (posthumous), Chief Watertender, U.S. Navy, USS *Neosho*, May 7, 1942.

Pharris, Jackson C., Lieutenant, U.S. Navy, USS *California*, [then Gunner], Pearl Harbor, December 7, 1941.

Pierce, Francis Jr., Pharmacist's Mate First Class, U.S. Navy serving with 2nd Battalion, 24th Marines, 4th Marine Division, Iwo Jima, March 15–16, 1945.

Powers, John J. (posthumous), Lieutenant, U.S. Navy, Bombing Squadron 5, Battle of Coral Sea, May 4–8, 1942.

Preston, Arthur M., Lieutenant, U.S. Navy Reserve, Torpedo Boat Squadron 33, Wasile Bay, Halmahera Island, September 16, 1944.

Ramage, Lawson P., Commander, U.S. Navy, USS *Parche*, Pacific, July 31, 1944.

Reeves, Thomas J. (posthumous), Radio Electrician (Warrant Officer) U.S. Navy, USS *California*, Pearl Harbor, December 7, 1941.

Ricketts, Milton E. (posthumous), Lieutenant, U.S. Navy, USS *Yorktown*, Battle of the Coral Sea, May 8, 1942.

Rooks, Albert H. (posthumous), Captain, U.S. Navy, USS *Houston*, Southwest Pacific, February 4–27, 1942.

Ross, Donald K., Machinist, U.S. Navy, USS *Nevada*, Pearl Harbor, December 7, 1941.

Schonland, Herbert E., Commander, U.S. Navy, USS *San Francisco*, Savo Island, November 12–13, 1943.

Scott, Norman (posthumous), Rear Admiral, U.S. Navy, Savo Island, October 11–12, November 12–13, 1942.

Scott, Robert R. (posthumous), Machinist's Mate First Class, U.S. Navy, USS *California*, Pearl Harbor, December 7, 1941.

Street, George L. III, Commander, U.S. Navy, USS *Tiranle*, Harbor of Quelpart Island, off the coast of Korea, April 14, 1945.

Tomich, Peter (posthumous), Chief Watertender, U.S. Navy, USS *Utah*, Pearl Harbor, December 7, 1941.

Van Valkenburgh, Franklin (posthumous), Captain, U.S. Navy, USS *Arizona*, Pearl Harbor, December 7, 1941.

Van Voorhis, Bruce A. (posthumous), Lieutenant Commander, U.S. Navy, Bombing Squadron 102, Battle of the Solomon Islands, July 6, 1943.

Wahlen, George E., Pharmacist's Mate Second Class, U.S. Navy, serving with 2nd Battalion, 26th Marines, 5th Marine Division, Iwo Jima, Volcano Islands group, March 3, 1945.

Ward, James R. (posthumous), Seaman First Class, U.S. Navy, USS *Oklahoma*, Pearl Harbor, December 7, 1941.

Williams, Jack (posthumous), Pharmacist's Mate Third Class, U.S. Naval Reserve, serving with the 3rd Battalion, 28th Marines, 5th Marine Division, Iwo Jima Volcano Islands, March 3, 1945.

Willis, John H. (posthumous), Pharmacist's Mate First Class, U.S. Navy, serving with the 3rd Battalion, 27th Marines, 5th Marine Division, Iwo Jima, Volcano Islands, February 28, 1945.

Young, Cassin, Commander, U.S. Navy, USS *Vestal*, Pearl Harbor, December 7, 1941.

U.S. Coast Guard Recipients

Munro, Douglas A. (posthumous), Signalman First Class, U.S. Coast Guard, Point Cruz, Guadalcanal, September 27, 1942.

Source: Naval Historical Center

SELECTED PRESERVED WORLD WAR II–ERA SHIPS

No.	Name	Date	Location
Battleship			
BB-31 (AG-16)	Utah	1911	*in situ*, USS Arizona Memorial, Pearl Harbor, HI
BB-35	Texas	1914	San Jacinto Battleground Historic Park, LaPorte, TX
BB-39	Arizona	1915	*in situ*, USS Arizona Memorial, Pearl Harbor, HI
BB-55	North Carolina	1941	USS North Carolina Battleship Memorial, Wilmington, NC
BB-59	Massachusetts	1942	Battleship Cove, Fall River, MA
BB-60	Alabama	1942	Battleship Memorial Park, Mobile, AL
BB-63	Missouri	1944	USS Missouri Memorial Association, Pearl Harbor, HI
Aircraft Carriers			
CVS-10	Yorktown	1943	Patriot's Point Naval/ Maritime Museum, Mount Pleasant, SC
CVS-11	Intrepid	1943	Intrepid Sea-Air-Space Museum, New York, NY
CVS-12	Hornet	1943	USS Hornet Museum, Alameda, CA
AVT-16	Lexington	1943	Lexington on the Bay Museum, Corpus Christi, TX
Cruiser			
CL-92	Little Rock	1944	Buffalo & Erie County Naval & Military Park, Buffalo, NY
Destroyers/Destroyer Escorts			
DD-537	The Sullivans	1943	Buffalo & Erie County Naval & Military Park, Buffalo, NY
DD-661	Kidd	1943	Louisiana Naval War Museum, Baton Rouge, LA
DD-724	Laffey	1943	Patriot's Point Naval & Maritime Museum, Charleston, SC
DD-793	Cassin Young	1943	Boston National Historical Park, Boston, MA
DD-850	Joseph P. Kennedy, Jr.	1945	Battleship Cove, Fall River, MA
DD-886	Orleck	1945	SE Texas War Memorial & Heritage Foundation, Orange County, TX
DE-238	Stewart	1943	Seawolf Park, Galveston, TX
DE-766	Slater	1944	Destroyer Escort Historical Foundation, Albany, NY
Tank Landing Ships			
LST393		1943	Great Lakes Naval & Maritime Museum, Muskegon, MI
LST325			Battleship Memorial Park, Mobile, AL
Submarines			
SS-224	Cod	1943	Cleveland Coordinating Committee, Cleveland, OH
SS-228	Drum	1941	Battleship Memorial Park, Mobile, AL
SS-236	Silversides	1941	Great Lakes Naval & Maritime Museum, Muskegon, MI
SS-244	Cavalla	1944	Seawolf Park, Galveston, TX
SS-245	Cobia	1944	Wisconsin Maritime Museum, Manitowoc, WI
SS-246	Croaker	1944	Buffalo & Erie County Naval & Military Park, Buffalo, NY
SS-287	Bowfin	1943	Pacific Fleet Memorial Association, Pearl Harbor, HI
SS-297	Ling	1945	New Jersey Naval Museum, Hackensack, NJ
SS-298	Lionfish	1944	Battleship Cove, Fall River, MA
SS-310	Batfish	1943	Muskogee War Memorial Park, Muskogee, OK
SS-319	Becuna	1944	Independence Seaport Museum, Philadelphia, PA
SS-343	Clamagore	1945	Patriot's Point Naval & Maritime Museum, Charleston, SC
SS-383	Pampanito	1943	National Maritime Museum Association, San Francisco, CA
SS-423	Torsk	1944	Baltimore Maritime Museum, Baltimore, MD

No.	Name	Date	Location
Minesweeper			
AM-240	Hazard	1944	Military Historical Society, Freedom Park, Omaha, NE
Patrol Boats			
PT-309		1944	Admiral Nimitz Museum, Kemah, TX
PT-617		1945	Battleship Cove, Fall River, MA
PT-658		1945	USN/Save the PT Boat, Inc., Portland, OR
PT-659		1945	Oregon Military Museum, Portland, OR
PT-695		1944	American Patrol Boats Association, Rio Vista, CA
PT-728		1945	Bill Bohmfalk/Key West Brewery, Key West, FL
PT-796		1945	PT Boats Inc./Battleship Cove, Fall River, MA
Army Tugs			
ST-695	Angels Gate	1944	Los Angeles Maritime Museum, San Pedro, CA
LT-5		1944	H. Lee White Marine Museum, Oswego, NY
—	Marquette	—	Great Lakes Naval & Maritime Museum, Chicago, IL
Landing Craft			
LSM-45	LSM45	1944	Freedom Park/Omaha Military Historical society, Omaha, NE
Liberty Ship			
—	Jeremiah O'Brien	1932	National Liberty Ship Memorial, San Francisco, CA
—	John Brown	1942	Project Liberty Ship, Baltimore, MD
Victory Ship			
AK-235	Red Oak Victory	1944	Richmond Museum of History, Richmond, CA
—	American Victory	1945	American Victory Mariners Memorial & Museum, Tampa, FL
—	Lane Victory	1945	US Merchant Marine Veterans of WWII, San Pedro, CA
German U-Boat			
U-505		1941	Museum of Science & Industry, Chicago, IL
U-534		1942	Nautilus Maritime Museum, restoration, Birkenhead, UK
U-995		1943	Marine Memorial, Laboe, Germany
U-2540		1945	German Maritime Museum, Bremerhaven, Germany
German Midget Submarine			
—	"Seehund"	—	USN Submarine Force Museum, Groton, CT
—	"Seehund"	—	New Jersey Naval Museum, Hackensack, NJ
U-5090	"Seehund"	—	Naval Museum, Brest, France
Italian Midget Submarine			
—	"Maiale"	—	USN Submarine Force Museum, Groton, CT
Japanese Suicide Torpedo			
—	"Kaitin"	—	Pacific Fleet Submarine Memorial Assn., Pearl Harbor, HI
—	"Kaitin"	—	New Jersey Naval Museum, Hackensack, NJ
Japanese Midget Submarine			
—	HA-8	—	USN Submarine Force Museum, Groton, CT
—	HA-19	—	Admiral Nimitz Museum, Fredericksburg, TX

BIBLIOGRAPHY

Alden, John D. *U.S. Submarine Attacks During World War II*. Annapolis, Maryland. Naval Institute Press. 1989.

Blair, Clay. *Hitler's U-Boat War: The Hunters, 1939-1942*. New York. Random House. 1996.

_____. *Hitler's U-Boat War: The Hunted, 1942-1945*. New York. Random House. 1996.

_____. *Silent Victory: The U.S. Submarine War Against Japan*. Vols. I and II. Philadelphia, Pennsylvania. J.B. Lippincott Co. 1975.

Bonner, Kit and Carolyn Bonner. *Great Naval Disasters: U.S. Accidents in the 20th Century*. Osceola, Wisconsin. MBI Publishing Company. 1998.

Browning, Robert M., Jr. *U.S. Merchant Vessel War Casualties of World War II*. Annapolis, Maryland. Naval Institute Press. 1996.

Carter, Kit C. and Robert Mueller, *The Army Air Forces In World War II: Combat Chronology*. Washington, D.C.: Office of Air Force History, Headquarters U.S. Air Force, 1973.

Cohen, Stan. *East Wind Rain: A Pictorial History of the Pearl Harbor Attack*. Missoula, Montana: Pictorial Histories Publishing, 1981.

Craven, Wesley Frank and James Lea Cate. *The Army Air Forces In World War II*. Vols. 1-7. Washington, D.C., : Office of Air Force History, Headquarters U.S. Air Force, 1983.

Cressman, Robert J. *The Official Chronology of the U.S. Navy in World War II*. Annapolis, Maryland: Naval Institute Press, 2000.

Dull, Paul S. *A Battle History of the Imperial Japanese Navy (1941–1945)*. Annapolis, Maryland. Naval Institute Press. 1978.

Francillon, Rene. *Japanese Aircraft of the Pacific War*. Annapolis, Maryland: Naval Institute Press, 1988.

Gannon, Michael. *Operation Drumbeat: The Dramatic True Story of Germany's First U-Boat Attacks Along The American Coast In World War II*. New York. Harper: Perennial, 1990.

Gibbs, Jim. *Disaster Log of Ships*. New York: Bonanza Books, 1971.

Hammel, Eric. *Air War Europa: Chronology*. Pacifica, California: Pacifica Press, 1994.

_____. *Air War Pacific: Chronology*. Pacifica, California: Pacifica Press, 1998.

Harding, Stephen. *Great Liners at War: The Military Adventures of the World's Largest, Fastest and Most Famous Passenger Steamships*. Osceola, Wisconsin: MBI Publishing Company, 1997.

Hoehling, A. A. *The Franklin Comes Home*. Annapolis, Maryland: Naval Institute Press, 1974.

Kenney, George C. *General Kenney Reports: A Personal History of the Pacific War*. Washington, D.C: Air Force History and Museums Program, 1997.

Kimmett, Larry and Margaret Regis. *The Attack on Pearl Harbor: An Illustrated History*. Seattle, Washington: Navigator Publishing, 1999.

Lane, Frederic C. *Ships for Victory: A History of Shipbuilding Under The U.S. Maritime Commission in World War II*. Baltimore, Maryland: The Johns Hopkins Press, 1951.

McAulay, Lex. *Battle of the Bismarck Sea*. New York: St. Martin's Press, 1991.

Madsen, Daniel. *Forgotten Fleet: The Mothball Navy*. Annapolis, Maryland: Naval Institute Press, 1999.

Marshall, Donald B. *California Shipwrecks*. Seattle, Washington: Superior Publishing Co, 1978.

Morrison, Samuel Eliot. *The Two-Ocean War: A Short History of the United States Navy in the Second World War*. Boston, Massachusetts. Atlantic-Little, Brown. 1963.

Morrison, Samuel Eliot. *History of United States Naval Operations in World War II*. Vols. 1-15. Boston, Massachusetts: Atlantic-Little, Brown, 1948-1968.

Morton, Louis. *United States Army in World War II: The Fall of the Philippines*. Washington, D.C: Department of the Army, Office of the Chief of Military History, 1953.

Nelson, William T. *Fresh Water Submarines: The Manitowoc Story*. Manitowoc, Wisconsin: Hoeffner Printing, 1986.

Niestlé, Axel. *German U-Boat Losses During World War II*. Annapolis, Maryland: Naval Institute Press, 1998.

Olynyk, Frank. *Stars and Bars: A Tribute to the American Fighter Ace, 1920–1973*. London: Grubb Street, 1995.

Polmar, Norman and Samuel Loring Morison. *PT Boats at War: World War II to Vietnam*. Osceola, Wisconsin: MBI Publishing Company, 1999.

Prange, Gordon W. *At Dawn We Slept: The Untold Story of Pearl Harbor*. New York: Penguin Books, 1981.

_____. *Miracle at Midway*. New York: McGraw Hill. 1982.

_____. *Pearl Harbor: The Verdict of History*. New York: McGraw Hill, 1986.

Rohwer, Jürgen and Gerhard Hümmelchen. *Chronology of the War at Sea 1939–1945*. Annapolis, Maryland: Naval Institute Press, 1992.

_____. *Axis Submarine Successes of World War Two: German, Italian and Japanese Submarine Successes, 1939–1945*. Annapolis, Maryland: Naval Institute Press, 1999.

Roscoe, Theodore. *United States Submarine Operations in World War II*. Annapolis, Maryland: Naval Institute Press, 1949.

Sawyer, L. A. and W. H. Mitchell. *The Liberty Ships: The History of the "Emergency" Type Cargo Ships constructed in the United States during the Second World War*. London.: Lloyd's of London Press, Ltd, 1985.

Sharpe, Peter R. *U-Boat Fact File: Detailed Service Histories of the Submarines Operated by the Kriegsmarine 1935–1945*. Leicester, Great Britain: Midland Publishing Ltd, 1998.

Silverstone, Paul H. *U.S. Warships of World War II*. Garden City, New York: Doubleday and Company, 1965.

Stewart, Adrian. *The Battle of Leyte Gulf.* New York: Charles Scribner's Sons, 1979.

Tuleja, Thaddeus V. *Climax at Midway: The Story of the Battle That Changed the Course of the Pacific War.* New York: W.W. Norton and Co, 1960.

Veronico, Nicholas A. with John M. and Donna Campbell. *F4U Corsair: The Combat, Development, and Racing History of the Corsair.* Osceola, Wisconsin: MBI Publishing Company, 1993.

_____. *Japanese Attacks on California: December 7, 1941 to February 25, 1942.* San Carlos, California: Pacific Aero Press, 1996

Wallin, Homer N. *Pearl Harbor: Why, How, Fleet Salvage and Final Appraisal.* Washington, D.C.: Naval History Division. U.S. Government Printing Office, 1968.

Webber, Bert. *Silent Siege III: Japanese Attacks on North America in World War II.* Medford, Oregon: Webb Research Group, 1992.

Wollenberg, Charles. *Marinship at War: Shipbuilding and Social Change in Wartime Sausalito.* Berkeley, California: Western Heritage Press, 1990.

Unknown. *Ships in Gray: The Story of Matson in World War II.* San Francisco, California: Matson Navigation Co, 1946.

_____. *Life Library of Photography.* New York: Time-Life Books, 1970. (Volumes: *Light and Film, The Camera, Color, The Great Themes, Photojournalism.*)

Government Publications

Navy Department, Office of the Chief of Naval Operations. *Dictionary of American Naval Fighting Ships.* Vols. 1–8. Washington, D.C.: U.S. Government Printing Office, 1959–1977.

Navy Department, Department of Ordnance and Gunnery. *Naval Ordnance and Gunnery, Vol. I: Naval Ordnance.* Washington, D.C.: U.S. Government Printing Office, 1955.

U.S. Senate. *Investigation of the Pearl Harbor Attack: Report of the Joint Committee on the Investigation of the Pearl Harbor Attack.* Washington, D.C.: U.S. Government Printing Office, 1946.

U.S. Senate. *Investigation of the Pearl Harbor Attack: Hearings Before the Joint Committee on the Investigation of the Pearl Harbor Attack.* Washington, D.C.: U.S. Government Printing Office, 1946. Parts 1 38.

U.S. Strategic Bombing Survey (Pacific). *The Campaigns of the Pacific War.* Washington, D.C.: U.S. Government Printing Office, 1946.

U.S. Strategic Bombing Survey (Naval Analysis Division). *Interrogations of Japanese Officials.* Vols. I and II. Washington, D.C.: U.S. Government Printing Office, 1946.

Periodicals

"Barrage Over L.A. —Was Target Real?" *San Francisco Chronicle, 24 February 1942.*

Colton, F. Barrows. "How We Fight With Photographs." *National Geographic,* September 1944.

"House Survey: 'Americas Are Riddled With Axis Bases.' " *San Francisco Chronicle, 20 December 1941.*

"Jap Subs Off Coast: Three Dead, Five Missing In Four Raids." *San Francisco Chronicle 23 December 1941.*

Needam, Howard. "Captain Tells Own Story of Sub Raid." *San Francisco Chronicel 22 December 1941.*

"S.F. Sub Attack: Survivors Tell Gripping Story How U.S. Pilots Battled Raider." *San Francisco Chronicle, 23 December 1941.*

"Ship Sunk Dec. 7 Was S.F. Owned." *San Francisco Chronicle, 20 December, 1941.*

"Sub Shells California!" *San Francisco Chronicle,* 24 February 1942.

"The Sub Stories: Attacks on U.S. Freighters Occurred Off Santa Cruz, Eureka; One Ship In Port." *San Francisco Chronicle, 21 December, 1941.*

"Three U.S. Ships Missing In The Pacific." *San Francisco Chronicle,* 8 December 1941.

INDEX